COMPOSITION AND RHETORIC
IN CONTENTIOUS TIMES

COMPOSITION AND RHETORIC IN CONTENTIOUS TIMES

EDITED BY
RACHEL McCABE
AND JENNIFER JUSZKIEWICZ

UTAH STATE UNIVERSITY PRESS
Logan

© 2023 by University Press of Colorado

Published by Utah State University Press
An imprint of University Press of Colorado
1580 North Logan Street, Suite 660
PMB 39883
Denver, Colorado 80203-1942

All rights reserved

 The University Press of Colorado is a proud member of the Association of University Presses.

The University Press of Colorado is a cooperative publishing enterprise supported, in part, by Adams State University, Colorado State University, Fort Lewis College, Metropolitan State University of Denver, University of Alaska Fairbanks, University of Colorado, University of Denver, University of Northern Colorado, University of Wyoming, Utah State University, and Western Colorado University.

ISBN: 978-1-64642-464-1 (hardcover)
ISBN: 978-1-64642-465-8 (paperback)
ISBN: 978-1-64642-466-5 (ebook)
https://doi.org/10.7330/9781646424665

Library of Congress Cataloging-in-Publication Data

Names: McCabe, Rachel Anne, editor. | Juszkiewicz, Jennifer Warfel, editor. Title: Composition and rhetoric in contentious times / edited by Rachel McCabe and Jennifer Juszkiewicz.
Description: Logan : Utah State University Press, [2023] | Includes bibliographical references and index.
Identifiers: LCCN 2023021435 (print) | LCCN 2023021436 (ebook) | ISBN 9781646424641 (hardcover) | ISBN 9781646424658 (paperback) | ISBN 9781646424665 (ebook)
Subjects: LCSH: English language—Rhetoric—Study and teaching (Higher) | English language—Composition and exercises—Study and teaching (Higher) | Academic writing—Study and teaching (Higher) | Education, Higher—Aims and objectives. | Interdisciplinary approach in education.
Classification: LCC PE1404 .C624 2023 (print) | LCC PE1404 (ebook) | DDC 808/.0420711—dc23/eng/20230807
LC record available at https://lccn.loc.gov/2023021435
LC ebook record available at https://lccn.loc.gov/2023021436

Cover illustration © vellot/Shutterstock.

In honor of Drs. Christine Farris and John Schilb

CONTENTS

Acknowledgments ix

Foreword
    Krista Ratcliffe xi

Introduction
    Rachel McCabe and Jennifer Juszkiewicz   3

SECTION ONE: CRITICAL INTERROGATIONS

1. Composition, Critics, and Care Work: An Undisciplined Reflection on Disciplinary Expertise
    Jacob Babb and William Duffy   17

2. Trust, Truth, and the Erosion of Public Discourse: The Virtue of Reality in the First-Year Writing Classroom
    Matthew S. S. Johnson   35

3. Writing with Our Bodies: Recovering Pathos through Critical Embodiment Pedagogy
    Christina V. Cedillo   50

SECTION TWO: CAREFUL LEADERSHIP

4. Continuing Writing across the Curriculum Programs amid the Contraction of Higher Education: Vision, Mission, and Strategy
    Christopher Basgier   69

5. Building an Affective Infrastructure to Lead Writing Programs
    Nicole Khoury, Nicholas Behm, and Sherry Rankins-Robertson   90

6. On Non-scalability and Transformative Relationships in the First-Year Composition "Jumbo"
    Laura A. Sparks and Kim Jaxon   107

SECTION THREE: DRAWING TOGETHER

7. Rooting Our Teaching in the Change around Us: Growing an Anti-Racist, Community-Interdependent Course Model
   Zapoura Newton-Calvert   125

8. Writing with the Working Class: The Future of Public Rhetoricians
   Anna Barritt and Kalyn Prince   143

9. Generative Combination: A Guiding Principle for the Future of Composition
   Matthew Overstreet   161

SECTION FOUR: WRITING OUR WAY BACK

10. A Future without Thesis Statements
    Hannah J. Rule   183

11. Teaching toward a More Just Citation Practice
    Elizabeth Kleinfeld   197

12. Film in the Interdisciplinary Composition Classroom
    Rachel McCabe   215

13. Learning from Black Teachers: Ida B. Wells-Barnett and Implementing Critical Engagement Strategies in Writing Classrooms
    Jessica Edwards   231

Afterword: Timely Is Timeless
   Deborah H. Holdstein   242

   Index   249
   About the Authors   255

ACKNOWLEDGMENTS

The conversations that inspired this collection started at the 2019 Futures of Rhet/Comp Symposium hosted by Indiana University–Bloomington to honor Drs. Christine Farris and John Schilb. These conversations helped create our shared vision, so we wish to thank all the speakers that weekend: Deborah H. Holdstein, Krista Ratcliffe, Caddie Alford, Ira Allen, Christopher Basgier, Lavinia Hirsu, Laura Johnson, Matthew S. S. Johnson, Alan Kalish, Deanna Luchene, Lisa Ottum, Laura Sparks, Lydia Wilkes, and Miranda Yaggi; organizer Doug Paul Case; and supporting faculty Dana Anderson, John Arthos, Scot Barnett, Justin Hodgson, Katherine Silvester, Kathy O. Smith, Robert Terrill, Freya Thimsen, and Kurt Zemlicka. We also wish to thank Beverly Hankins.

Some from that group chose to expand their ideas in writing, contributing to this written collection even as their ideas also developed and changed as a result of time and world events. Others saw our CFP and joined in, deepening the insights and heightening the stakes of our consideration of current pedagogy and administration in the discipline of composition and rhetoric. These contributors drafted and revised their work over time, responding to each other so the chapters are intentionally interconnected. Krista Ratcliffe and Deborah H. Holdstein generously engaged in the conversation as well, further exploring the potential of the chapters through their foreword and afterword, respectively. Rachael Levay has been a wonderful press editor. In the end, this collection reflects years of thinking and rethinking among these many scholars as the academic landscape continues to change in anticipated and unanticipated ways.

We also wish to thank our family and friends. Rachel thanks her husband, Erich, for all his love and support throughout the stages of creating this collection. She also thanks her colleagues at La Salle

University; their commitment to the importance of student writing has been a source of ongoing motivation. Jennifer thanks Ryan, Javy, Mia, and Zella as well as her stalwart writing group at Saint Mary's College and her ATK family.

FOREWORD

Krista Ratcliffe

In 2020, when George Floyd's six-year-old daughter Gianna said "Daddy changed the world," I doubt she had in mind the field of composition and rhetoric studies and the teaching of writing. But she could have. The viral video of George Floyd's death instantiated a cultural call for change in the US that echoes today. As I write this foreword, questions about Black Lives Matter are intersecting with questions about BIPOC lives more broadly, #MeToo, LGBTQIA rights, voting rights, climate change, inflation, national sovereignty, and war. In this moment of cultural questioning, US writing classrooms have changed too, in ways that affect all students and teachers. Many undergraduate and graduate students are asking that we take our cultural moment seriously in the classroom. Such engagements, they believe, will help them both understand and change the world, including institutions of higher learning. As a result, teachers are finding that comfortable ways of teaching no longer work quite as well as they did in the past.

What to do?

Implement pedagogical changes that respond to our cultural moment, of course. Such pedagogical changes should be principled, carefully planned, and skillfully executed so that teachers and students develop tools for rethinking and re-feeling cultural commonplaces, for having difficult discussions about how these commonplaces inform both personal identity and systems of power, and for writing our ways forward.

But the real question is: *how?*

To that end, the chapters in this edited collection offer multiple options. The Critical Interrogations section reflects with readers on our discipline, classrooms, and bodies. The Careful Leadership section encourages readers to prioritize writing across the curriculum/

writing in the disciplines (WAC/WID) programs in universities, the role of affect in graduate composition and rhetoric programs, and the design of jumbo first-year courses reimagined outside a cultural logic of scalability. The Drawing Together section invites readers to extend the writing classroom into our communities and cultural arenas without leaving academic discourses and spaces behind. The Writing Our Way Back section calls readers to rethink teachers' and students' classroom practices in hopes of transforming not just writing classrooms and writing standards, not just students and cultural values, but also the world and our praxes of justice. The hope threaded throughout this collection has driven composition teachers for many decades, an idea captured by Cheryl Glenn in *Rhetorical Feminism and This Thing Called Hope*.[1]

When asked to contribute a foreword to this collection, I reflected not only on its sections and chapters but also on problems and questions I have noted as a writing teacher and as chair of a very large English department at Arizona State University—problems/questions that, given our cultural moment, are haunting all classrooms, not just writing ones. The one I want to talk about here is: *how do teachers and students discuss difficult topics within the context of cancel culture and its competing discourses?*

The term *cancel culture* was entered into dictionary.com in 2016, defined as "the phenomenon or practice of publicly rejecting, boycotting, or ending support for particular people or groups because of their socially or morally unacceptable views or actions."[2] This process of exiling or ostracizing (i.e., cancelling) people, ideas, cultural artifacts, and practices with whom or with which one disagrees emerged just as polarization in US culture was becoming even more entrenched.

Cancel culture manifests across the US political spectrum. In conservative political discourses, cancel culture has emerged as arguments against "the left's" employing identity politics to cancel "the right's" ideas, practices, and revered cultural artifacts. Critical race theory, it is claimed, cancels the individualism that undergirds the American Dream. Queer studies, it is claimed, cancels religious beliefs. Taking down Civil War monuments valorizing the confederacy, it is claimed, cancels history. In more progressive political discourses, cancel culture has emerged as arguments against groups and people standing in the way of cultural reckoning and decolonization. Misusing personal pronouns, it is claimed, cancels the gender authenticity of the people being discussed. Ignoring race in any situation, it is claimed, cancels anti-racist efforts, thus promulgating racism. Denying class differences in the US, it is claimed, cancels efforts toward economic equity, thus perpetuating the increasing economic divide among people living in the US.

How valid are these claims—and for whom? What are the stakes in these claims—and for whom? These questions haunt students' lives and, as such, should certainly be investigated in writing classrooms. But for such discussions to succeed, students need to be given tools. To that end, they could benefit from learning rhetorical concepts and tactics for identifying and analyzing situated discourses as well as for talking and writing across differences. Students already use many rhetorical concepts and tactics and simply need to be made aware of them, but they could benefit from being offered new ones—whether Cedric Burrows's rhetorical crossover, Lisa Blankenship's rhetorical empathy, Lisa Flores's racial rhetorical criticism, and more.[3] And students would benefit from learning not just how to express their thoughts and feelings but also how to address their thoughts and feelings to different audiences *in ways these audiences can actually hear them*. It will be up to students, of course, to decide in particular situations whether to implement any of these rhetorical tools. But knowledge of them provides students with agency for making such decisions.

During the November 2021 ASU Common Read (which invites first-year composition students to interact with an author whose book they have all read), Georgetown University sociology professor Michael Eric Dyson, in his discussion of his 2020 book *Long Time Coming: Reckoning with Race in America*, cautioned about cancel culture.[4] When discussing its emergence among progressives, Dyson pinpointed its danger as "the inability to acknowledge that human beings are flawed and have foibles and make mistakes."[5] Echoing his ministerial training, he argued for belief in the possibility of redemption: "Even actions alone that feel hostile may ultimately be redemptive . . . We should be redeemed. We should redeem each other. We should have enough space to have nuance and complication and [to] overcome the things we do that are horrible."[6] To those who would too quickly jump to condemn others, Dyson advised: "Slow down . . . Give somebody a chance to develop . . . to do the wrong thing, then do the right thing."[7] If they do the right thing, that is great. If they do not, well, that will soon be evident. To such ends, he advocated for classrooms in which a wide variety of views are engaged and interrogated even as he admitted that such discussions are difficult, rife with possibilities for mistakes. Given my interest in rhetorical listening, particularly my interest in pausing to reflect rather than rushing to judgment, Dyson's comments resonate with me and seem to travel across political spectra.

Take, for example, the case of comedian Stephen Colbert. As *New Yorker* writer Jay Caspian Kang explains, Colbert was subject to a #CancelColbert campaign for a satiric but a-contextual tweet about Asians.[8] When asked about cancel culture in a 2021 podcast interview, Colbert replied, "I can control my intention but not your interpretation. That said, [long pause] I also value humility, and that is something that I have not always associated with my work."[9] He delineates his responsibility as a comedian as "I never hide behind, 'It's just a joke.' "[10] But his main point in response to the question about cancel culture is: "I have come to believe that saying to historically marginalized people . . . 'You all gotta take a joke' is a little Olympian [or loftily detached]. You can say it, but I think it might be a little solipsistic to think that your intention is more important than the effect of your work"[11]—especially, he implies, when the *you* doing the intending belongs to a non-marginalized group. In short, while Colbert believes we can say anything we want, he emphasizes that we have to live with the consequences. Again, given my interest in rhetorical listening to better understand and, when necessary, to revise our actions, Colbert's reflections resonate with me and strike me as the kind of response Dyson calls for.

For *how we act and react in relation to others* is important. Our actions and reactions should be well thought out and grounded, according to Colbert, in humility and, according to Dyson, in the possibility of redemption. With these ideas in mind, writing classrooms may be imagined as spaces where students learn that what counts as knowledge and what counts as cultural currency change over time. For example, Ovid is no longer de facto in all literature surveys; in fact, the literature survey as a form of curricular delivery is being called into question. For another example, mode-based curricula are no longer de facto in composition courses; in fact, modes such as definition, classification, and comparison/contrast are being reimagined as they were originally used, as parts of Aristotle's twenty-eight common topics or habits of mind that can be combined within one text.[12] Bottom line: things change. But they usually change slowly through negotiations among people. Our current moment is encouraging quick change, understandably so. But as Dyson cautions, immediate moves to cancel just might need to be slowed down sometimes, especially for (writing) classroom discussions.

There are, of course, other problems/questions that teachers and students are also engaging at this contentious cultural moment. The following list offers only a few:

- How will we define *writing* in the twenty-first century—and what are the implications for the study of rhetoric in K–12 as well as in colleges and universities?
- How do we rethink standards that define *good writing* as well as best practices for teaching writing?
- How do we navigate impulses that attempt to essentialize identity politics?
- How do we rethink codeswitching as a pedagogical tactic?
- How do we ground feminism and feminist theory in the face of proliferating categories of sex and gender?
- What does the flailing economic model of public higher education indicate for the future of composition as a university requirement?
- What exactly does it mean *and what concrete actions will it take* to decolonize the writing classroom . . . and the university . . . and the world, for that matter?
- And how has the Covid-19 pandemic generated technologies, pedagogies, and, let's be honest, traumas that will forever change our lives in the academy?

Yes, the US is in the middle of a fraught cultural moment; so too is much of the world.

As global citizens, we honestly do not know where we will land on all the issues that confront us in different ways. Given our cultural moment, we have our work cut out for us as teachers of rhetoric and writing, as residents of nations, and as citizens of the world. Many of our problems are not new exactly; it is just that in our moment they take particular forms—and, frankly, assume a particular urgency. Our students know this, indeed feel this. So even if we all differ in how we answer the above questions (and countless other unstated ones) and in how we define problems and design solutions, we must find ways to live together and in harmony with the planet and all its inhabitants. An easy claim, but a challenging project to which humanities thinking should contribute.

In all the uncertainty haunting our current moment, one thing seems fairly certain to me. The question to debate is not *whether* the US should be a diverse nation: as biologists and cosmologists tell us, diversity is endemic to life and, frankly, always has been. The question to debate, rather, is *how* we as individuals, as nations, as a global community will respond to our diversity—specifically, to the diverse and competing cultural logics in which we function, cultural logics about people, nations, genders, sexualities, races, religions, aesthetics, education, financial systems, climate threats, etc., etc., etc. In answer to this question of *how,* former president Barack Obama offers optimism. When addressing attendees at a Bill and Melinda Gates Foundation event, he exhorted, "Your response has to be to reject cynicism and reject pessimism and push forward, with a certain infectious and relentless optimism . . . Not blind optimism, not one that ignores the scale and scope of our challenges, but that hard-earned optimism, that's rooted in the stories of very real progress that have occurred throughout human history."[13]

Riffing on the former president, I argue that what is needed at this point are pedagogies of optimism (even though, and perhaps because, at this particular moment burnout is very, very real). What are examples of pedagogies of optimism?

I think of Notre Dame composition professor John Duffy, who in 2021 called for students and teachers to participate in a writing initiative called Write to Vote (WTV). As Duffy explains, "WTV will encourage student writing on the subject of voting rights, broadly defined. Students may write on historical topics, such as essays addressing the women's suffrage movement, or on contemporary issues, such as the effects of gerrymandering. While participating institutions will define for themselves the types of writing students undertake, the primary motivation for WTV is encouraging students to write op-eds on voting-related issues that writers can submit for publication in local and campus newspapers and on various social media platforms. In this way does WTV seek to inform students and non-students about the critical importance of protecting voting rights."[14]

I also think of Anishinaabekwe and SUNY environmental biology professor Robin Wall Kimmerer who calls for her students and, really, for all of us to reorient our relationships with the land. In her book *Braiding Sweetgrass,* she recounts a field trip with biology students to the Great Smoky Mountains: "I had given them so much information, all the patterns and processes laid on so thick as to obscure the most important truth. . . . How will people ever care for the fate of moss spiders if we don't teach students to recognize the world as gift"[15]—as *gift* that offers us both sustenance and lessons for living. In this way, Kimmerer's work introduces the term *gift* into discourses of biology. We should introduce it into the discourses of composition and rhetoric as well.

When performing pedagogies of optimism to enact changes in the classroom and beyond, students and teachers may find it useful to proceed by performing a generosity of spirit, granting goodwill when ascribing motives to others, being honest about what is and is not possible, and embracing a willingness to do better because, as I have heard so often these days, we have all made mistakes and we will all make more. But as I have tried to teach my daughter, mistakes (both our own and others') need not be imagined as failures that determine our identities for all time; rather, mistakes are opportunities to learn and to do better.

So what gifts did writing this foreword to *Composition and Rhetoric in Contentious Times* offer me?

Humility. Redemption. Optimism. My new trifecta of tropes . . . and hopes.

NOTES

1. Glenn, *Rhetorical Feminism and This Thing Called Hope*.
2. "Cancel Culture," Dictionary.com.
3. Burrows, *Rhetorical Crossover*; Blankenship, *Changing the Subject*; Flores, "Between Abundance and Marginalization," 4–24.
4. Dyson, *Long Time Coming*.
5. Dyson, "Discussion of *Long Time Coming*."
6. Dyson, "Discussion of *Long Time Coming*."
7. Dyson, "Discussion of *Long Time Coming*."
8. Kang, "The Campaign to 'Cancel' Colbert."
9. Colbert, "Stephen Colbert Talks Cancel Culture."
10. Colbert, "Stephen Colbert Talks Cancel Culture."
11. Colbert, "Stephen Colbert Talks Cancel Culture."
12. Aristotle, *On Rhetoric*, 194, 196, 198.
13. Mejia, "Barack Obama Says You Should Embrace 'Relentless Optimism.'"
14. John Duffy, personal email, November 29, 2021.
15. Kimmerer, *Braiding Sweetgrass*, 221.

REFERENCES

Aristotle. *On Rhetoric: A Theory of Civic Discourse*. Trans. George Kennedy. Oxford, UK: Oxford University Press, 1991.

Blankenship, Lisa. *Changing the Subject: A Theory of Rhetorical Empathy*. Logan: Utah State University Press, 2019.

Burrows, Cedric. *Rhetorical Crossover: The Black Presence in White Culture*. Pittsburgh, PA: University of Pittsburgh Press, 2020.

Colbert, Stephen. "Stephen Colbert Talks Cancel Culture, Dave Chappelle, and the Insurrection." *Offline with Jon Favreau*, November 21, 2021. https://www.youtube.com/watch?v=KJopQ3vPmkk.

Duffy, John. Personal email. November 29, 2021.

Dyson, Michael Eric. "Discussion of *Long Time Coming*." ASU Common Read. Hosted by Mitchell Jackson and Safiya Sinclair. Uploaded by Arizona State University Department of English, November 1, 2021. https://www.youtube.com/watch?v=ObWk4_Ezktg.

Dyson, Michael Eric. *Long Time Coming: Reckoning with Race in America*. Manhattan, NY: St. Martin's, 2020.

Flores, Lisa. "Between Abundance and Marginalization: The Imperative of Racial Rhetorical Criticism." *Review of Communication* 16, no. 1 (2016): 4–24.

Glenn, Cheryl. *Rhetorical Feminism and This Thing Called Hope.* Carbondale: Southern Illinois University Press, 2018.
Kang, Jay Caspian. "The Campaign to 'Cancel' Colbert." *New Yorker,* March 30, 2014. https://www.newyorker.com/news/news-desk/the-campaign-to-cancel-colbert.
Kimmerer, Robin Wall. *Braiding Sweetgrass: Indigenous Wisdom, Scientific Knowledge, and the Teachings of Plants.* Minneapolis, MN: Milkweed, 2015.
Mejia, Zomeena. "Barack Obama Says You Should Embrace 'Relentless Optimism' to Be Successful." *CNBC Make It,* September 22, 2017. https://www.cnbc.com/2017/09/22/barack-obama-says-you-should-embrace-relentless-optimism.html.

COMPOSITION AND RHETORIC
IN CONTENTIOUS TIMES

INTRODUCTION

Rachel McCabe and Jennifer Juszkiewicz

We live in a moment of national polarization. While a number of key moments in American history have been marked by ideological and political differences, the *feeling* of division has hit a high point.[1] Over the past forty years, the political landscape of the United States has shifted, with citizens becoming both calcified in their support of their chosen political party and simultaneously more afraid of their party's opposition.[2] In the process, the political has also become the personal as Americans increasingly consider political party membership a key piece of an individual's identity.[3] The implications of this polarization for the teaching of writing have compounded: some students are increasingly concerned that their college courses are indoctrinating them into "leftist" thinking, while others fear their universities are condoning the right by allowing Republicans to engage in debate or dialogue on their campus.[4]

This polarity extends to the interpretation of major events, including the 2016 and 2020 elections, the #MeToo and Black Lives Matter Movements, the January 6, 2021, attack on the US Capitol, and the Covid-19 pandemic. As one of our contributors notes, the elections had the effect of both freezing family discussions and electrifying media coverage.[5] The #MeToo and Black Lives Matter Movements began in this media environment, as they seek to uncover, come to terms with, and stop violence and injustice. Retelling history is burdensome work, though, especially when facts themselves are up for debate. Unlike national traumas such as the assassination of President John F. Kennedy or the terrorist attacks of September 11, the 2021 attack on the US Capitol was not unanimously considered a tragedy; further, the Covid-19 pandemic has not been collectively considered a problem requiring federal intervention.

Many Americans see these events as a necessary step in the fight toward freedom and fair representation, making it difficult to engage with such monumental issues in the writing classroom—classrooms where communication methods and rhetorical strategies are at the core of most curricula. That said, to ignore such moments is to do our students a great injustice. Composition courses, designed to help students find their voices and enter the academic community, often hinge on building complex arguments that acknowledge multiple perspectives and voices, trust reputable sources, and effectively communicate student ideas about the world beyond the classroom. These pedagogical choices, then, are fraught at every turn, particularly for non-tenured university faculty.

Therefore, at its core, this collection responds to the problems of our polarized world for students, faculty, and administrators in higher education. While previous collections in rhetoric and composition have contended with major historical shifts, this collection considers the political *and* educational factors of the last decade while seeing these changes not as temporary obstacles but as sites of learning that will help us navigate future challenges. Authors in this collection look to break down division in favor of models and practices that encourage compassionate exploration to help students work through ambiguity and reductive logics. The focus of many of these chapters is explicit binary thinking: the classroom versus the larger community, the traditional essay versus multimodal production, academic text versus real-world artifact, personal identities versus public ones, faculty versus administration, or fiscal responsibility versus humanism. However, others look at incendiary but less explicit themes of division, exclusion, or oversimplification. Regardless of specific focus, each of the chapters in this collection seeks to break down assumed divisions or assumptions to find common ground through best practices for all members of the educational community.

In the process, *Composition and Rhetoric in Contentious Times* poses critical questions of representation, accessibility, social justice, affect, and labor to evaluate and better understand the futures of composition and rhetoric. This collection considers how the multiple current crises of and surrounding composition and rhetoric can be met in the near future with generosity and cautious optimism. In differing ways, each chapter provides an answer to the question, "How can our courses help students become stronger writers while contending with current social, environmental, and ethical questions posed by the world around them?" Authors consider this question from numerous perspectives, recognizing the important ways power and privilege impact our varying means of addressing this question. In doing so, authors engage with social constructivist, critical, critical race, socioeconomic, and activist pedagogies. This collection includes contributors from diverse institutions and utilizes both rhetorical theory and pedagogical case studies to propose answers to the current concerns about the longevity of the humanities.

Composition and Rhetoric in Contentious Times addresses our current national and global context; it is also a testament to how rhetoric and composition has long been preparing students to become engaged global citizens. The scholars in this collection have been building their pedagogy in a crucible of pressures that certainly predate the 2016 election—the market pressures of the Great Recession, the contraction of the humanities and higher education generally. These contributors and their work are evidence of how the field is and has been committed to pedagogy that meets students where they are, that celebrates students and faculty for their neuro-, cultural, racial, gender, economic, and linguistic diversity. We have far to go, each contributor acknowledges, but we have a great deal on which to build.

This collection offers comprehensive, innovative approaches for socially attuned learning in this complex environment, approaches that support faculty, administrator, and student development. Relying on both theory and practice, this collection centers writing courses within the wider university and society, as the field of composition and rhetoric has changed dramatically in the last decade. In addition to the curricular debates that have been occurring for decades, shifts in teaching modalities have necessitated new types of learning for both instructors and students. While these changes have occurred, dramatic fluctuations in course enrollment have put additional pressure on faculty to justify their methods of instruction. These localized questions are also mirrored by major institutional shifts. The humanities, where many writing courses are located, are increasingly underfunded. Departments and schools are merging or being eliminated in record numbers.[6] All of these challenges raise questions about the importance and place of writing courses and writing instructors.

Composition and Rhetoric in Contentious Times considers the larger questions about equity, representation, and accessibility highlighted by the tragedies of 2020. The Covid-19 pandemic, the murders of George Floyd and many other people of color at the hands of police, more gun violence than ever before,[7] and a record-breaking number of natural disasters across the United States highlighted the severity and immediacy of our national dysfunction and its impact on the globe. These events directly affected universities: many universities moved online, some students and faculty went on strike, and schools across the country trimmed operational costs to run on a deficit.[8] While this collection addresses the impacts of these events on higher education, authors also look at this pivotal moment as an opportunity for growth, a chance to implement major changes to our educational infrastructure and theory to address underlying problems. In addressing the challenges of binary thinking, our hope is that a more generous model can be championed by the field of composition and rhetoric. This collection looks forward to a vision of higher education that has learned from the mistakes of the early 2000s and 2010s and creates a more inclusive, supportive, and just educational space.

Composition and Rhetoric in Contentious Times is ordered telescopically: beginning with broad, disciplinary concerns and then moving into specific programmatic, curricular, and classroom-based strategies and approaches. In the process, this collection offers best practices to support administrators and instructors to empower students to write effectively and prepare for their role as global citizens.

SECTION ONE: CRITICAL INTERROGATIONS

This collection begins by asking wide-ranging questions about the discipline's position in and responsibility to the wider world. The chapters here look at how rhetoric and composition must continue to assert its importance in higher education and reckon with the place of public, political discourse in our classrooms. These chapters utilize a historical perspective to argue for the discipline's positioning in public discourse about literacy now and into the future.

Chapter 1, "Composition, Critics, and Care Work: An Undisciplined Reflection on Disciplinary Expertise," by Jacob Babb and William Duffy, calls for a rethinking of composition and rhetoric's ownership of student writing. The authors examine the kinds of uninformed arguments about students' writing that frequently appear in venues such as the *Chronicle of Higher Education* and *Inside Higher Education*. Rather than seeing these prompts as proof of a lack of education about student writing, the authors provide a look at what it might mean to respond to both students and public statements on writing with care. Their call for "care work" in the classroom and outside it stresses that disciplinarity be recognized while including the knowledge other fields have generated, and continue to generate, about how to best support student writers.

The second chapter, "Trust, Truth, and the Erosion of Public Discourse: The Virtue of Reality in the First-Year Writing Classroom," by Matthew S. S. Johnson, is written from the perspective of an educator in the midst of a crisis of truth. Johnson resists the lure of handling "fake news," "alternative facts," and "junk science" with anything less than scare quotations. He shows how the terms worked their way into his own classroom, affecting his students' engagement and his teaching practice and theory. In the end, Johnson calls us all to action: if we are to challenge and reverse the trends toward rhetorical and political divisiveness, the treatment of facts as "facts," he contends, writing instructors must accept the political nature of the classroom and their responsibility as educators to teach students to recognize truth as such.

Such recognition—of truth, of each other, of the political nature of the classroom—carries into Christina V. Cedillo's chapter, "Writing with Our Bodies: Recovering Pathos through Critical Embodiment Pedagogy." Cedillo reweaves the history of rhetoric, showing how it has tried to capture and control the body even as it elides, hides, and shames the body. Building on critical race theory and disability theory, Cedillo explores how the body is necessary for memory. The body enables a more fulsome accounting of living, teaching, and learning in the midst of diverse social, cultural, political, and material forces that both include and exclude some scholars, some students. Without such an honest accounting, Cedillo argues, composition and rhetoric abandons the body, allowing it to continue as a whitestream nonentity. Such abandonment is an erasure of the violence against those who have been marginalized, differentiated, or punished due to their bodies.

SECTION TWO: CAREFUL LEADERSHIP

There is a risk in a collection such as this to think that the current, highly pressurized moment is a surprise. The truth is, many of our challenges and many of our strengths are sedimentary. Composition and rhetoric has long provided the educational background for writing program administrators, writing center directors, and committee/department directors because of their theoretical grounding in civic engagement and social responsibility. This section shows how this training ground needs to be approached more praxically, rather than assuming that either theory or practice can fully support the development of future administrators. The authors in this second section note that such administrative work requires the same deployment of theoretically responsive, civic-minded, ethical, and pragmatic pedagogies as does classroom teaching.

"Continuing Writing across the Curriculum Programs amid the Contraction of Higher Education: Vision, Mission, and Strategy," by Christopher Basgier, details the ongoing demographic and structural disruptions in higher education and considers the role writing across the curriculum (WAC) can play amid those changes. The ongoing contraction of higher education has manifested as disinvestment in public colleges and college closures. Simultaneously, higher education is witnessing changes in student demographics in terms of race, ethnicity, and age. Basgier demonstrates how the WAC program at Auburn University expanded its purview beyond writing-intensive courses and writing-enriched curricula by engaging actively with high-impact practices (HIPs).

In "Building an Affective Infrastructure to Lead Writing Programs," by Nicole Khoury, Nicholas Behm, and Sherry Rankins-Robertson, the authors address the gap in research on mental wellness for writing program administrators and instructors. This chapter responds to this situation, offering ways to help graduate students—a particularly vulnerable demographic within higher education—develop a sustainable work life by theorizing and describing a pedagogy of self-care that can be integrated in writing program administration and composition theory graduate courses. The authors build on the rhetoric of vulnerability and rhetorical empathy to offer strategies for cultivating wellness and an administrative philosophy of self-care.

Laura Sparks and Kim Jaxon negotiate administrative and pedagogical priorities in their chapter, "On Nonscalability and Transformative Relationships in the First-Year Composition 'Jumbo.'" They describe a course at their institution called the "Jumbo," a large-enrollment model of composition instruction that is premised on distributed learning among a community of students, mentors, and instructors. Sparks and Jaxon push back against the pressure to make such models a matter of scalability. The Jumbo is not scalable: it is a re-conception of a writing community model that creates new possibilities for students' participation and authorization, mentors' professional development, and instructors' engagement. This model enables those in the course to take up, together, meaningful issues and questions about both the content of the course and the writing process itself. Sparks and Jaxon's model offers possibilities for rethinking the field's adherence to small class sizes as the ideal writing and learning communities, offering a way to extend the students' action-oriented engagement beyond a class of eighteen or twenty or even thirty into a class of ninety and into a campus and local community of many more.

SECTION THREE: DRAWING TOGETHER

Composition and rhetoric's curriculum has long been an interdisciplinary conversation: writing courses are often designed by scholars with differing pedagogical and theoretical investments. Our students come from across the university and, potentially, the community. The scholars in this section demand that writing courses come to terms with the existing links between our students and our community. They also consider composition and rhetoric as a site that can bridge disjunctions within K–12 education.

"Rooting Our Teaching in the Change around Us: Growing an Anti-Recist, Community-Interdependent Course Model" by Zapoura Newton-Calvert examines the "intentional adaptation" process occurring in the community-based Social Justice in K–12 Education Capstone course at Portland State University in response to a convergence of simultaneous and interwoven pandemics (Covid-19 and racism/white supremacy). Informed by adrienne maree brown's emergent strategy models and Ibram X. Kendi's work on anti-racism, this writing describes emerging practices; the way remote learning encouraged a positive breakdown of traditional roles; the impact of a focus on racial and literacy justice on the writing, editing, and learning processes in the course; and the relationship building required to allow deep inquiry and accountability to ourselves and each other.

Anna Barritt and Kalyn Prince argue that composition and rhetoric scholars need to speak *with* rather than speak *to* or *about* those in the working class. In their chapter, "Writing with the Working Class: The Future of Public Rhetoricians," Prince and Barritt suggest two settings where the field can engage with these publics: the classroom and public, local arenas of concern. They rely on their own experience as scholars from working-class backgrounds to explore the first, and they use the example of Oklahomans' debates about fracking to explore the second. They prompt their students to reconnect with and contribute to their home publics, they encourage public-facing scholarship, and they advocate for revising graduate student pedagogical training to embrace a future as public humanitarians. They hail rhetoric and composition, as the discipline that trains scholars to analyze and communicate, to take up the standard of serving as activists within our own communities and training our students to do the same.

In "Generative Combination: A Guiding Principle for the Future of Composition," Matthew Overstreet argues that the future of composition entails generative combination. To meet modern literacy challenges, he claims that writers need familiarity with a variety of genres and modes. Integrally, they also need to be able to deploy such tools in combination to create wholes larger than the sum of their parts. A similar logic applies to writing instruction. Writing teachers shouldn't see themselves as teaching either academic writing or non-academic multimodal forms. Instead, we should teach both and do so in ways that allow for synergy between genres and modes. Toward this end, he suggests that transmediation—the translation of meaning between sign systems—might be of particular use. The act of translating meaning from textual, academic forms to popular multimodal forms, for instance, can make real the varied affordances of mode and genre. It can also reveal points of synergy between disparate forms, thus helping move composition beyond a simplistic text/multimodal binary.

SECTION FOUR: WRITING OUR WAY BACK

In the final section of this collection, authors are thinking critically about the writing that happens in writing courses. They consider how to keep that writing authentically reflective of students' complex and evolving thoughts. They are also concerned with the voices and narratives we invite into our classrooms. The aim of all four chapters here is to revise the way students engage with texts through writing, which is the heart of the discipline of rhetoric and composition.

While many of the chapters in this collection embrace the discipline, Hannah J. Rule uses her chapter, "A Future without Thesis Statements," to suggest that we move on from that history. Specifically, she argues that we should move on from the reductive, limiting practice of teaching students to write thesis statements. She acknowledges the difficulty of questioning what is perhaps one of the most universalized features of composition writing instruction; however, as thesis statement logic is at the heart of reductive, formulaic, conformist writing, she argues that such abandonment is necessary. Not only does requiring thesis statements teach students to contain their writing within arbitrarily proscribed limits, it also demonizes other forms of effective communication and potential approaches to writing instruction. Moving beyond thesis statements opens writing to possibilities, exploration, and uncertainty. It allows students to work within the complex and, yes, uncertain world in which they actually live.

Elizabeth Kleinfeld joins Rule in holding the field to a higher, more just standard. Traditional citation practices have remained abelist, racist, and patriarchal despite recent, limited efforts to incorporate more diverse authors in our field through other avenues (expanding the canon, for example). Kleinfeld's chapter, "Teaching toward a More Just Citation Practice," relies on multiple authors to uncover the layered biases that continue in current citation practices. She advocates for incorporating more diverse voices in our bibliographies. Her argument asks for more than a simple shift in appearances, though. She pushes us to take this work to heart, coming to terms with it and integrating it substantively into our arguments and considerations of who we are and what we can do. If citations are a genealogy of thought, Kleinfeld demonstrates that our current work is stunted by a disciplinary resistance to acknowledging our scholarly relations.

In "Film in the Interdisciplinary Composition Classroom," Rachel McCabe explores the opportunities afforded composition and rhetoric as a field with a fluctuating location within higher education. This interdisciplinary location and the diverse people who teach writing courses have led to the use of interdisciplinary texts. This chapter explores one such medium—film—and its beneficial relationship to student writing within the interdisciplinary structure of the modern and future composition course. McCabe considers the ways theories of identification can illustrate the power and potential of writing about film. To do so, she looks at the pedagogical maneuvers necessary to successfully bring both superficially simple films and more complex works into the writing classroom.

Jessica Edwards's chapter, "Learning from Black Teachers: Ida B. Wells-Barnett and Implementing Critical Engagement Strategies in Writing Classrooms," looks at the ways the personal and the professional are inextricably linked for Black instructors. By studying the pedagogical practices as well as the communication techniques of Ida B. Wells, Edwards posits that contemporary scholars can see both a model for Black pedagogies and a look at the work of an early technical communicator. Using critical race theory's understanding of counterstory, Edwards demonstrates how rhetorical understandings of story in Wells's work provide both an important text for teaching and an empowering model for educators.

CONCLUSION

The work collected here has grown over time, beginning from conversations at the Futures of Rhet/Comp Conference in the spring of 2019. At that conference, hosted by John Schilb and Christine Farris, scholars—a few of whom also contributed to this collection—sought to build a new vision for the future. Deborah Holdstein noted in her presentation surveying *College Composition and Communication* that many of the concerns first published in the journal are concerns we still share: questions about diversity and access, instructor and student control, racism, and sexism. She called on those present and the discipline more widely to be as attentive to our histories as to our futures, as each of the contributors in this collection does as well. Each author here refuses to concede the field, even when the obstacles are so many and so high. At the same conference, Krista Ratcliffe asked a pivotal question, one this collection continues to seriously consider as we look ahead. It is a question about the audacity of foresight: how can we think we can prepare students for a future we can't predict? Many conversations in the field have hinged on determining what skills, what knowledge our students will need once they leave our classes, our institutions. How can we prepare them for their majors? For their careers? For a world on fire? In the end, we cannot. We cannot know their futures. As Ratcliffe implies, that is not the point. Our task is to know the kind of world we want to build from the materials we see around us and to teach students to build as well. Reading the writing on the wall isn't the question at hand; the question at hand is how to write for ourselves and with our students.

Our goal is to leave readers of *Composition and Rhetoric in Contentious Times* with a sense of this cautious optimism, with a commitment to finding out *how* to move forward. We and our contributing authors recognize the obstacles, which include (but aren't limited to) increasingly limited enrollment numbers, pressure from administrators, and students who struggle to see the value of a college education in a world plagued by continued racism, sexism, ableism, and economic disparity. We simultaneously see opportunities for growth and evolution in our field. In acknowledging the deep polarization of our current sociopolitical moment, we hope this collection provides strategies to reveal complexity and embrace compassion in every aspect of our work.

NOTES

1. Najle and Jones, "American Democracy in Crisis."
2. Bishop, "If We Can't Polka Together, We Can't Govern Together"; Pew Research Center, "Amid Campaign Turmoil, Biden Holds Wide Leads on Coronavirus."
3. Fredrick, "Welcome to the Fractured States of America."
4. Flaherty, "Students, Professors, and Politics"; Wermiel and Blackman, "Thwarting Speech on College Campuses," 20–21.
5. Johnson, chapter 2, this volume.
6. Lederman, "The Number of Colleges Continues to Shrink."
7. Chiwaya, "Gun Violence Is Up"; Della Cava and Stucka, "Mass Shootings Hit a Record High in 2020"; Thebault and Rindler, "Shootings Never Stopped during the Pandemic."
8. Snyder, "Haverford College Students Launched a Strike Last Fall after a Racial Reckoning"; Schifrin and Tucker, "College Financial Grades 2021."

REFERENCES

Bishop, Bill. "If We Can't Polka Together, We Can't Govern Together." CNN, November 21, 2019. https://www.cnn.com/2019/11/21/opinions/self-segregation-america-geography-bishop/index.html.

Chiwaya, Nigel. "Gun Violence Is Up; It's Been Up for More than a Year." NBC News, April 26, 2021. https://www.nbcnews.com/news/amp/ncna1265201.

Della Cava, Marco, and Mike Stucka. "Mass Shootings Hit a Record High in 2020; Can COVID-19 Vaccines Bring Peace in 2021?" *USA Today*, February 26, 2021. https://www.usatoday.com/story/news/nation/2021/02/26/mass-shootings-soared-covid-black-lives-matter-fears-2020/6784339002/.

Flaherty, Colleen. "Students, Professors, and Politics." *Inside Higher Education*, March 3, 2020. https://www.insidehighered.com/news/2020/03/03/some-students-do-feel-political-pressure-their-professors-few-change-their-views.

Fredrick, Yaffa. "Welcome to the Fractured States of America." CNN, 2019. https://www.cnn.com/interactive/2019/11/opinions/fractured-states-of-america/part-one-fredrick/.

Lederman, Doug. "The Number of Colleges Continues to Shrink." *Inside Higher Education*, August 2, 2021. https://www.insidehighered.com/news/2021/08/02/number-colleges-shrinks-again-including-publics-and-private-nonprofits.

Najle, Maxine, and Robert Jones. "American Democracy in Crisis: The Fate of Pluralism in a Divided Nation." Public Religion Research Institute, February 19, 2019. https://www.prri.org/research/american-democracy-in-crisis-the-fate-of-pluralism-in-a-divided-nation/.

Pew Research Center. "Amid Campaign Turmoil, Biden Holds Wide Leads on Coronavirus, Unifying the Country." Pew Research Center, October 2020. https://www.pewresearch.org/politics/2020/10/09/voters-feelings-about-the-election-and-possible-outcomes//#many-see-lasting-harm-if-the-other-partys-candidate-wins-in-november.

Schifrin, Matt, and Hank Tucker. "College Financial Grades 2021: Will Your Alma Mater Survive Covid?" *Forbes*, February 22, 2021. https://www.forbes.com/sites/schifrin/2021/02/22/college-financial-grades-2021-will-your-alma-mater-survive-covid/?sh=7b8c5bf84916.

Snyder, Sam. "Haverford College Students Launched a Strike Last Fall after a Racial Reckoning; the Impact Still Lingers." *Philadelphia Inquirer*, April 25, 2021. https://www.inquirer.com/news/haverford-college-strike-division-racism-wallace-20210425.html.

Thebault, Reis, and Danielle Rindler. "Shootings Never Stopped during the Pandemic: 2020 Was the Deadliest Gun Violence Year in Decades." *Washington Post*, March 23, 2021. https://www.washingtonpost.com/nation/2021/03/23/2020-shootings/?outputType=amp.

Wermiel, Stephan, and Josh Blackman. "Thwarting Speech on College Campuses." *Human Rights Magazine: American Bar Association* 43 no. 4 (n.d.): 20–21. https://www.americanbar.org/groups/crsj/publications/human_rights_magazine_home/the-ongoing-challenge-to-define-free-speech/thwarting-speech-on-college-campuses/.

SECTION ONE

Critical Interrogations

1
COMPOSITION, CRITICS, AND CARE WORK
An Undisciplined Reflection on Disciplinary Expertise

Jacob Babb and William Duffy

In November 2020, *Inside Higher Ed* (*IHE*) published an essay vaguely titled "Next-Generation Writing Instruction" that included this not-so-vague sub-headline: "How to Bring All Students to an Acceptable Level of Writing Proficiency Cost-Effectively."[1] The responses by writing studies specialists on social media were predictably harsh. "Oh goodness," begins one of the more tempered comments we saw on Twitter, a comment that ends with a reminder about the value of writing across the curriculum programs. Another comment, one less tempered, ends with this retort: "IHE is trash, y'all." This latter comment reflects what ended up being a common refrain, indicating frustration that *IHE* would publish this essay in the first place. As another commenter pointed out, "Next-Generation Writing Instruction" is just the latest iteration of an essay published regularly in venues like *IHE* and the *Chronicle of Higher Education* (*CHE*) that either purports to discover pedagogical strategies compositionists have been using for decades or bemoans the fact that college students don't get enough grammar instruction. As this last commenter pointed out, "Next-Generation Writing Instruction," an essay written by a history professor conspicuously unaware that the discipline of rhetoric and composition exists, manages to do both.

As Donald McQuade reminds us, "Composition studies remains one of the few academic disciplines in which outsiders insist on naming and authorizing its activities, without accepting the intellectual responsibility—and institutional consequences—of doing so."[2] The frustration compositionists feel when our expertise seems to be either invisible or invalid in public discourse is hardly new. We understand this frustration, and we fully appreciate the desire our colleagues feel to gnash their teeth and tear out their hair when another contemporary instantiation of "Why Johnny Can't Write" pops up. *CHE* published a column less than a year prior to the above-mentioned essay titled "Why We Must Get Back to the Basics in Teaching Composition;"[3] the title says everything one needs to know about its argument. As with the *IHE* piece, many responses by compositionists directed criticism less toward the essay itself and more on *CHE* for publishing it. Setting aside the economics of "clicks" and "reads" to which these periodicals are beholden, do we expect such periodicals to stop publishing essays that a small number of readers who specialize in that subject area find questionable or shortsighted? Does expressing displeasure on social media or posting the occasional comment at the bottom of these pieces make a difference? While there may be epideictic value in some of these expressions of displeasure, surely it is fleeting. Indeed, such demonstrations may prove harmful, as professors' public displays may further alienate academics from the public, as Anna Barritt and Kalyn Prince argue in chapter 8 of this collection.

But these aren't our only two avenues for response. Not only can we write our own op-eds, we can also be more deliberate about how we market ourselves to the various publics with which we regularly engage. At least since the publication of Linda Adler-Kassner's *The Activist WPA* and Shirley K. Rose and Irwin Weiser's edited volume *Going Public*, compositionists have been encouraged to claim their disciplinary expertise as they engage with critics who don't understand or are otherwise unaware of what exactly writing studies specialists do. As Rita Malenczyk, Susan Miller-Cochran, Elizabeth Wardle, and Kathleen Blake Yancey note in *Composition, Rhetoric, and Disciplinarity*, "If we are a discipline, we have both a right and a responsibility to change popular understandings of and practices regarding writing."[4]

Consider, for instance, how Doug Hesse has modeled such public advocacy. "Complaints about student writing have a long lineage," notes Hesse in a 2017 essay published in *CHE* a few months after it published Joseph Teller's "Are We Teaching Composition All Wrong?" Hesse was frustrated with Teller's piece, and for good reason. In addition to doubling down on tired canards about students' inability to write clear sentences and how "social justice" has taken over composition curricula, Teller professes a naive view of student writing: not only is it possible to assess good writing from bad, he says, it's also not hard to teach students to write correctly. "I don't ignore the experience of individual teachers like Teller," Hesse concedes. "However, I can't let pass unchallenged general claims about the way 'we' are 'wrongly' teaching composition, especially when they so dramatically misrepresent, even ignore, the field they would aspire to correct."[5] A careful reading of Hesse's essay is as close to a master class as one could find on how to refute flawed arguments about the supposed inadequacy of college students' writing abilities. Not only does Hesse employ sound counterarguments to correct Teller's faulty claims, he does so without the tacit insults or character jabs that are characteristic of responses in social media posts or professional listserv discussions when pieces like Teller's get published.

With that said, how effective are arguments like Hesse's? Is such public writing capable of sufficiently countering the continual stream of publications like Teller's in ways that might prove persuasive? In this chapter, we sidestep such questions to instead suggest the value of what we're calling an "undisciplined" approach to public engagement, one that focuses less on our disciplinary expertise and more on the values we bring to our work—including how these values manifest in practices that *reflect* but don't necessarily *claim* our expert status as teachers and scholars of writing. At the same time, we forward what might for some readers be an impertinent argument about our disciplinary expertise—namely, that our field does not "own" the academic study of writing, let alone the teaching of it. We put "own" in scare quotes because this argument harks back to another piece of writing by Hesse, his 2005 Conference on College Composition and Communication (CCCC) chair's address, in which he reflects on the question of who owns "the content and pedagogy of composition."[6] As he sees it, "Those who *teach* writing must affirm that we, in fact, *own* it," a claim he follows with this qualification: "The question is what we should aspire to own—and how."[7] While we do question the ownership stakes Hesse claims about the teaching of writing, it's that second question about what "we" as disciplined insiders want disciplinary outsiders to understand about effective writing pedagogy that motivates our writing here.

We write this chapter after two years of the Covid-19 pandemic. The impact the pandemic has had on our pedagogical approaches, including the subsequent sharpening of our sense of the values at the heart of our discipline, only strengthens our sense that we need to put care at the core of what we do as writing instructors and that care should also be extended to how we respond to critics like Teller and Mintz. That is, we are not arguing for or against any one pedagogical approach. Instead, we advocate for writing teachers to commit to teaching with care, which includes promoting dispositions that inspire students to want to learn about writing. In fact, we believe the content of a writing course is secondary in importance to the dispositions toward writing that students develop. These dispositions, what we describe below in terms of care work, are what mark the "undisciplined" stance to public engagement that we argue for in this chapter.

In short, we argue that the teaching of writing has been and always will be an undisciplined enterprise—even within a robust and healthy academic discipline—that is at its best when instructors engage students with care and promote the values of risk taking and experimentation, both of which are necessary for developing confident students who can own their own development and identity as writers.

We first consider rhetoric and composition's proclivity for disciplinary self-exploration, in particular insiders' need to demonstrate their status as experts when responding to the kinds of public utterances about writing we describe above. We argue that this need has instilled in us a defensive posture that ultimately does not aid the discipline in its mission to improve writing instruction. Then, we present "undisciplined expertise" as a concept intended to reinvest experience with generative force within and beyond the field as disciplined insiders engage in public arguments about writing. Finally, we argue for approaching the teaching of writing as care work, which we believe is essential both to the discipline's pedagogical mission and to finding ways to make more effective arguments about writing instruction in public discourse.

MOVING FROM DEFENSIVE DISCIPLINARITY TO UNDISCIPLINED EXPERTISE

Before we explore undisciplined expertise, we acknowledge the long struggle of rhetoric and composition to garner recognition as a legitimate academic discipline. In the opening passage of their article about the Visibility Project, an effort to inscribe the disciplinarity of rhetoric and composition through recognition with the National Research Council (NRC) and the federal Classification of Instructional Programs (CIP), Louise Wetherbee Phelps and John M. Ackerman write that an enduring desire of scholars in rhetoric and composition "is for the academy and the public to acknowledge that what we do . . . is worthy of disciplinary status."[8] Phelps and Ackerman's work represents a significant breakthrough for the disciplinary recognition of our field. Receiving recognition as an academic discipline comes with important material benefits. For example, academics apply for funding at multiple levels, and having their disciplinary labor inscribed in recognizable codes makes it easier for members of the discipline to receive such funding.

As a pedagogically oriented field, rhetoric and composition has had its work cut out for it in cultivating the kinds of institutional and professional space necessary to be recognized as a discipline, and so far we have represented only a few of the teacher-scholars who have engaged these debates precisely because it is difficult to represent all the voices that have challenged or supported our disciplinarity over the past several decades. Among the most prominent examinations of our disciplinarity is Stephen M. North's *The Making of Knowledge in Composition*, a book in which he critiques the field's lack of a unified methodology and too much reliance on what he calls "lore." Janice M. Lauer characterizes rhetoric and composition as a "dappled discipline" because of its reliance on multiple approaches to research, noting that for rhetoric and composition scholars, "many of their most important problems can be properly investigated only with multiple research methods."[9] In other words, the field's methodological diversity has been used by some to challenge its disciplinarity and by others to clarify how it makes the field unique.[10]

One of the few constants in the scholarship on disciplinarity is an ongoing sense of identity crisis. In a reflection on how the field has evolved since North's critiques, Lance Massey notes that "who we are and what we do remain fuzzy, contestable categories."[11] Massey argues that as writing studies continues to grow, it should retain its self-reflexive habit to construct itself as an interdisciplinary field—something Karen Kopelson would say is likely given that scholars in rhetoric and composition are "unrivaled in our proclivity for self-examination."[12]

An additional complication in the disciplinary identity of rhetoric and composition is its long engagement with management and labor. Sidney Dobrin implicates the discipline in shaping itself as a "juggernaut in the American university" by convincing institutions there is "a need for a required course in writing, a need for large staffs of instructors to teach the required courses, and a need for a validated administrator to oversee these instructors."[13] Other scholars such as Donna Strickland, Collin Craig and Staci Perryman-Clark, Nancy Welch and Tony Scott, and Seth Kahn, William Lalicker, and Amy Lynch-Biniek argue that we must acknowledge the complex contextual situations of writing programs in institutions and our own direct involvement in the sustained casualization of academic labor, including the role of gender and race in that labor.[14] Disciplinarity, then, comes with significant challenges that shouldn't be ignored.

Because of the discipline's pedagogical roots, it's no surprise that dedication to both teaching and service is a source of resilience and pride for the discipline even as it binds us to exploitative labor practices. In a special issue of *College Composition and Communication* focused on "The Future of Rhetoric and Composition," Gregory G. Colomb writes, "No discussion of the future of composition—or its past, for that matter—can avoid the evident fact of our 'service' mission."[15] Colomb argues that our status as a service discipline complicates our disciplinary arguments. "When we use *service* to frame our thinking about who we are and our planning for what we do, we mislead both ourselves and others about our accomplishments and our possibilities,"[16] Colomb says, noting that when we publicly claim our service mission, "we and our work are too readily disrespected, both undervalued and undercompensated."[17]

For Keith Rhodes, composition professionals should unite around a branding strategy that conveys "the true nature of our best work," which "remains largely unknown by the public that, ultimately, pays for our services."[18] While Rhodes notes that we "should question and contest those trends to commodify higher education,"[19] rhetoric and composition "should understand them as of a piece with larger intellectual movements that many of us embrace."[20] Just as Colomb does, Rhodes insists we have a product (quality writing instruction) that we offer to customers (our students). While this transactional view might make some of us feel smarmy, we should defend this work and our expertise to do it. Or as Rhodes says, "Branding at its best and most effective can be conceived in part as treating customers as stakeholders in a common enterprise with sellers—a vision clearly compatible with teaching writing."[21]

Even though this brief overview of scholarship on rhetoric and composition's disciplinarity barely scratches the surface of work in this area, what matters is that writing studies practitioners have expended significant energy in justifying their place in academia. To be clear, we are not asserting that rhetoric and composition needs to surrender its proclivity for self-reflection; rather, we need to avoid allowing our deeply ingrained habit of disciplinary self-examination to shape our responses to criticisms that come from beyond our discipline.

We want to parse a crucial difference here. The disciplinary status of composition is paramount to its continued growth, but our concern is about reinvesting value in the experience writing teachers bring to their work, not just their disciplinary expertise. We assert that defaulting to a defensive posture about our expertise is rarely the best rhetorical strategy for engaging with public audiences around questions of writing instruction.

We have chosen to identify our approach to public debates about the teaching of writing by claiming a position of undisciplined expertise, a term we use in this particular context because we wish to highlight how the best practices we've adopted in our teaching stem less from the researched knowledge composition scholars have produced and more from the trial-and-error testing of that knowledge through experience in the classroom. That is, we acknowledge the important work of composition research, especially when it comes to understanding how writers develop through acts of revision, peer engagement, and critical reading practices. But we also acknowledge that writing is an idiosyncratic practice that becomes "disciplined" as we are enculturated into the various conventions and practices of those communities to which our writing is directed.

As scholars in rhetoric and composition, we do not ever want to dismiss the importance of disciplinary knowledge; ongoing research is vital to the field. Instead, we are suggesting that undisciplined expertise serves to provide a different perspective on public discourses about writing. We are advocating for a shift in how we think about ourselves as experts and how we feel called upon to defend that expertise. Undoubtedly, many of us have been called upon to defend our expertise in different ways, such as when we argue with administrators about the need to maintain lower course caps for first-year writing classes. But when it comes to engaging with publics outside these insider spaces, we think it is advantageous to step away from a defensive posture and ground such engagement in an ethics of care.

TEACHING WRITING AS CARE WORK

"Undisciplining" writing instruction is important for understanding some of the practices we believe make the most difference in encouraging the writing development of our students. Whether one utilizes a writing-about-writing approach, a literature approach, a rhetoric approach, or any other specific content-focused pedagogy, effective writing instructors understand that successful writers develop over time and across contexts. There's no single class, how-to book, or seminar series that can turn us into successful writers, just as there's no assignment sequence, textbook, or incentive structure that can convince us to exercise the creative muscles that ultimately contribute to our development as writers. Accordingly, we believe students are best served when courses are designed to cultivate the agency required to recognize and harness opportunities to compose as occasions to experiment and take risks.

Cultivating students' sense of agency is critical to their development as writers. Too often students have been enculturated to approach writing as something that is either "correct" or "incorrect," "good" or "bad"—ideas that not only misrepresent writing as a rhetorical activity but also demonstrate what Sheri Rysdam notes when she argues that "a deficit approach to writing pedagogy still abounds."[22] This deficit approach all but demands that students engage the writing they undertake in school as a "textual transaction," one through which they demonstrate to an instructor what they know or have learned.[23] In such a transactional context, it's difficult to parse what a student has learned from what a student has performed for a grade. But even when the performance is the point, such as when an instructor expects student writing to conform to a set of generic parameters, this doesn't change the fact that "one of the first lessons writers learn, one that may be either frustrating or inspiring, is that they will never have learned all that can be known about writing and will never be able to demonstrate all they do know about writing."[24] What Rose describes as the "imperfectability of writing ability" underscores the reality that just because a student might be able to effectively demonstrate their writerly chops in one context doesn't mean their writing will be effective in a different context.[25]

Indeed, it is because writing is an imperfectible skill that as instructors, both of us are more invested in helping students navigate this imperfectability as an opportunity to discover possibilities for what their writing can be and can do. In practical terms, this means we approach the courses we teach following the advice of Theodore Baird, the Amherst professor who is the subject of Robin Varnum's *Fencing with Words*: "The best we can do is treat writing—and the writer—with respect and imagination."[26] Popular fiction writer Stephen King offers similar, if perhaps sterner, advice in *On Writing*: "If you can take it [writing] seriously, we can do business."[27] We want our students to take writing seriously, but serious writing can and should leave space for creativity and play.

These might be easy concepts to invoke, but our experience tells us that in practice this kind of teaching is difficult and can hardly be standardized. As Tara Roeder and Roseanne Gatto write, "We don't believe in prescriptions or generalities; we believe in a localized, context-specific pedagogy where one size never fits all. And we fiercely value our students and the complex embodied knowledge they bring to our classroom."[28] Respecting students' "complex embodied knowledge" while also making room for imagination are the conditions around which we have come to imagine the teaching of writing as a kind of care work. We use the term care work not only because it speaks to Nel Noddings's (1984) well-known explication of an ethics of care and bell hooks's (2003) proposition that teaching is ultimately a caring profession but also because it speaks to the pedagogical commitments Catherine Denial (2020) promotes in "A Pedagogy of Kindness"—one of the chapters included in an open-access book that aims to remind instructors, per the editors' introduction, that no matter what or how we teach, "care has to be at the center of this work."[29]

The Covid-19 pandemic has made putting care at the center of our pedagogy that much more vital. When we proposed this essay in May 2020, college students and their instructors were wrapping up a semester marked by the sudden switch to remote instruction. Many instructors, including us, had to negotiate struggles that made teaching substantially more challenging—including the loss of childcare, layoffs and furloughs, prolonged illness, and, of course, the loss of friends and family members to the virus. As instructors struggled with their own physical and mental health challenges, many of them recognized that their students were experiencing the same struggles. Now as the pandemic shifts toward a new normal, we have no desire to return to a pre-Covid frame of mind in our teaching. That's because we (Jacob and Will) recognize that we're better educators when we approach teaching as care work. As bell hooks reminds us, "Students want us to see them as whole human beings with complex lives and experiences rather than simply as seekers after compartmentalized bits of knowledge."[30] In short, to teach writing from a position of care is to engage with students as whole human beings.

What does it mean for us to approach the teaching of writing as care work? First and foremost, it means we don't view students as antagonists. As Denial confesses, and as we can verify from our own experiences, much of our enculturation into postsecondary teaching taught us "to be on the lookout for plagiarism, to be vigilant for cheaters, to assume that the students wouldn't do the reading, and to expect to be treated as a cog in a consumerist machine."[31] We were also convinced that we needed to maintain strict attendance policies, including detailed and ableist expectations for class participation. Without such stringent behavioral standards, it is believed that students might take advantage of teachers or that our classes might lack "rigor," a term that over the past decade has become more commonplace in policy discussions about academic achievement. But we no longer believe rigor is something our teaching should aspire to. If anything, we are more inspired by Denial's commitment to kindness, which she says "as [a] pedagogical practice distills down to two simple things: believing people, and believing *in* people."[32]

Compositionists should hear traces of Peter Elbow's "believing game" analogy in Denial's description of a pedagogy of kindness. As Elbow explains, " 'Believing' is my shorthand for listening, affirming, entering into, trying to experience more fully, and restating—understanding ideas from the inside."[33] Believing *in* students, as Denial notes, "means seeing them as collaborators—believing they have valuable contributions to make to the way in which syllabi, assignments, and assessments are designed, and [have] life experiences that should be respected in the classroom."[34] We'll add to these descriptions about what it means to believe in our students and why an attitude of kindness is important for understanding the teaching of writing as care work.

First, we don't just agree with Denial that we should view students as collaborators; we also believe students should have opportunities to shape how a writing course plays out. There's no right or wrong way to go about this as long as we build in opportunities to listen to students. For example, in a recent technical communication course Will taught, students could choose from three project prompts in each unit, or they could propose their own. While offering three project opportunities per unit required more planning on Will's part, the payoff for students was obvious: they could select the projects that most appealed to them, increasing the potential that they would engage with those projects meaningfully.

Second, we believe students should have opportunities to experiment with their writing without also assuming added levels of anxiety about their performance in our courses. One way we do this is through the practice of un-grading, which is like the concept of labor-based grading in that it removes the burden of inventing generic standards against which to assess a student's work.[35] Gone are rubrics with point breakdowns, hairsplitting explanations for why a paper earned a B+ instead of an A, and arbitrary standards about what constitutes good writing from bad.[36] Too often, grades become "a false currency that, over time, seems to override students' intrinsic desire for mastery and personal sense of purpose."[37] Mitchell R. James describes grading as a "silent, one-way evaluation"[38] that always carries a load of hidden meanings and biases.[39] Our experience has so far confirmed what James says about how when grades are removed from the equation, "the desire to evade punishment or failure can dissolve into the desire to seek knowledge and learn something new."[40]

Third, we believe students are best served in our courses when we "abolish cop shit," as Jeffrey Moro phrased it in a viral blog post from February 2020. Cop shit, Moro explains, is "any pedagogical technique or technology that presumes an adversarial relationship between students and teachers"[41]—which includes plagiarism detection software like Turnitin, tracking students' activity on LMSs, remote proctoring services, and strict attendance policies that infantilize or might otherwise embarrass students. Not only do many of these technologies and policies create an antagonistic relationship between teachers and students; they limit the agency required to teach and learn. No one benefits from such an arrangement except the companies hawking these services. Shifting away from cop shit and toward care work undercuts an adversarial teacher-student relationship that advocates of plagiarism detection and similar surveillance services assume. Such a move also invites more room for experimentation and play. As Stephanie Vie argues when discussing the concept of remix, for example, "The advantage here of casting aside the hunt for plagiarists and embracing a remix culture is that we can embrace the idea that nothing we create will be entirely new and that's okay."[42]

As we say above, focusing on care work as a pedagogical framework doesn't shirk the best practices informed by research in writing studies. Indeed, we would argue that centering care work is not a radical suggestion, especially given the discipline's engagement with critical pedagogy. As Mike Rose memorably put it, "Students will float to the mark you set."[43] According to the authors of the *Elon Statement on Writing Transfer*, moreover, students benefit when instructors structure various "enabling practices" into the curriculum, including:

- Constructing writing curricula and classes that focus on study of and practice with concepts that enable students to analyze expectations for writing and learning within specific contexts. These include rhetorically-based concepts (such as genre, purpose, and audience);
- Asking students to engage in activities that foster the development of metacognitive awareness, including asking good questions about writing situations and developing heuristics for analyzing unfamiliar writing situations; and
- Explicitly modeling transfer-focused thinking and the application of metacognitive awareness as a conscious and explicit part of a process of learning.[44]

When instructors let students have a say over the "what" of the curriculum, even if that means simply giving them a range of options for completing assignments, those discussions can "enable students to analyze expectations for writing and learning within specific contexts." When students are free to compose and experiment with their writing without the pressure of grades, how much more potential does this open for encouraging students to recognize and "foster the development of metacognitive awareness"? Finally, when we don't marshal "cop shit" in our classes but instead treat students as curious, capable, complex human beings who deserve our trust and respect—when we believe and believe *in* our students, to echo Denial—we increase the efficacy of our efforts to promote "transfer-focused thinking and the application of metacognitive awareness."

The *Elon Statement* is a useful piece of scholarship—a *disciplined* resource—for any instructor interested in writing pedagogy because it emphasizes that disciplinary standards are not universal, which, as Linda Adler-Kassner and John Majewski explain, can come as a surprise to many educators: "This is especially true in regard to writing because faculty members sometimes regard writing as a universal skill applicable in all contexts rather than a series of particular disciplinary conventions."[45] If we acknowledge that writing is not a universal skill, it makes sense to acknowledge that *teaching* writing doesn't require a set of universal skills, let alone disciplinary credentials. Yes, we believe trained compositionists who have accrued expert knowledge are inevitably better qualified and prepared writing teachers. But we don't believe these credentials alone are what make a quality writing instructor.

CONCLUSION: WHAT ABOUT COMPOSITION'S CRITICS?

We began this chapter by considering how rhetoric and composition specialists respond to critics of student writing in public discourse. Disciplined insiders often read such articles as attacks on the discipline, while the authors of those articles often seem oblivious to our field. We have argued that responding from a defensive posture does not help the discipline. Instead, we posit that writing studies would be better served by responding from an undisciplined expertise by drawing on the deep well of our pedagogical experiences. Such a stance does not call for us to surrender our disciplinary expertise but rather to consider how to frame our responses less defensively and more generously.

Instead, we suggest framing our responses based on our pedagogical experience grounded in care work. To return to the opening of our chapter, what happens if we extend a similar ethics to the critics of composition who publish essays like "Next-Generation Writing Instruction," essays that can and often do come across as dismissive of the care work we discuss here? We are suggesting that if such critics want to complain about student writing, they need to invest in learning about teaching writing; as disciplinary insiders, we can invite critics to learn. Consider this example from outside the discipline, which demonstrates an openness to learn about writing pedagogy. In her introduction to *Writing*

Anthropology, Carole McGranahan reminds readers that "there is no right way to write, no magic formula," but what does matter is experience and practice.[46] She continues, "Writing moves your thinking forward, writing improves your writing. The more you do it, the more you think about it; the more you seek out guidance, the better your writing gets."[47] McGranahan isn't a comp/rhet insider, but she and the dozens of anthropologists who contributed essays to *Writing Anthropology* have pedagogical perspectives about writing that warrant consideration and engagement across disciplinary lines.

Likewise, for the past several years, Jacob has facilitated a faculty writing program on his campus that uses psychology professor Paul J. Silvia's *How to Write a Lot* as a central text. Silvia notes in the preface to the second edition that his specialized knowledge informs his approach to the book because the book's purpose is to encourage writers to change their dispositions toward writing: "Helping people change, fortunately, is what we do in the meddlesome field of psychology, my intellectual home."[48] Certainly, we can quibble with some of the epistemological assumptions Silvia makes about how writing works, but the text has helped many faculty writers become more productive. Like the authors in *Writing Anthropology*, Silvia is not a comp/rhet specialist, but he is teaching writing. These are just two examples, of course, and they do not touch on the day-to-day work faculty members do on our campuses to incorporate writing instruction into their courses.[49] But by extending the frame of care work beyond our classrooms to colleagues in our institutions, we can find ways to help faculty learn more about teaching writing, and we as the "specialists" can learn more about writing and writing instruction in the process.

Our discipline is rooted in the teaching of writing, the commonality that holds together multiple threads of composition and rhetoric. Whether we are teaching first-year writing, professional or technical writing, multimodal composition, or graduate seminars in writing pedagogy, we are focused on writing, and that is where our expertise lies. We have argued that we need to step away from that expertise to reframe our responses to critics who challenge this work. While we fully honor the disciplinary expertise that put us in the position to write this chapter to begin with, we also want to recognize a simple fact: composition and rhetoric specialists are not the only people teaching writing in higher education. In chapter 9 of this collection, Matthew Overstreet emphasizes the need for generative combination in writing instruction, to expose students to "a variety of genres and communicative modes." As Overstreet asserts, writing instruction should keep pace with changing and proliferating communicative modes, and we would add that an effective avenue for addressing that proliferation is working with faculty across the disciplines who teach writing in its various forms. Disciplined insiders can provide aid to instructors who have no formal training in writing pedagogy and who may work from flawed assumptions about how writers develop, and therein lies the value of our expertise. However, we maintain that disciplined insiders can also learn about writing instruction from these disciplinary outsiders, particularly in light of the ongoing evolution of genres and modes in which our students need education and experience.

We spent a year meeting via Zoom to talk about this chapter, working through what we wanted to write while we learned to write with one another. Throughout those meetings, we realized that what we wanted to say in this chapter continued to evolve, shifting from an earlier, almost cynical argument that composition and rhetoric is at best symbiotic and at worst parasitic in its relationship with neoliberal critiques of "bad" writing to a far more hopeful perspective anchored in care work. Although the complex relationship between writing studies and higher education certainly requires further scrutiny, we realized throughout our collaboration that we needed the sustaining concept of care work just as much as we think our students do. This realization ultimately changed our argument into a more expansive, optimistic one about how disciplined insiders should engage with disciplinary outsiders in public arguments about writing and writing instruction. We saw that we need to undiscipline ourselves, that we need to draw just as much on our experiences as teachers and writers as we do on our field knowledge. As our own perspective about these ideas changed during a life-altering pandemic, we kept asking ourselves a question we think is central to our argument, and it is the question Hesse posed in his 2005 CCCC chair's address: who owns writing?

This chapter has responded to the frustration so many of us feel when we see complaints about student writing published in venues like CHE and IHE. We sympathize with this defensiveness, ingrained as it is in our discipline's history. However, we also share Adler-Kassner's reminder that "while many speak for writing, not all understand writing in the same ways."[50] After all, while scholar-teachers in composition and rhetoric quite rightly lay claim to expertise in writing, we must conclude that writing does not belong to our discipline alone. The mission of composition and rhetoric, rooted in care work, should be to support the education of as many writers as we can reach. Who owns writing? Writers do.

NOTES

1. Mintz, "Next-Generation Writing Instruction."
2. McQuade, "Composition and Literary Studies," 484.
3. Jenkins, "Why We Must Get Back to the Basics in Teaching Composition."
4. Malenczyk et al., *Composition, Rhetoric, and Disciplinarity*, 337.
5. Hesse, "We Know What Works in Teaching Composition."
6. Hesse, "Who Owns Writing," 459.
7. Hesse, "Who Owns Writing," 459, original emphasis.
8. Phelps and Ackerman, "Making the Case for Disciplinarity in Rhetoric, Composition, and Writing Studies," 180.
9. Lauer, "Composition Studies," 26.
10. Other significant historical works that either argue for or question the disciplinarity of rhetoric and composition include Berlin, *Writing Instruction in Nineteenth Century American Colleges*; Harris, *A Teaching Subject*; Crowley, *Composition in the University*; McComiskey, *Microhistories of Composition*; Malenczyk et al., *Composition, Rhetoric, and Disciplinarity*, to name just a few.
11. Massey, "The (Dis)Order of Composition," 306.
12. Kopelson, "Sp(l)itting Images," 775.
13. Dobrin, *Postcomposition*, 118.
14. Strickland, *Managerial Unconscious*; Craig and Perryman-Clark, "Troubling the Boundaries"; Welch and Scott, *Composition in the Age of Austerity*; Kahn, Lalicker, and Lynch-Biniek, *Contingency, Exploitation, and Solidarity*.
15. Colomb, "Franchising the Future," 11.
16. Colomb, "Franchising the Future," 11, original emphasis.
17. Colomb, "Franchising the Future," 12.
18. Rhodes, "You Are What You Sell," 59.
19. Rhodes, "You Are What You Sell," 62.
20. Rhodes, "You Are What You Sell," 63.
21. Rhodes, "You Are What You Sell," 64.
22. Rysdam, "The Economy of Expressivism," 282.
23. Eodice, Geller, and Lerner, *The Meaningful Writing Project*, 136.
24. Rose, "All Writers Have More to Learn," 59.
25. Rose, "All Writers Have More to Learn," 60.
26. Varnum, *Fencing with Words*, 250.
27. King, *On Writing*, 107.
28. Roeder and Gatto, "Re-Imagining Expressivism," 8.
29. Noddings, *Caring*; hooks, *Teaching to Transgress*; Denial in Stommel, Friend, and Morris, *Critical Digital Pedagogy*.
30. hooks, *Teaching to Transgress*, 15.
31. Denial, "A Pedagogy of Kindness."
32. Denial, "A Pedagogy of Kindness," original emphasis.
33. Elbow, *Everyone Can Write*, 77.
34. Denial, "A Pedagogy of Kindness."
35. Blum, *Ungrading*; Danielewicz and Elbow, "A Unilateral Grading Contract"; Inoue, *Labor-Based Grading Contracts*.
36. We don't have the space to unpack the various meanings and methods associated with un-grading, but we do want to note that un-grading practices aren't always an option, especially for contingent faculty who are expected to follow standardized grading policies.
37. Chiaravalli, "Grades Stifle Student Learning," 83.
38. James, "Grading Has Always Made Writing Better," 257.

39. All assessment practices can carry biases, even labor-based grading and similar practices (Carillo, *Hidden Inequities*), a point we want to make even though we don't have the space to elaborate in this discussion.
40. James, "Grading Has Always Made Writing Better," 257.
41. Moro, "Against Cop Shit."
42. Vie, "Plagiarism Detection Services Are Money Well Spent," 291.
43. Rose, *Lives on the Boundary*, 26.
44. *Elon Statement on Writing Transfer*.
45. Adler-Kassner and Majewski, "Extending the Invitation," 190.
46. McGranahan, *Writing Anthropology*, 7.
47. McGranahan, *Writing Anthropology*, 7–8.
48. Silvia, *How to Write a Lot*, ix.
49. We both frequently tell our colleagues to visit the WAC Clearinghouse website (https://wac.colostate.edu/) to access resources for promoting sound writing instruction across the disciplines. We also appreciate the work being published in the new open-access journal *Prompt: A Journal of Academic Writing Assignments* for the way it demonstrates how instructors from a range of disciplines incorporate writing instruction into their courses.
50. Adler-Kassner, "Looking Outward," 304.

REFERENCES

Adler-Kassner, Linda. *The Activist WPA: Changing Stories about Writing and Writers*. Logan: Utah State University Press, 2008.

Adler-Kassner, Linda "Looking Outward: Disciplinarity and Dialogue in Landscapes of Practice." In *Composition, Rhetoric, and Disciplinarity*, edited by Rita Malenczyk, Susan Miller-Cochran, Elizabeth Wardle, and Kathleen Blake Yancey, 303–30. Logan: Utah State University Press, 2018.

Adler-Kassner, Linda, and John Majewski. "Extending the Invitation: Threshold Concepts, Professional Development, and Outreach." In *Naming What We Know: Threshold Concepts of Writing Studies*, edited by Linda Adler-Kassner and Elizabeth Wardle, 186–202. Logan: Utah State University Press, 2015.

Berlin, James. *Writing Instruction in Nineteenth Century American Colleges*. Carbondale: Southern Illinois University Press, 1985.

Blum, Susan, ed. *Ungrading: Why Rating Students Undermines Learning (and What to Do Instead)*. Morgantown: West Virginia University Press, 2020.

Carillo, Ellen C. *The Hidden Inequities in Labor-Based Contract Grading*. Logan: Utah State University Press, 2021.

Chiaravalli, Arthur. "Grades Stifle Student Learning: Can We Learn to Teach without Grades?" In *Ungrading: Why Rating Students Undermines Learning (and What to Do Instead)*, edited by Susan Blum, 82–88. Morgantown: West Virginia University Press, 2020.

Colomb, Gregory G. "Franchising the Future." *College Composition and Communication* 62, no. 1 (2010): 11–30.

Craig, Collin Lamont, and Stacy M. Perryman-Clark. "Troubling the Boundaries: (De)Constructing WPA Identities at the Intersection of Race and Gender." *WPA: Writing Program Administration* 34, no. 2 (2011): 27–58.

Crowley, Sharon. *Composition in the University: Historical and Polemical Essays*. Pittsburgh, PA: University of Pittsburgh Press, 1998.

Danielewicz, Jane, and Peter Elbow. "A Unilateral Grading Contract to Improve Learning and Teaching." *College Composition and Communication* 61, no. 2 (2009): 244–68.

Denial, Catherine. "A Pedagogy of Kindness." In *Critical Digital Pedagogy*, edited by Jesse Stommel, Chris Friend, and Sean Michael Morris. Washington, DC: Hybrid Pedagogy, 2020. https://hybridpedagogy.org/critical-digital-pedagogy/.

Dobrin, Sidney. *Postcomposition*. Carbondale: Southern Illinois University Press, 2011.

Elbow, Peter. *Everyone Can Write: Essays toward a Hopeful Theory of Writing and Teaching Writing*. New York: Oxford University Press, 2000.

Elon Statement on Writing Transfer. Elon University, 2015. https://www.centerforengagedlearning.org/elon-statement-on-writing-transfer/.

Eodice, Michele, Anne Ellen Geller, and Neal Learner. *The Meaningful Writing Project: Learning, Teaching, and Writing in Higher Education*. Logan: Utah State University Press, 2016.

Harris, Joseph. *A Teaching Subject: Composition since 1966*. 2nd ed. Logan: Utah State University Press, 2012.

Hesse, Doug. "We Know What Works in Teaching Composition." *Chronicle of Higher Education*, January 3, 2017. https://www.chronicle.com/article/we-know-what-works-in-teaching-composition/.

Hesse, Douglas. "Who Owns Writing?" In *Views from the Center: The CCCC Chairs' Addresses 1977–2005*, edited by Duane Roen, 457–72. Boston: Bedford/St. Martin's, 2006.

hooks, bell. *Teaching Community: A Pedagogy of Hope*. New York: Routledge, 2013.

hooks, bell. *Teaching to Transgress: Education as the Practice of Freedom*. New York: Routledge, 1994.

Inoue, Asao B. *Labor-Based Grading Contracts: Building Equity and Inclusion in the Compassionate Writing Classroom*. Fort Collins and Boulder: WAC Clearinghouse and University Press of Colorado, 2019.

James, Mitchell R. "Grading Has Always Made Writing Better." In *Bad Ideas about Writing*, edited by Cheryl E. Ball and Drew M. Loewe, 255–58. Morgantown: West Virginia University Libraries Digital Publishing Institute, 2017.

Jenkins, Rob. "Why We Must Get Back to the Basics in Teaching Composition." *Chronicle of Higher Education*, January 29, 2020. https://www.chronicle.com/article/why-we-must-get-back-to-basics-in-teaching-composition/.

Kahn, Seth, William Lalicker, and Amy Lynch-Biniek, eds. *Contingency, Exploitation, and Solidarity: Labor and Action in English Composition*. Fort Collins, CO, and Anderson, SC: WAC Clearinghouse and Parlor Press, 2017.

King, Stephen. *On Writing: A Memoir of the Craft*. New York: Scribner, 2010.

Kopelson, Karen. "Sp(l)itting Images: Or, Back to the Future of (Rhetoric and?) Composition." *College Composition and Communication* 59 no. 4 (2008): 750–80.

Lauer, Janice M. "Composition Studies: Dappled Discipline." *Rhetoric Review* 3, no. 1 (1984): 20–29.

Malenczyk, Rita, Susan Miller-Cochran, Elizabeth Wardle, and Kathleen Blake Yancey, eds. *Composition, Rhetoric, and Disciplinarity*. Logan: Utah State University Press, 2018.

Massey, Lance. "The (Dis)Order of Composition: Insights from the Rhetoric and Reception of *The Making of Knowledge in Composition*." In *The Changing of Knowledge in Composition: Contemporary Perspectives*, edited by Lance Massey and Richard C. Gebhardt, 305–22. Logan: Utah State University Press, 2011.

McComiskey, Bruce, ed. *Microhistories of Composition*. Logan: Utah State University Press, 2016.

McGranahan, Carole, ed. *Writing Anthropology: Essays on Craft and Commitment*. Durham, NC: Duke University Press, 2020.

McQuade, Donald. "Composition and Literary Studies." In *Redrawing the Boundaries: The Transformation of English and American Literary Studies*, edited by Stephen Greenblatt and Miles G. Gunn, 482–519. New York: Modern Languages Association, 1992.

Mintz, Steven. "Next-Generation Writing Instruction." *Inside Higher Ed*, November 20, 2020. https://www.insidehighered.com/blogs/higher-ed-gamma/next-generation-writing-instruction.

Moro, Jeffrey. "Against Cop Shit." February 13, 2020. https://jeffreymoro.com/blog/2020-02-13-against-cop-shit/.
Noddings, Nel. *Caring: A Relational Approach to Ethics and Moral Education*. Berkeley: University of California Press, 1984.
North, Stephen M. *The Making of Knowledge in Composition: Portrait of an Emerging Field*. Portsmouth, NH: Heinemann, 1987.
Phelps, Louise Wetherbee, and John M. Ackerman. "Making the Case for Disciplinarity in Rhetoric, Composition, and Writing Studies: The Visibility Project." *College Composition and Communication* 62, no. 1 (2010): 180–215.
Rhodes, Keith. "You Are What You Sell: Branding the Way to Composition's Better Future." *WPA: Writing Program Administration* 33, no. 3 (2010): 58–77.
Roeder, Tara, and Roseanne Gatto. "Re-Imagining Expressivism: An Introduction." In *Critical Expressivism: Theory and Practice in the Composition Classroom*, edited by Tara Roeder and Roseanne Gatto, 7–11. Fort Collins, CO, and Anderson, SC: WAC Clearinghouse and Parlor Press, 2014.
Rose, Mike. *Lives on the Boundary: A Moving Account of the Struggles and Achievements of America's Educationally Underprepared*. New York: Penguin, 1989.
Rose, Shirley K. "All Writers Have More to Learn." In *Naming What We Know: Threshold Concepts of Writing Studies*, edited by Linda Adler-Kassner and Elizabeth A. Wardle, 59–61. Logan: Utah State University Press, 2015.
Rose, Shirley K., and Irwin Weiser, eds. *Going Public: What Writing Programs Learn from Engagement*. Logan: Utah State University Press, 2010.
Rysdam, Sheri. "The Economy of Expressivism and Its Legacy of Low/No-Stakes Writing." In *Critical Expressivism: Theory and Practice in the Composition Classroom*, edited by Tara Roeder and Roseanne Gatto, 281–88. Fort Collins, CO, and Anderson, SC: WAC Clearinghouse and Parlor Press, 2014.
Silvia, Paul J. *How to Write a Lot: A Practical Guide to Productive Academic Writing*. 2nd ed. Washington, DC: American Psychological Association, 2018.
Stommel, Jesse, Chris Friend, and Sean Michael Morris, eds. *Critical Digital Pedagogy: A Collection*. Hybrid Pedagogy, 2020. https://hybridpedagogy.org/critical-digital-pedagogy/.
Strickland, Donna. *The Managerial Unconscious in the History of Composition Studies*. Carbondale: Southern Illinois University Press, 2011.
Teller, Joseph. "Are We Teaching Composition All Wrong?" *Chronicle of Higher Education*, October 3, 2016. https://www.chronicle.com/article/are-we-teaching-composition-all-wrong/.
Varnum, Robin. *Fencing with Words: A History of Writing Instruction at Amherst College during the Era of Theodore Baird, 1938–1966*. Urbana, IL: National Council of Teachers of English, 1996.
Vie, Stephanie. "Plagiarism Detection Services Are Money Well Spent." In *Bad Ideas about Writing*, edited by Cheryl E. Ball and Drew M. Loewe, 287–93. Morgantown: West Virginia University Libraries Digital Publishing Institute, 2017.
Welch, Nancy, and Tony Scott, eds. *Composition in the Age of Austerity*. Logan: Utah State University Press, 2016.

2
TRUST, TRUTH, AND THE EROSION OF PUBLIC DISCOURSE
The Virtue of Reality in the First-Year Writing Classroom

Matthew S. S. Johnson

Researchers at Stanford University were "shocked into reality" when they discovered that the assumption "because young people are fluent in social media[,] they are equally savvy about what they find there" was rather wide of the mark.[1] What is really shocking is that the researchers were shocked.

Between 2015 and 2016, the Stanford History Education Group (SHEG) "prototyped, field tested, and validated a bank of assessments that tap civic online reasoning—the ability to judge the credibility of information that floods young people's smartphones, tablets, and computers."[2] But composition teachers have been educating students to assess online sources and develop media literacy skills for some time. While helping "young people judge the credibility of information" seemed a sensible pursuit at the end of SHEG's study, such a solution relies on students' interest in credibility in the first place—or at least their willingness to exercise reason. Which is reasonable.

Yet nearly simultaneously with the conclusion of this study, a political culture emerged in which opinion is too often given the same weight as fact, pathos is as sustainable as logos, and persuasion is the art of talking to an audience already in agreement. The impact in politics was immediate and obvious: above all else, this new political culture championed division accompanied by vitriol, animosity, contempt. Sadly, in such an environment, assertive, aggressive, loud, combative, and dismissive rhetors thrive. In this atmosphere, exercises in source assessment begin to seem quaint. Comp/rhet organizations were swift to respond to this dismaying shift. By late 2016, the Conference on College Composition and Communication (CCCC), the Rhetoric Society of America (RSA), and the Council of Writing Program Administrators (CWPA) had issued statements to reaffirm their organizations' core values;[3] however, as

Bruce McComiskey reminds us, the very reaffirmation "signifies . . . anxiety that Trump's successful rhetoric represents a direct challenge" to their missions.[4]

Within a year, McComiskey published the timely *Post-Truth Rhetoric and Composition*, a passionate call to action and a text whose clear focus is largely on one individual: President Donald Trump. This hyper-focus is by itself significant. McComiskey's goal, in a fiery text with space too limited "to explore specific pedagogical strategies," is to "confront post-truth rhetoric head-on" by "doubl[ing]-down on the values we have already articulated and publicized."[5] However, even those news sources that seem to strongly support comp/rhet organizations' missions of diversity, inclusiveness, respect, collaboration, equality, and reason have been, along with the comp/rhet organizations themselves, subtly sliding into a new mission: not just continuing to fight for the values we hold dear but now having to simultaneously spend much time addressing the unreasonable—even the absurd—at enormous opportunistic cost. Vitriolic political rhetoric spilling into everyday public discourse is alarming enough. The situation worsens with the rise in irrational thinking in the form of willful susceptibility to fake news, acceptance of "alternative fact," and the proud dismissal of science. There is a serious possibility of forced conflation of teaching and indoctrination should teachers acknowledge unreason as a valid perspective to be addressed in higher education—an institution that values reason, evidence-based analysis, and the scientific method. Flagrant unreason is a phenomenon that cannot be ignored but that also has no place in serious pedagogical engagement in the classroom.[6]

In the spring of 2017, I was teaching a largely elective intermediate composition course that focuses on writing in the disciplines and public discourse. The course is required for social work majors and designed for students across the university. President Trump had just delivered his inaugural address to a crowd that he claimed was the largest ever generally and (I think important to him) larger than President Barack Obama's was. He declared[7] that "1.5 million people had attended his inauguration," "a claim that photographs disproved."[8] What happened next made me entirely rework the next two weeks of my syllabus: Kellyanne Conway, senior counselor to President Trump (and previously his campaign manager), uttered the phrase "alternative facts" in defending White House press secretary Sean Spicer's lie about the inaugural address's number of attendees.[9] I need not explain the stunning implications of the phrase "alternative facts." To put it in perspective, though, I've only ever immediately and substantially rewritten a syllabus due to current events two other times: after the terrorist attacks on the US on September 11, 2001, and in August 2014 when Michael Brown was shot by a police officer (one of the events that put the Black Lives Matter movement into the national spotlight) in Ferguson, Missouri, which is twenty miles from my campus.

When I raised the topic of "alternative facts" as related to the inaugural address with my students, much of the class was lively—not necessarily because of the thoroughly interesting subject matter but because some students in the room reacted so defensively. That's not even the right term: they were not merely defensive but immobile. They would not listen, would not hear, would not entertain discussion. And there was an undeniable, if then undefinable, tension. This circumstance was unusual.

A few words about the institutional demographic of Southern Illinois University Edwardsville (SIUE): it is situated on the Illinois side of the Mississippi River, just across from St. Louis, Missouri. Within minutes of driving, one can be in urban St. Louis, rural Illinois and Missouri, or suburbia. Our students come from all these areas—from urban Chicago and St. Louis, from their suburbs (which, socioeconomically, vary extremely widely), and from genuinely rural regions. Politically, the population runs the gamut, and the students and the university population generally reflect that spectrum. What this means for the classroom is that discussion of politics—which students immediately read as "Democrat *versus* Republican"—has always been ardent, generally not fervid, certainly not furious. The students' inaccessibility in this instance was new: loud, resistant Trump supporters took center stage. Others were either silent or felt silenced.

Even when I tried to limit our focus to the rhetorical situation of inaugural addresses generally or to the implications of making an unsubstantiated claim about media coverage as opposed to accusing journalists of intentionally manipulating photographs (that is, not about Trump, not about the current political fervor), the situation persisted. This unwillingness to speak generally was unusual: classroom participation is often fueled by speaking around and not directly about a specific object of analysis. Regardless, students seemed to be having trouble conceptualizing the complete fabrication taking place, so in an effort to indicate that there was no debate here, no "equal sides," but rather the reality and a falsehood, I introduced FOX News coverage. FOX News, my students had previously acknowledged without protest or controversy, is conservative leaning, just as they had identified MSNBC as liberal leaning; this is a conventional part of source assessment pedagogy not unlike SHEG suggests. FOX News had also stated unambiguously that "Trump is wrong."[10] The students still wouldn't have it, remaining energetically immobile or silent. Photographs didn't matter. Statistical analysis conducted by neutral parties, even those versed in crowd estimation, didn't matter. What quickly became clear is that any statement that contradicted the lie was interpreted as an anti-Trump "argument" by the boisterous present; Trump supporters went on the offensive while others seemed unwilling to engage. There was no refocusing the conversation on rhetorical moves, concepts, or general implications such as the rhetorical difference between questioning journalists' claims and accusing them of intentionally manipulating data. It was Whatever versus Trump.

Composition instruction at its best has long motivated students to think beyond binaries—to relocate them, to challenge them, to recognize complexity and intricacy, to see situations as multifaceted, and to view them from numerous perspectives—despite our knowledge that students (and many others) want desperately to simplify. Ellen C. Carillo bemoans this condition: "Unfortunately, . . . as a field we are beholden to largely impoverished models of argumentation that circulate widely within secondary and postsecondary institutions."[11] Carillo acknowledges, and it merits repeating here, that such practices are largely due to problematic working conditions (undercompensated and overworked teachers assigned too many students, and many of those teachers—in postsecondary education in the form of teaching assistants—lack experience): "Simplistic argumentative essays are relatively easy to teach and easy to grade."[12] These traditional high school and often college pro/con assignments are problematic. When students are asked to "choose a side" (which is often accompanied by the assumption that there are only two) in the effort to teach them "argument," there is already a binary—usually overly simplistic and created for that simplicity. This instruction is often issued before any research is done, which also means that such a project is essentially telling students "have a knee-jerk reaction to a cultural 'debate' and support that reaction." When research *is* introduced in these circumstances, it's often either through the teacher's explicit instruction or the students' assumption that source vetting must be done merely to find sources that "support" one's view. Frustrating. In this particular classroom situation, the binary was always the same. Criticism of "alternative fact" = anti-Trump. Value of the free press = anti-Trump. Any utterance not repeating what Trump said at any given moment = anti-Trump. Even if not voiced by the majority of my students but a loud minority, this immobility was atypical, where any debate was suddenly reclassified as pro- or anti-Trump.

Such a situation could be caused by and lead to unintentional willingness to use (on the teachers' and students' parts) seemingly innocuous language that is actually subversive or sinister—a serious threat to foundations we thought, perhaps only assumed, were solid. Over the last few years, it has been revealed that these foundations are spongy: the fact ("fact?") that the phrases "fake news" (which by definition isn't news), "alternative facts" (which by definition aren't factual), and "junk science" (which by definition isn't scientific) have entered into common parlance should give us pause but best not for long, as our response needs, as McComiskey contends, ferocious action: "The effects of post-truth rhetoric may devastate composition studies if left unchecked" and "xenophobia will replace social justice, isolationism will invalidate cultural freedom, shouting will trump listening, disruption will drown out response, insults will replace respect, exclusion will dimmish diversity, divisiveness will preclude negotiation, invective will erode support, fear will challenge safety, and success at all costs will invalidate responsible inquiry . . . and it is already happening."[13]

We have had a little time since McComiskey's prediction to see how his argument has played out: three years more of the Trump administration led to increasingly divisive politics (and two impeachments); severe anti-immigration sentiments; violence against Asian Americans (Covid-19's country of origin used as an ignorant excuse to perpetuate violence); race-related violence (often exacerbated by a president seemingly unwilling to speak strongly against it, if not condone it); conspiracy theories so passionately supported that they are spotlighted in mainstream media; the dismissal of science, which has stunted civilization-saving agendas from curtailing global warming to protecting—and then vaccinating—populations from a deadly, global pandemic; unsupported and widespread accusations of voter fraud; and the storming of the US Capitol, an incident energized, if not inspired, by the president's own inflammatory rhetoric. Worth noting is that "post-truth" certainly did not end with the Trump administration and the election of President Joe Biden:[14] the venomous political expression was *and is* clear for all to see, whether one celebrated such drama or lamented the damage it caused.

Less apparent is the sinister nature of the reaction to such poisonous rhetoric: the troubling and inadvertent harm those contesting it perpetuate in their desperation to sincerely discourse. In January 2017, Joshua Johnson on *1A* expressed his views on "fake news" clearly: "Now I am on record, and I want to disclaim my bias first of all, I am strongly on record as being against the term fake news. There is no such thing as fake news, because if it is fake, by definition, it is not news. News is an honest brokerage of information. So for the rest of the hour, I want you listening to know, I hate that term. But it's a commonplace for talking so we'll start there."[15]

I wanted to say "hear, hear!" And I applauded, initially, this statement. While the injury caused by constant acrimonious public discourse is apparent, however, the infection incubates quietly: what is the effect of a "disclaimer" being necessary for a "bias" that "fake news" isn't a thing? That Johnson is *biased* against the undermining of journalistic freedom and integrity? Certainly, Johnson didn't quite mean a "bias," which was merely an available term, even a slip. Johnson's motive, I think, in deciding to continue using the term—even if the anti-concept is then disseminated, preserved in the form of a shorthand to address the issue—is that he wants and needs to engage, which is not something the "alternative fact" group is interested in doing. Rather, it prefers quick agreement or silence, not discourse. Yet all listeners should be concerned about any acknowledgment that "fake news" is a "commonplace" and thus we should proceed to use the term.

Commonplaces, many of which are untrue, have a nasty habit of becoming perspectives through which we view the world.[16] It's not the acknowledgment that fake news doesn't exist that listeners are likely to remember. It's the phrase. Repeat "vaccinations cause autism" too frequently to negate the claim, and such nonsense accidentally becomes an "argument" that needs to be addressed. To repeat that Obama was born in Kenya, even to refute it, elevates such twaddle to a level that it needs to be refuted—again. Language can define our reality. Now that I've repeated these commonplaces, does it give them more force? More staying power? I hope not, but my audience isn't a general public consuming news or a mass audience casually browsing social media. And I'm certainly not going to ask the editors of this collection to include a facsimile copy of Obama's birth certificate.

In February 2019, Joshua Johnson interviewed Democratic National Committee chair Tom Perez about "what people think when they think democratic." Perez responded, in part, that Democrats "believe that climate change is real" and added that Republicans are "denying the science."[17] Here, Perez is, however unintentionally, playing into climate change denial by couching climate change as a belief and juxtaposing it with denying science as a political stance that perhaps one might hold as reasonably as fiscal conservativism or small government. This dangerous kind of discourse will not be addressed through source assessment, the otherwise useful pedagogy and activities that SHEG developed in response to its "discovery" that students are so susceptible to uncritically accepting information they access through social media. And listeners are not likely to engage in serious close reading or rhetorical analysis when listening to the news—*especially* if writing and rhetoric teachers must spend time "justifying" facts and arguing that science is a comparatively objective method to determine what reality is like.

Several weeks after Johnson's interview of Perez, Audie Cornish interviewed GOP senator Lamar Alexander of Tennessee on *All Things Considered*. They were talking about the Republican response to the Green New Deal, a response called the "New Manhattan Project," a title whose problematic implications seemed entirely lost on the senator. Cornish says: "You started this conversation by saying you believe in climate change. You believe that humans have contributed to it. And that is not always how members of your party have spoken at all. Do you see Republicans as ready to start a real conversation about climate change?"[18]

I praise Cornish for use of the term real—a *real* conversation as opposed to a ridiculous "debate" when it comes to global warming. Yet I also would point out that like Perez, Cornish and many other fine journalists mistakenly cater to this notion that somehow global warming is a "belief." Still, Cornish refuses to let Alexander off easily: she asks Alexander how he conceives of the Green New Deal as "bizarre" (his word) and of the Republican plan, despite clear overlaps, as "more straight ahead" (his phrase). He responds that the Green New Deal "focuses on cows, combustion . . ." and Cornish interrupts "cows are not mentioned in the resolution, senator," unapologetically letting laughter enter her voice—a none-too-subtle calling out of the senator's ludicrousness. The senator attempts to backtrack with some vague notion of it being about "agriculture" and "cow burping" and, speaking over his evasive stumbling, Cornish interrupts again: "So I'm looking at the proposal, and it says, 'working collaboratively with farmers to eliminate pollution and greenhouse gas emissions, supporting family farming.' It doesn't say anything about attacking cows." Alexander finally says, "Wuh . . . well . . . they . . . they've cleaned it up a little bit," to which Cornish responds "oookay," a clear indication that having a real conversation just wasn't going to happen. I found myself laughing as I listened to Cornish laugh: it's genuinely funny in its absurdity. But I sobered up, as it reveals a serious circumstance. *The Daily Show*—yes, the news satire program—is sometimes at its most humorous when there is no comedic spin put on the news. That's *The Daily Show* and it can be hilarious. But the NPR interview of a US senator is *the news*. I'm listening to the actual news, and I'm hearing *The Daily Show*. That's not funny at all. Despite Cornish's clear desire to have that real conversation, the interview reveals the sheer impossibility of doing so when one conversant cannot even get basic facts straight: here, the actual content of the written bill, let alone the reality of global warming. The senator is among those responsible for vetting this bill, and yet he clearly either has only vague notions of what it contains or doesn't really care because it seems contrary to what is assumed to be Republican thinking: it is immediately and irretrievably branded "anti." There's an unwillingness to confront the issue (global warming) and the text (the literal black-and-white words). The sobering thought that doused my initial amusement is that it feels as though Cornish is talking as a parent to a toddler. Actually, it's not just sobering; it's chilling.

What is revealed through these instances is that there is a severe divide—not the traditional Democrat/Republican one, even at its most vicious, but one between reason and unreason. The latter is sinister in its subtlety and is shockingly seductive. It enables a reasonably minded, moderately critically aware public—composed even of those vehemently opposed to these anti-concepts—to spread them when instead we (by which I mean an inclusive, reasonable, if passionate, public) need to adamantly reveal not just their irrationality but their absurdity. We must "scuttle the euphemisms" (as my colleague put it). Such euphemisms frame facts as beliefs and hide the process of doing so. Contrarily, a deepfake is called what it is: *fake*.[19] It does not have a reputable, rhetorical counterpart. An "alternative fact" isn't a fact; it's a lie that misrepresents. "Fake news" isn't news; it's fiction pretending factuality. "Junk science" isn't science; it's untested, absurd nonsense.

To resist and, it is hoped, arrest this trend, McComiskey proposes to "double-down on the values we [comp/rhet scholars and teachers] have already articulated."[20] I add the need to be critically aware of and careful about the way those values are rearticulated, remaining wary of elevating ignorance to the level of debate. Leah Ceccarelli (2011), writing about how groups create scientific controversy where there is none (as in climate change), analyzes non-rhetoric scholars' "focus on the manufacture of scientific *uncertainty*" in the effort to "demonstrat[e] how conventional ignorance claims in scientific articles are taken out of context, data is cherry-picked, and statistical methods are manipulated with evaluations standards being strengthened for studies that have inconvenient results."[21] The problem, Ceccarelli argues, is that by concentrating on "*uncertainty* production, rather than *controversy* production, these scholars . . . turn their analytic gaze away from some of the most significant rhetorical dynamics involved in manufacturing an ongoing scientific debate in the face of overwhelming scientific consensus."[22] There is even slippage in Ceccarelli's claim: neither "scientific uncertainty" nor "ongoing scientific debate" is manufactured. Rather, it's the *appearance* of scientific uncertainty and ongoing debate that is manufactured in *non-scientific* discourse. The opportunistic cost of such concentration is significant. The more time spent dealing with "fake news," the less time spent rhetorically analyzing news. We can see that source assessment—a common strategy in helping students separate the reliable from the unreliable and the strategy that SHEG offers—won't work. Or at least we will have to build strong foundations before it will,[23] for the simple reason that an assessor must accept the premise that reliability can be determined by more than instinct or opinion: otherwise, a reliable source can be declared "fake news" and scientific evidence can be summarily discounted.

Comp/rhet teachers must still reject starting at that point (persuading that characteristics of reliable sources are determined primarily by logos and ethos and that the scientific method is an effective measure of reality) because doing so problematically assumes that our students come to classes rejecting reputable news and science (most don't, although the few who do have become brasher in recent years). It also acknowledges post-truth as a viewpoint worth pursuing in higher education, which I assume we would like to avoid. Just as Ceccarelli warns against shifting the conversation to uncertainty when it comes to scientific debate, we must be wary of entertaining any notion of "alternative fact" when we're using facts. We are here to teach, not indoctrinate; however, if we have even a minority population who accepts, for instance, science as "belief," then teaching and indoctrination become the same, at least from the perspective of that population. The more we even entertain unreason in the press and with our students, the more false binaries are created and the more troubling they become.

In my neighborhood, one sees "Thin Blue Line" flags and before and during (and after, as it happens) the 2020 presidential election, plenty of pro-Trump "God, Guns, and Country" signs. One also sees variations of signs that say "In this house we believe in" followed by a women's power emblem (a fist in a Venus sign), "Black Lives Matter," "Science," "Diversity," and "Love Is Love." These are beliefs? It is clear what is generally meant here, but as with some of my students, caught in simplistic and inaccurate binary "thinking" on the topic of the inaugural address, these signs display how distressingly easily worrying binaries are asserted. Such a contentious political climate has rendered it apparently necessary for numerous media outlets—*The Atlantic, New York Times,* NPR, FOX News, CNN, and others all had their particular versions—to publish articles not only about how to talk politics when views differ but how to have a dinner conversation at Thanksgiving with family (for several Thanksgivings running, I should add). Apparently, science is now a political belief (as is, apparently, "love") when it must be declared that "in this house we believe in science." Not just political beliefs but support of particular candidates have been revealed to be essential to identity itself.

Thus, some students in my class would not (could not?) engage in discussions of the dangers of undermining confidence in our institutions, the consequences of repeated accusations of journalistic corruption, or the perils of constantly crying out about unsubstantiated voter fraud. There was no critical distance present, academic or personal, that would enable a real discussion. John Fletcher, a social change performance researcher, explains: "Social-psychological consensus . . . leans toward the view that we acquire beliefs and attachments first, pre-rationally, and that we justify them post-hoc, constantly, by filtering evidence (often unconsciously) through interpretive lenses. For issues that we detect as salient to our identities, we ignore, highlight, or weight input about those issues to maintain identity coherence."[24] There is a performance of identity when one refuses to wear a mask during a pandemic whose virus is spread through air particulates, despite clear scientific evidence that indicates that wearing a mask would protect to a degree both the wearer and others from contracting and spreading SARS-CoV-2. With more than 270,000 dead Americans (at the time I initially wrote this sentence)[25] due to Covid-19, not even cold, rational numbers sway audience members who instead need to perform their political identities—even if it means denying science and putting themselves and others in potential danger: as Fletcher states, to preserve our sense of "us," "we detect and shun evidence and interpretations that we identify with 'them.' "[26]

Carillo argues, throughout *Teaching Readers in Post-Truth America,* that understanding the psychology of how emotions are strongly related to beliefs is essential, or at least highly beneficial, for comp/rhet teachers moving forward: "Research from the field of psychology offers insight into the relationship among mental functions. Most striking in the psychological research on how people are persuaded is the degree to which emotion and beliefs are bound up with one another, intertwined, and thought to be largely inseparable."[27] In addition, she refers to "findings from several experiments indicating that people cannot articulate or provide evidence for why they believe what they believe."[28] Part of me, here, wants to assert that people need neither evidence nor reason to believe what they believe: that's why it's a belief. There are educational spaces for that, but they aren't university classrooms. But Carillo and McComiskey and others, including me, are writing in reaction to a shift in the rhetorical situation that has already taken place and to which we must adapt as teachers, rethinking the role pathos might play in rhetorical instruction: "Another challenge that emerges . . . as we consider resisting and responding to the current climate is our field's oversimplification of the relationship between thought and emotion, between logos and pathos. If 'we, as a community of scholars and teachers,' are going to ' "double down" on the tools we have to combat post-truth rhetoric' (McComiskey 2017:38), we had better be working from more complex understandings of the varied relationships between these mental processes."[29]

As a starting point, I refrain from teaching ethos, pathos, and logos as separate. They are certainly not mutually exclusive,[30] and it is not difficult to get students to begin to consider the overlap and relationships between the appeals: "If a writer has a strong reputation (ethos) does it reasonably (logos) follow that we might pay attention?" "If we lose a loved one, does it not make sense (logos) that we would feel sad and express that sadness (pathos)?" "Given an event in someone's life, can you not reasonably surmise how they might feel? And if so, might this indicate that emotions follow a certain, predictable logic?"[31] Personal experience as expressed through storytelling often brims with emotional and ethical appeal while simultaneously communicating an event that may eventually become shared knowledge (logos).[32]

Psychological research enables Carillo to revisit pedagogies proposed in early comp/rhet, including Patrick Sullivan's "pedagogy of listening,"[33] Rogerian approaches,[34] and Peter Elbow's "Doubting and Believing Game"[35]—all in the effort to promote a better understanding of how emotion (specifically empathy, on which these approaches focus) is tied to beliefs. Furthermore, we "are asking [students] to reject the very psychological systems that are set up to protect them (all of us) from having to entertain any ideas that do not fit neatly into their worldview."[36] Even so, Carillo acknowledges that "one can't help but wonder, though, if dialogue is even possible in a post-truth culture, since 'the facts' cannot even be agreed upon,"[37]—and thus one turns to psychology to help.[38]

I've joked that I appreciate being in my field because unlike others—such as medicine, for example—"if students choose not to learn what we teach in rhetoric courses, nobody dies." I've meant it in part as encouragement to many first-year writing teachers because when a class doesn't go according to plan, they experience considerable anxiety. But when mask wearing in the effort to protect oneself and others from a deadly coronavirus became a rhetorical, political expression of identity in 2020, I was reluctant to jest in this way. I have also quipped, paraphrasing a former (problematic) secretary of defense, "We go to class with the students we have, not the students we might want." If students are susceptible to the rhetoric of "fake news," "alternative facts," and "junk science," or at least if students will continue to be surrounded by rhetors who promote these anti-concepts, then comp/rhet teachers will need to devote more time to pathos because it can masquerade as logos. Pathos has traditionally been viewed as subordinate to logos in the university, where research methods are evidence-based and argumentative strategies favor reason, where reason is scientific and scholarly currency. Yet we also understand that pathos is implicated in reason—and in news and in science. Logos is not as favored elsewhere; rhetorically if not academically, pathos is as powerful as logos, even potentially as sustainable, contrary to much of its teaching. Pathos is used in legal and political argumentation. And as Christina V. Cedillo (chapter 3, this volume) reminds us, "Pathos determines many of our reasons for communicating"—it is tied to our motives in arguing in the first place. Teachers, even in logos-favoring universities, need to help students understand pathos-as-motive if they're going to help prepare their students to be active citizens, a mission comp/rhet has taken on. As teachers of rhetoric, we must enable pathos to sit beside its siblings, logos and ethos, at the same level and not let our pedagogies favor overly much academic persuasion and academic audience "in service" to other fields/departments. The university *already* favors these; we need to engage rhetorical contexts of diverse varieties "in service" to our own field.

And while we have long embraced classroom spaces as political, even as we avoid assessing students on their own politics, we're going to have to be comfortable being "political" and "ideological" and even "indoctrinating" in our classrooms *if facts are understood to be beliefs* by some in our audiences. We must also "situate ourselves clearly and acknowledge what we can know from our specific perspective,"[39] institutionally and, perhaps, personally. By insisting on agreed-upon realities (which we should) while others refuse (which they do), we will be unable to avoid bringing politics, or that which is perceived as political, directly into the classroom. For the time being at least, stating a fact may also be stating a political position from certain audience members' perspectives.

Facts, even of the scientific variety, "all depend on an agreement," as astrophysicist Adam Frank eloquently put it.[40] The foundations of these agreements have begun to show cracks that need to be mended and the mends constantly maintained: facts cannot be alternative, news cannot be fake, and science is certainly not junk.

NOTES

1. Wineburg et al., "Evaluating Information," 7.
2. Wineburg et al., "Evaluating Information," 3.
3. As of December 2020, the three statements were available as follows: "Statement on Language, Power, and Action," CCCC, November 2016, https://cccc.ncte.org/cccc/language-power-action; "Message from the President," RSA, November 2016, https://associationdatabase.com/aws/RSA/pt/sd/news_article/130762/_PARENT/layout_details/false; "Statement on Supporting a Diverse and Inclusive Environment," CWPA, November 2016, https://lists.asu.edu/cgi-bin/wa?A1=ind1611&L=WPA-L.
4. McComiskey, *Post-Truth*, 4.
5. McComiskey, *Post-Truth*, 44, 43.
6. Not to be confused with emotion: unreason is not synonymous with emotion, as much as emotion is commonly set as opposed to reason. More about that in a moment.
7. The quotation and its refuting were widely reported similarly by other news outlets.
8. Davis and Rosenberg, "With False Claims."
9. Conway, interview by Chuck Todd, January 22, 2017.
10. Associated Press, "FACT CHECK"; FOX News, "Trump Reportedly Wanted Additional Photos of Inauguration Day Crowd Size." The Associated Press article published by FOX News indicated bluntly, "Trump is wrong." An article posted six days later to the FOX News website—and attributed to FOX News itself—asserts, "Photos taken that day made clear that crowds didn't extend to the Lincoln Memorial as Trump later asserted and that his claim of 1 million to 1.5 million people in attendance was wrong" (terms such as reportedly and allegedly do appear, I should mention, which makes for a more interesting source assessment discussion).
11. Carillo, *Teaching Readers*, 99.
12. Carillo, *Teaching Readers*, 100.
13. McComiskey, *Post-Truth*, 43.
14. Toxic rhetoric aside, even the election itself may never be over for some: as late as May 21, 2021, months after the election, NPR reported that some mail-in ballots in Georgia (narrowly won by Joe Biden) might be counted again: "The order marks the latest challenge for Fulton County in a seemingly never-ending election cycle [as] the former president and his allies made Fulton County a target of a disinformation campaign with the goal of overturning the state's election results" (see Kauffman, "Why 2020 Mail-in Ballots from One Georgia County May Be Scanned Again"). The danger of keeping the accusations going (and entertaining them) can undermine confidence in a secure voting system; it also diverts limited resources potentially needed elsewhere to pointless activities.
15. "Fighting for the Facts."
16. They emerge even from childhood: "sticks and stones will break my bones, but names will never hurt me," many children are taught to say (because names hurt a great deal); "it's what's on the inside that counts," many are told, perhaps in part to deny that appearance matters and there's less that we can do about it. While well-intentioned, these statements, designed to protect, also cloud the reality that underlies

17. "Left Field."
18. "GOP Sen. Lamar Alexander Wants to Address Climate Change."
19. Like "fake news," deepfakes are forecast by some to be a catalyst enabling the refutation of journalistic integrity (see Floridi, "Artificial Intelligence"; also see Fletcher, "Deepfakes").
20. McComiskey, *Post-Truth*, 43.
21. How easily I could have written "the climate change debate" here to capture that entire phenomenon in simple shorthand. How commonplace it would have sounded: but there is no scientific debate.
22. Ceccarelli, "Manufactured Scientific Controversy," 197 (original emphasis).
23. Even while writing it, I hoped that my argument in this chapter would be moot by the time it made it to print. Sadly, it is not moot, but perhaps we're moving in the right direction? On August 12, 2021, NPR reported that "Illinois will require news literacy courses at every high school" (see Medlin, "Illinois Is the First State").
24. Fletcher, "Deepfakes," 466.
25. The number was 662,249 as of September 14, 2021, as I revised the chapter (and 1,001,603 during a subsequent revision, May 20, 2022). I felt the previous numbers were worth preserving. Given the now wide distribution of three vaccines and the vaccination of 38 percent of the US population (65 percent as of March 17, 2022), the CDC has lightened its mask-wearing recommendations for the vaccinated (again). And yet mask wearing is still a political issue (news articles and memes supporting those who continue to wear masks and reminding those who don't to respect those who do are legion).
26. Fletcher, "Deepfakes," 466.
27. Carillo, *Teaching Readers*, 95.
28. Carillo, *Teaching Readers*, 97.
29. Carillo, *Teaching Readers*, 99.
30. In my graduate-level pedagogy classes, I instruct future composition teachers likewise. During teaching observations and demonstrations, I have seen many secondary and postsecondary teachers present an excerpt from a text and then ask students to classify it as logos, ethos, or pathos. Some textbooks seem to promote the appeals as classification (as opposed to analytical) tools.
31. Emotion and pathos (and, for that matter, affect, which has its own theory and even studies) are not synonymous but are related; these admittedly quite simple questions merely help students reveal (largely by themselves, with little prodding from the teacher) the nebulous nature of the boundaries among logic, emotion, and character and aid in seeing them, together, as human.
32. Also see Cedillo, chapter 3, this volume.
33. Carillo, *Teaching Readers*, 101–3.
34. Carillo, *Teaching Readers*, 37, 103.
35. Carillo, *Teaching Readers*, 47–50, 111–12.
36. Carillo, *Teaching Readers*, 108.
37. Carillo, *Teaching Readers*, 104.
38. I understand that Carillo is here calling attention to the phrase "the facts" when she puts them in scare quotes, perhaps additionally emphasizing the dangers of declaring disagreements with them; however, I might also pose that so marking facts recognizes an argument when there isn't one (not unlike Joshua Johnson and Audie Cornish inadvertently do with "fake news" and climate change as a "belief," respectively, above).
39. Cedillo, chapter 3, this volume.
40. Frank, "Science and Facts."

REFERENCES

Associated Press. "FACT CHECK: Trump Overstates Crowd Size at Inaugural." FOX News, January 21, 2007. http://www.foxnews.com/us/fact-check-trump-overstates-crowd-size-at-inaugural.

Carillo, Ellen C. *Teaching Readers in Post-Truth America*. Logan: Utah State University Press, 2018.

Ceccarelli, Leah. "Manufactured Scientific Controversy: Science, Rhetoric, and Public Debate." *Rhetoric and Public Affairs* 14, no. 2 (2011): 195–228.

Conway, Kellyanne. Interview by Chuck Todd. *Meet the Press*, NBC News, January 22, 2017. https://www.nbcnews.com/meet-the-press/meet-press-01-22-17-n710491.

Davis, Julie Hirschfeld, and Matthew Rosenberg. "With False Claims, Trump Attacks Media on Turnout and Intelligence Rift." *New York Times*, January 21, 2017. https://www.nytimes.com/2017/01/21/us/politics/trump-white-house-briefing-inauguration-crowd-size.html.

"Fighting for the Facts: How to Tell What's News and What's Fiction." *1A*, NPR, KWMU St. Louis, January 23, 2017. https://the1a.org/shows/2017-01-23/fighting-for-the-facts-and-how-to-tell-whats-news-and-whats-fiction.

Fletcher, John. "Deepfakes, Artificial Intelligence, and Some Kind of Dystopia: The New Faces of Online Post-Fact Performance." *Theatre Journal* 70, no. 4 (2018): 455–71.

Floridi, Luciano. "Artificial Intelligence, Deepfakes and a Future of Ectypes." *Philosophy and Technology* 31, no. 3 (2018): 317–21.

FOX News. "Trump Reportedly Wanted Additional Photos of Inauguration Day Crowd Size." FOX News, January 27, 2017. https://www.foxnews.com/politics/trump-reportedly-wanted-additional-photos-of-inauguration-day-crowd-size.

Frank, Adam. "Science and Facts, Alternative or Otherwise." NPR, January 24, 2017. https://www.npr.org/sections/13.7/2017/01/24/511348618/science-and-facts-alternative-or-otherwise.

"GOP Sen. Lamar Alexander Wants to Address Climate Change without the Green New Deal." *All Things Considered*, NPR, KWMU St. Louis, March 26, 2019. https://www.npr.org/2019/03/26/706969356/gop-sen-lamar-alexander-wants-to-address-climate-change-without-the-green-new-deal.

Kauffman, Johnny. "Why 2020 Mail-in Ballots from One Georgia County May Be Scanned Again." NPR, May 21, 2021. http://www.npr.org/2021/05/21/999312771/why-2020-mail-in-ballots-from-one-georgia-county-may-be-scanned-again.

"Left Field: The 2020 Democratic Nominees for President, According to Voters." *1A*, NPR, KWMU St. Louis, February 21, 2019. https://the1a.org/shows/2019-02-21/left-field-the-2020-democratic-nominees.

McComiskey, Bruce. *Post-Truth Rhetoric and Composition*. Logan: Utah State University Press, 2017.

Medlin, Peter. "Illinois Is the First State to Have High Schools Teach News Literacy." NPR, August 12, 2021. https://www.npr.org/2021/08/12/1026993142/illinois-is-the-first-state-to-have-high-schools-teach-news-literacy.

Wineburg, Sam, Sarah McGrew, Joel Breakstone, and Teresa Ortega. "Evaluating Information: The Cornerstone of Civic Online Reasoning." Stanford History Education Group, November 22, 2016: 1–29. https://purl.stanford.edu/fv751yt5934.

3
WRITING WITH OUR BODIES
Recovering Pathos through Critical Embodiment Pedagogy

Christina V. Cedillo

In "*Memoria* Is a Friend of Ours," Victor Villanueva connects memory to experience and authority.[1] Unfortunately, Villanueva notes, "Memory simply cannot be adequately portrayed in the conventional discourse of the academy."[2] Academic language permits us to make sense of ideas and analyze arguments, but such discourse is "very weak in pathos," tied as it is to the "Aristotelian ideal of being completely logocentric."[3] Rereading Villanueva's essay, I am drawn to the term's double meaning: "logocentric," meaning the privileging of words but also the privileging of logic, as if logic alone creates communicative meaning. Words can never fully capture lived experience. While they can represent reality and reflect organizational frameworks, pathos determines many of our reasons for communicating. In addition, as Matthew S. S. Johnson argues in chapter 2 of this volume, pathos is "as powerful as logos, even potentially as sustainable," meaning that academia's singular focus on logical discourse can obscure the power of pathos to deleterious effect. By continuing to ignore or discount the affective dimensions of rhetoric, we also fail to account for how people imbue words with meaning based on emotions.

Therefore, our efforts to reclaim memory require that we recuperate pathos as a crucial element of building knowledge. Although words cannot render our realities in their totality, people from marginalized communities share our stories to remind one another that we are not alone, that we are still here, and that we shall endure. We receive and interpret each other's "incomplete" stories (by logical standards) by filling in gaps using shared affective repertoire, a "nonarchival system of transfer" built experientially that permits us to detect vital resonances despite differences in the details.[4] We know firsthand that "language is not the only medium or material that speaks."[5] It is vital that we reclaim not only ancestral and communal memories but all of the rhetorical dimensions

https://doi.org/10.7330/9781646424665.c003

used to communicate them. Yet feelings and the bodies that experience them are often equated with a lack of reason and the basest forms of persuasion. This framing of emotions as patently illogical and bodies as "mere matter" is used to disparage marginalized communities who use embodiment and pathos to enact story and relationship. Normative rhetorical instruction thus becomes a means to save us from ourselves.

Consequently, I argue for the use of critical embodiment pedagogies in the composition classroom as a means to make more inclusive learning spaces for students from marginalized communities. Such pedagogies center bodies' being in the world as the source of epistemological knowledge, and so they regard pathos as a valued rhetorical architectonic rather than a crude appeal to be unethically exploited. First, working from a de-colonial cultural rhetorics perspective, I deliberately trace a corpo-centric thread within the discipline characterized by cultural rhetorics and composition scholarship that recovers bodies and affect as key elements in communication. These cumulative critiques illustrate how the disregard for real bodies renders "the body" a monolithic whitestream notion that erases forms of violence faced by bodies that are made to embody difference. Then, I explain how an orientation toward critical embodiment can help rhet/comp instructors invite memory, bodily knowing, and pathos into the classroom and the discipline through the use of story.

RECLAIMING BODY KNOWLEDGE

Story is not a simple diversion but a vital rhetorical technology that permits cultural groups to cohere. Storying as teaching engages generations' worth of reflection on stories to build consubstantiality, or, in Indigenous terms, to enact peoplehood. In an often-cited passage, Daniel Heath Justice reminds us that "kinship isn't a static thing; it's dynamic, ever in motion . . . something that's done more than something that simply is."[6] Part of that doing includes sharing stories. Indeed, storying is both a vital relational technology and a crucial act in creating and sustaining culture and identity. For that reason, it's important to think of storytelling's ethical dimensions. As Andrea Riley-Mukavetz states in "Developing a Relational Scholarly Practice," Indigenous intellectual tradition exemplifies how "being a good storyteller means creating an intimate and participatory relationship with the audience."[7] Thus, storying, as I use it here, is less about talking at others and more about inviting them into mutually respectful, mutually sustaining conversation. It's about practicing relationality and being accountable to one another, recognizing that (as they say in Spanish) every person is a whole world, autonomous but akin, and that every person inhabits a complex respective reality. What determines much of that reality is embodied identity—shaped by power dynamics, relational networks, and the body's signification and significance within event-spaces.[8] All of these factors create and are created by the identities we know as race, gender, dis/ability, and so on.

Within composition and rhetoric studies, select critics have argued that bodies matter in meaning making—indeed, that they enmatter meaning—and that we should not discount their analytical relevance. In *Rhetorical Bodies*, Barbara Dickson explains how actual living bodies connect to both material rhetorics and the social construction of bodies, explaining that this corporeal-theoretical nexus teaches us about invention, agency, and persuasion.[9] Kristie S. Fleckenstein's work on somatic mind, which "fus[es] materiality and discourse without totalizing or essentializing identity and meaning," and imageword, the "embodiment of literacy through imagery," shows why we cannot ignore the body's influence on learning and writing.[10] Debra Hawhee's research, from ancient Greek athletics to Kenneth Burke's interest in the body, reveals that "rhetoric isn't just a cerebral, conscious process" but a process that is "messy, unpredictable" and that unavoidably involves corporeality.[11] More recently, scholars like A. Abby Knoblauch and Karma R. Chávez have helped hone our understanding of the bodily dimensions of writing and communication by refining critical terminology and clarifying vital distinctions. Knoblauch distinguishes among "embodied language," "embodied knowledge," and "embodied rhetoric"—terms often conflated or elided by researchers.[12] Chávez provides a survey of feminist scholarship that shows that the abstract notion of the body undergirding most of rhetorical criticism and praxis is actually the very real, material bodies of white men.[13] In addition, Chávez notes the contributions to rhetorical studies by Black and women of color feminists such as Olga Idriss Davis and Bernadette Marie Calafell, as well as disability rhetorics scholars like Jay Timothy Dolmage and performance studies scholars like Phaedra C. Pezzullo—whose collective works can help researchers and teachers reorient their theoretical, historical, and methodological approaches.[14]

Given my purpose here of tying bodies to storying and the recovery of pathos, however, I deliberately turn to scholars working within cultural rhetorics, a subfield that emphasizes the need to disrupt "the facility of canonical Western rhetorical theories and practices to account for the experiences of non-Western peoples" and highlight "the cultural specificity of all rhetorical practices/productions."[15] For cultural rhetoricians like myself, issues of place and space, constellations and communities, stories and counterstories cannot be separated from writing or rhetoric. As the members of the Cultural Rhetorics Theory Lab explain, "The practice of story is integral to doing cultural rhetorics," although "these may not be the kinds of stories you're used to hearing, or the kinds of things you're used to recognizing as story."[16] Much of cultural rhetorics scholarship promotes de-linking from colonial matrices of knowledge production and identity formation. Cultural rhetorics approaches invite those of us from marginalized communities to contest dominant cultural narratives about who we are as human beings and to reclaim our culturally situated frameworks and praxes. Cultural rhetorics scholars stress the centrality of affect and bodies to understanding how and why people communicate, meaning that we eschew appeals to neutrality and objectivity in favor of foregrounding the particularities of embodied experience. This crucial difference ensures that bodies cannot be automatically theorized as white, male, able-bodied, cis, and so on, and that the very real violences faced by bodies made to embody difference cannot be ignored. The whitestream body typically universalized, along with its attendant privileges and experiences, must be recognized as just as contingent as "diverse" bodies. Furthermore, the stories any one body can tell depend on the specific intersections of access that body inhabits.

Conversely, stories are an embodying technology. Scholarship by Villanueva, Lois Agnew and colleagues, M. Remi Yergeau, and others represents just some of the works that demonstrate why researchers, teachers, writers, and readers must account for the diverse social, cultural, political, and material forces that constrain and marginalize certain bodies.[17] Villanueva examines how white supremacist tropes make their way into everything from politics to student papers, informing how people are "read" racially; Powell (in Agnew) calls out the larger discipline's tendency to prioritize logocentric texts over materiality, bodies, or the meaning that either produces; and Yergeau firmly grounds their analysis of autism rhetorics (how autistics communicate and how nonautistics speak over people with autism) in the stimming, messy, beautiful disabled body in motion.[18] Bodies are wherever communication occurs, or at least they should be, except they are often erased under the dominance of the Word even among those of us who can never ignore our racialized, (non-)gendered, or disabled bodies. Hence, Eli Clare writes that "there are disability thinkers who can talk all day about the body as metaphor and symbol but never mention flesh and blood, bone and tendon—never even acknowledge their own bodies"—even though "without the lived bodily experience of identity and oppression, we won't truly be able to refigure the world."[19] We are taught to ignore our bodies while writing—"deadlines don't care if you're sick or in distress"—and in writing—"don't you dare use I or write for people like you"—just like everyone else. However, a cultural rhetorics praxis demands that we situate ourselves clearly and acknowledge what we can know from our specific perspective. Stories are not pulled from the aether (ancient Greek pun intended); real people tell them.

Rhetoric and writing teach us how to instigate movement—emotional, intellectual, and physical. For that reason, we cannot ignore the body's importance in sharing the stories that make us who we are, whether we are the tellers or the listeners. Otherwise, we risk losing layers of meaning that are especially vital to projects of re-humanization and survivance undertaken by Black, Indigenous, and people of color (BIPOC). Colonization frames BIPOC as "ruled by impulses and superstition," lacking in moral and ontological integrity.[20] These deliberately constructed fantasies are typically transposed onto the body so that BIPOC are described as overly physical and barbarous. Such Othered bodies stand in contrast to the white "rational" subject ostensibly ruled by the mind rather than by sensuality and whose body consequently disappears. This erasure renders the white subject as "dis/embodied" objectivity, meaning it personifies the omnipresent voice of immanent truth and reason while all other bodies become hyper-visible or conspicuously racialized. While these issues may seem to some far afield of basic composition's wheelhouse, their effects have major implications for how we teach writing. Below are just a few examples that show how a cultural rhetorics focus on bodies in relationship to stories can enhance our analytical repertoire.

A cultural rhetorics praxis stresses that embodied perspectives matter because rhetoric finds its grounding in real bodies living within complex networks of relations. For that reason, ethical writers must be careful of the tropes and assumptions they use, and they must understand how writing interacts with other modalities to affect real human beings. For example, the racializing tropes that target immigrants are created through language use, visual depiction, and spatial regulation. In "Containment and Interdependence," V. Jo Hsu connects the current Covid-19 pandemic to smallpox outbreaks in the late 1800s to show how historically, Chinese communities have been blamed for spreading sickness. Hsu explains, "When epidemics appeared in the city—even though Chinatown experienced fewer smallpox cases per capita than the rest of San Francisco—Chinese patients were barred from public hospitals for fear of contamination. Rhetorical containment did not actually prevent the spread of disease, but it did render Chinese populations disproportionately vulnerable to illness and death."[21] Although white authorities tried to "contain" the disease by constricting Chinese people's mobility, the white economy relied heavily on Chinese labor, revealing borders between communities as "far more permeable than racism and classism would have us believe."[22] During this time, official policies and communal institutions pushed reforms with far-reaching consequences for disabled people and other minority communities, marking disabled bodies as needing to be hidden from public view and helping to create a "model minority" wedge group that could be used to affirm Black and Native inferiority. Along similar lines, J. David Cisneros shows how Latinx immigrants have been associated with pollution and disorder, framed as a threat to the fabric of white society.[23]

These cases reveal how whitestream group identity is established against that of other groups, often through processes of rhetorical denigration. As a result, dominant culture histories are sustained not only by the frequent exclusion of minoritized groups from the official record but by actual segregation. Immigrants and racialized people are tied to contamination so that their presence is seen as threatening to living ("clean") bodies, the body politic, and the story of exceptionalism that says these groups did nothing as opposed to being prevented from doing anything. Hence, the stories laid bare by a focus on how Othered bodies are demonized teach us that silences are usually the result of silencing and that we must ask ourselves who we are speaking over as we ourselves write. In addition, we must acknowledge that rhetorics do not occur in isolation but ripple outward to affect more than their intended audiences.

Cultural rhetorics also asks us to consider how the body affects the way we learn, write, and experience the world through our connections to our surroundings. Research on embodied literacies, particularly land-based rhetorics, reveals that our culturally oriented bodies allow us to make sense of things and to speak accordingly as we inhabit different spaces. Kristin L. Arola writes about the look of social media interfaces, noting that their seemingly inconspicuous aesthetics become obvious when viewed through a non-dominant culture lens. Since the look and usability of an interface attract particular users, Arola wonders what an Indigenous interface might look like, and a group of respondents makes suggestions that Arola interprets as promoting "a visible promise of Indianness."[24] Regardless of whether respondents' responses are tribally informed, they point to a problem with her original question regarding design and being Indian. Rather than an interface "looking Indian," an interface should allow users to engage in "doing Indian," that is, facilitate composition based in rhetorical sovereignty "within a preexisting and shifting web of relations."[25] Arola concludes that designs that ostensibly demonstrate cultural affinity are "intimately connected to issues of embodiment and race" for most audiences.[26]

These connections hold for other forms of rhetoric, too. In "Cultivating Land-Based Literacies and Rhetorics," Gabriela Raquel Ríos explains how perspectives on literacy are usually "bound up in notions of race, labor, productivity, and even 'humanity.'"[27] Listening to farm laborer organizers like Gerardo Reyes of the Coalition of Immokalee Workers, Ríos notes that rhetors like Reyes also acknowledge literacy's connections to these notions, albeit as critique: their rhetorics are read by the dominant culture through frameworks of traditional Euro-Western literacies that fetishize print rather than traditional Indigenous literacies that demand skilled knowledge of and interaction with the land. This difference has major implications for the teaching of composition. As Ríos points out, "Though in Rhet-Comp we tend to locate a link between citizenship and literacy (often as a relatively recent phenomenon), scholars in Indigenous studies locate that same link as one between settler-colonialism and literacy, citing a different historical trajectory and locus for understanding formations of literacy."[28] Writing courses usually treat writing as though it happens in a vacuum or is only about what makes it onto the page while overlooking the critical importance of bodies and/in spaces to composition. How our bodies are construed, how the forms of communication we are able to embody are valued—these matters determine what spaces we are able to enter or feel safe in, what conversations we have access to, and whether we are "heard."

Finally, by recognizing the body's centrality in communicating, we can properly account for the power of affective rhetorics. In writing about Black women's rhetorical impatience as a tactic that challenges misogynoir, Tamika L. Carey states, "Rhetorics of impatience are performances of frustration or dismissal and time-based arguments that reflect or pursue haste for the purpose of discipline . . . These rhetorics foreground the assumption that equity and justice for one's self, Black women, and Black communities is already overdue and, thus, requires speed and decisive action."[29] Rhetorical impatience demands concrete action and change by highlighting the physical and material circumstances that undermine Black women's dignity and humanity. In analyzing the public rhetorics of figures including Fannie Lou Hamer,

Carey finds that performing impatience enhances the grounds of argumentation by disrupting a degrading status quo; in Hamer's case, the affective dimension of her speech reveals that "the disrespect of racism is a dehumanizing systemic disease" even as her verbal style stokes the public's compassion.[30]

Ersula Ore also highlights the multifaceted character of Black women's affective rhetorics in "Pushback: A Pedagogy of Care," where she defines pushback as "a strategic counterrhetoric" that permits the rhetor to "actively and aggressively respond to injustice by consciously disrupting acts of implicit racism as they operate within the historical, social, and political sphere of America's post–civil rights era."[31] In our historical moment, identity-avoidant racism stresses overt civility toward BIPOC while leaving oppressive social structures in place.[32] Pushback serves a pedagogical purpose by leading people to question how the warrants of their thinking bolster whiteness and white privilege. Pathos, or the appeal to emotion, has usually been discounted by traditional (white, masculine) rhetoric as simple manipulation or a cheap ploy. However, Carey and Ore teach us that emotions can provide the basis for rhetorical methodologies that prioritize humanization and signify resistance to unjust conditions.

Cultural rhetorics approaches recognize that knowing always engages the body and emotions because they inform how and why we transmit and receive information. They also provide the foundations for collective knowledges based in "diverse but interconnected bodily histories and memories."[33] Conversely, "Every act by the so-called self involves profound and complex collective histories."[34] Circumstances personally experienced can become a source of corporeal identification or dissociation owing to their affective resonances. We speak, write, and act through a desire to connect, contest, or just be seen as human. Our writing pedagogies should reflect these realities.

CRITICAL EMBODIMENT PEDAGOGIES

Different bodies inhabit radically different worlds even as we navigate the same spaces. Writing must adapt to those worlds rather than students conforming to whitestream standards of composition. When instructors demand that writing happen through a one-size-fits-all model, they force on students the idea that there is only one right way of knowing. As Nicole Khoury, Nicholas Behm, and Sherry Rankins-Robertson explain in chapter 5 of this collection, this alienating notion helps create a "culture . . . that produces so much angst, anxiety, and fear." Writing about a lack of "affective infrastructure" in graduate programs, Khoury, Behm, and Rankins-Robertson explain that attending to students' emotional and bodily needs can help us "reconfigure dominant norms and revise the competitive culture" too prevalent in academia. Bodies, identities, epistemologies, and rhetorical customs emerge through social networks that constellate space, time, culture, gender, language, dis/ability, and other categories that establish the norm and difference; positionality changes depending on context. Writing pedagogies must be receptive of diverse ways of being and knowing and introduce students to composition practices that also accommodate such diversity. Recognizing that each student is their own world requires making room for the goals they themselves deem important too, based on who they are and want to be, not on who we believe they should be.

Rhetorics establishes how bodies take on meaning in relation to each other, bodies determine how we engage in rhetorical activity, and affect informs this reciprocal process by guiding our uses of rhetoric to safeguard our humanity. Our teaching should allow students opportunities to practice analysis that centers this nexus. One way to do this is by employing pedagogies based in critical embodiment. I define critical embodiment pedagogies as approaches that center the body in response to various epistemological concerns including the habituated mind-body divide, the invisibility and hyper-visibility of Othered bodies, and the phenomenological backgrounding of bodies in writing—and how these issues ensure the erasure of marginalized groups from (and through) dominant histories, traditions, and practices. This approach does not advocate the use of specific methods, intended instead to provide a framework through which instructors may build up a personal repertoire that works for them and helps them adapt their praxes as needed depending on the unique circumstances of teaching contexts. Plainly stated, a critical embodiment writing praxis welcomes lived experiences and identities into the classroom and onto the page/screen.

My take on critical embodiment pedagogy draws theoretically from feminist rhetorics, disability studies, critical race theory, de-colonial studies, and critical pedagogy. In *Feminist Rhetorical Practices*, Jacqueline Jones Royster and Gesa E. Kirsch argue that the task of rhetorical recovery demands innovative means by which to define our subjects and alternative methodologies for analyzing their modes of communication. They urge us to "take into account the internal journey toward discovery—acknowledging the bodily effects, the visceral changes in mind, heart, backbone, and stomach that the discovery process occasions."[35] The sensorial body is a communicative and interpretive medium, capable of receiving, transmitting, creating, and deflecting meaning based on reactions we have and inspire in others. Feminist rhetoricians advance the body as a medium of meaning making but also focus on social norms that influence how we weigh the rhetorical value of said making. Working from a feminist/disability studies angle, Jay Timothy Dolmage and Cynthia Lewiecki-Wilson argue that "we must examine the ways that [the] body shapes possibilities for expression by disciplining bodily difference or enforcing bodily norms."[36] Furthermore, as Subini Ancy Annamma, David J. Connor, and Beth A. Ferri argue, race determines much regarding access for those with disabilities, and race is constructed within a framework predicated on dis/ability.[37]

No matter how disembodied we pretend that writing is, our analyses depend on our judgment of the bodies that produce it. Thus, to further nuance the way social, cultural, and political factors influence how we learn and delimit access to knowledge, I also draw on critical race theory (CRT). CRT "originated in schools of law in the late 1980s with a group of scholars seeking to examine and challenge race and racism in the United States legal system and society."[38] CRT recognizes that race and racism determine much about life in the US, challenges claims of neutrality based on identity-avoidant frameworks that deny the existence or salience of race, advances education as a social justice tool, acknowledges the firsthand knowledge intrinsic to genres employed by people of color and other marginalized groups, and analyzes -isms from historical and interdisciplinary angles.[39] Within critical embodiment pedagogies, CRT reminds us to train our attention on real-world conditions that students may or may not be working in, which we may or may not be aware of, so we can teach from a perspective of generosity rather than deficit. For members of Black, Indigenous, and other communities of color, many of the oppressive constraints we face began with colonization. Hence, critical embodiment pedagogies must also emphasize critical themes highlighted by de-colonial projects. Five hundred years later, those of us of Indigenous and African descent struggle to understand why we find it difficult to fit in at school, why our thinking and approaches to learning might not mesh with whitestream expectations even when we speak and write in Standard Written English. Addressing issues of issues of colonization and coloniality as we teach writing is so vital because "to speak now, and teach now, is to try to give all of us a new chance."[40] Furthermore, as Ernest Stromberg argues, "If we limit the definition of rhetoric to a system of techniques for achieving eloquence and effective argumentation," we discount or ignore communicative traditions outside the Euro-Western canon.[41] Cultures maintain different paradigms for what constitutes proof, argument, and exchange; as teachers of writing, we cannot be familiar with them all. However, we can become attuned to welcoming knowledges students bring with them into the classroom through respectful exchange and a genuine interest in combatting erasure.

Finally, these orienting influences merge with practical application provided by critical pedagogy. Educators like Paulo Freire and Donaldo Macedo, Henry A. Giroux, and Antonia Darder and Luis F. Mirón advocate for teaching that empowers students and positions them as co-creators of knowledge alongside their instructors.[42] Critical pedagogy's main goal is to "humanize schools so that they become more hospitable to the lives, interests, backgrounds and aspirations of young people (especially those from 'disadvantaged' or challenging contexts), rather than institutions of incarceration, fear, punishment and retribution."[43] While these are noble goals, we must still be wary lest we engage in *uncritical* forms of critical pedagogy. Using terms like empowerment and social change can easily re-inscribe the same power dynamics and hierarchies we wish to contest unless we clearly articulate what social issues we mean to address.[44] And our methods and practices should be established by the real needs of our students rather than by dominant culture assumptions regarding deficit or empowerment.

A critical embodiment approach promotes the creation of student-centered pedagogies suited to instructors' individual teaching styles. This comprehensive theoretical grounding can productively guide instructors seeking to invent methodologies and strategies rooted in visions of equity, access, and student dignity. Still, we can distill the insights provided by these different fields of study into a set of principles to which we should all be attuned.

Embodiment determines a lot about our lives, from questions of access to concerns about safety to concepts of literacy. Foregrounding embodiment in composition allows us to highlight literacy's social functions as performance and interrelationship. Tony Mirabelli provides an expansive view of literacy that includes the ability to "read" and respond to others' body language. He states, "The concept of multiliteracies supplements traditional literacy pedagogy by addressing the multiplicity of communications channels and the increasing saliency of cultural and linguistic diversity in the world."[45] Fields like business and technical writing already consider embodied and material contexts—reports must account for people's time; directions are succinctly given to avoid accidents on the factory floor or lab. Other composition courses could benefit from a focus on bodies.

Identity informs how, why, and when we compose. Students should be provided with opportunities to critique identity's impact on composition. Racial and class distinctions are often based in the denigration of particular dialects and registers. Audiences are welcomed or excluded by our rhetorical choices. Genres do not work because they're intrinsically effective; we're trained to favor certain speech forms to enter discourse communities framed as advantageous or respectable. We must analyze our own participation in sociolinguistic systems because through our own uncritical use of these forms, we help bolster the impression that a group's privileged status is based in fact rather than social hierarchy.

Privilege must be addressed openly. Students may be reluctant to discuss privilege, whether they are members of privileged groups who argue that they don't benefit from anything "extra" or members of marginalized groups hoping to circumvent discussions that underscore their hyper-visibility. But the issue of privilege is a fundamental aspect of rhetorical analysis as we make decisions about who matters in terms of audience and who usually gets left out of important conversations. Conversations about the use of stories and counterstories, like those provided by CRT-guided writing studies,[46] can teach students to deploy their respective forms of privilege to make room for others less often heard. They can also learn how to establish rhetorical presence in contesting the social inequities that create oppositional privilege-deficit dynamics. As they engage in these exercises, they come to realize the power of writing.

Writing has real-world impact. Thus, we must take responsibility for our uses of language. Rhetoric never occurs in an ethical vacuum but engages people's material, mental, and affective lives. A relentless elevation of logos over pathos proves a major problem for members of minoritized communities who are already hyper-corporealized by dominant culture norms. BIPOC are characterized as "hysterical," "angry," and "irrational." These stereotypes uphold an oppressive order, and they don't always do their work in grand gestures but through everyday inscription, in what is said and not said.[47] Persuasion may occur through the conventional use of language, but it affects audiences in mental and emotional realms that escape an author's intent, highlighting the slippage between the tractability and the unruliness of language.

Pathos matters and must be reclaimed. Communication happens across multiple literacies and modalities, all of which are received through the body. Affect can help us gauge whether we feel like strangers in the conversations we enter with our writing. How or what do we feel as we write? As Villanueva points out, pathos is discounted in favor of reason, yet it proves "an essential element in the intellect" and of interpretation.[48] Acknowledging our own feelings can allow us to conceive of our audiences as embodied persons too rather than as vague impressions. What do we want our audiences to experience and feel? Using emotion, we might ask if readers are being invited into the spaces created by our writing or whether we are unintentionally "pushing" them out. And we can use such corporeal empathy to more carefully compose pathos-based appeals that are ethical and respectful.

Critical embodiment approaches to pedagogy center students' real-life knowledges and purposely examine how teaching practices sustain injustices targeting those of us who do not experience life in whitestream bodies. Our bodily diversity is overwritten by erasure of the corporeal even as cultural discourses deem us less qualified for intellectual activity, but writing can empower us to declare presence through self-affirmation and self-assertion. As with any pedagogy, developing a teaching praxis based on critical embodiment might not be easy and will take time, but denial of the bodily and material dimensions of writing upholds coloniality and dominance through unawareness or indifference. Every body/Everybody is their own world, so our pedagogies must acknowledge the "pluriverse" present in the classroom and beyond to create spaces of heterogeneous community and possibility. This goal cannot be based in intellectualism. Affective goals, so often excluded from our curricula, must be taught as foundational components of rhetoric and writing praxes. Perhaps in this way, we may not only invite memoria into our individual praxes but ensure that it always holds an honored place.

NOTES

1. This chapter was composed on the historic homelands of the Karankawa and Akokisa peoples.
2. Villanueva, "*Memoria*," 12.
3. Villanueva, "*Memoria*," 12.
4. Taylor, *The Archive and the Repertoire*, xvii.
5. Selzer, "Habeas Corpus," 8.
6. Justice, "Go Away, Water," 352.
7. Riley-Mukavetz, "Developing a Relational Scholarly Practice," 547.
8. Puar, "I Would Rather Be a Cyborg than a Goddess," 60–61.
9. Dickson, "Reading Maternity Materially," 298.
10. Fleckenstein, "Writing Bodies," 286; Fleckenstein, Embodied Literacies, 6.
11. Hawhee, "Rhetorics, Bodies, and Everyday Life," 157.
12. Knoblauch, "Bodies of Knowledge."
13. Chávez, "The Body," 244.
14. Chávez, "The Body," 245–46.
15. Bratta and Powell, "Introduction to the Special Issue."
16. Cultural Rhetorics Theory Lab, "Our Story Begins Here."
17. Villanueva, "Blind," "*Memoria*"; Agnew et al., "Octalog III"; Yergeau, Authoring Autism.

18. Villanueva, "Blind"; Agnew et al., "Octalog III"; Yergeau, *Authoring Autism.*
19. Clare, "Stolen Bodies, Reclaimed Bodies," 364.
20. Hokowhitu, "Haka," 279.
21. Hsu, "Containment and Interdependence," 126–27.
22. Hsu, "Containment and Interdependence," 127.
23. Cisneros, "Contaminated Communities."
24. Arola, "Indigenous Interfaces," 213.
25. Arola, "Indigenous Interfaces," 217.
26. Arola, "Indigenous Interfaces," 214.
27. Ríos "Cultivating Land-Based Literacies and Rhetorics," 62.
28. Ríos, "Cultivating Land-Based Literacies and Rhetorics," 63.
29. Carey, "Necessary Adjustments," 270.
30. Carey, "Necessary Adjustments," 272–73.
31. Ore, "Pushback," 12, 21.
32. See Cedillo, "On Surveillance."
33. Spoel, "Re-inventing Rhetorical Epistemology," 208.
34. Escobar, *Pluriversal Politics,* 21.
35. Royster, and Kirsch, *Feminist Rhetorical Practices,* 87.
36. Dolmage, and Lewiecki-Wilson, "Refiguring Rhetorica," 28.
37. Annamma, Connor, and Ferri, "Dis/ability Critical Race Studies (DisCrit)."
38. Yosso, *Critical Race Counterstories,* 6.
39. Solorzano, Ceja, and Yosso, "Critical Race Theory, Racial Microaggressions, and Campus Racial Climate."
40. King, Gubele, and Anderson, "The Story That Follows," 212.
41. Stromberg, "Rhetoric and American Indians," 2.
42. Freire and Macedo, *Literacy*; Giroux, "When Schools Become Dead Zones of the Imagination"; Darder and Mirón, "Critical Pedagogy in a Time of Uncertainty."
43. Smyth, *Critical Pedagogy for Social Justice,* 56.
44. Ellsworth, "Why Doesn't This Feel Empowering."
45. Mirabelli, "Learning to Serve," 146.
46. See Martinez, *The Rhetoric and Writing of Critical Race Theory.*
47. See Bonilla-Silva and Forman, "I'm Not a Racist but . . ."
48. Villanueva, "*Memoria.*" For more concrete examples of how to reclaim pathos in the classroom, see Carillo, *Teaching Readers in Post-Truth America.*

REFERENCES

Agnew, Lois, Laurie Gries, Zosha Stuckey, Vicki Tolar Burton, Jay Dolmage, Jessica Enoch, Ronald L. Jackson II, LuMing Mao, Malea Powell, Arthur E. Walzer, Ralph Cintron, and Victor Vitanza. "Octalog III: The Politics of Historiography in 2010." *Rhetoric Review* 30, no. 2 (2011): 109–34. https://www.jstor.org/stable/23064002.

Annamma, Subini Ancy, David J. Connor, and Beth A. Ferri. "Dis/ability Critical Race Studies (DisCrit): Theorizing at the Intersections of Race and Dis/ability." *Race, Ethnicity, and Education* 16, no. 1 (2013): 1–31. https://doi.org/10.1080/13613324.2012.730511.

Arola, Kristin L. "Indigenous Interfaces." In *Social Writing/Social Media: Publics, Presentations, and Pedagogies,* edited by Douglas M. Walls and Stephanie Vie, 211–26. Boulder: WAC Clearinghouse, 2017.

Bonilla-Silva, Eduardo, and Tyrone A. Forman. " 'I'm Not a Racist but . . .': Mapping White College Students' Racial Ideology in the USA." *Discourse and Society* 11, no. 1 (2000): 50–85. https://doi.org/10.1177%2F0957926500011001003.

Bratta, Phil, and Malea Powell. "Introduction to the Special Issue: Entering the Cultural Rhetorics Conversations." *Enculturation* 21 (2016). http://enculturation.net/entering-the-cultural-rhetorics-conversations.

Carey, Tamika L. "Necessary Adjustments: Black Women's Rhetorical Impatience." *Rhetoric Review* 39, no. 3 (2020): 269–86. https://doi.org/10.1080/07350198.2020.1764745.

Carillo, Ellen C. *Teaching Readers in Post-Truth America*. Louisville, CO: Utah State University Press, 2018.

Cedillo, Christina V. "On Surveillance, Social Media, and Identity-Avoidant Frameworks." In Privacy Matters: Conversations about Surveillance within and beyond the Classroom, edited by Estee Beck and Les Hutchinson Campos, 129–49. Louisville, CO: Utah State University Press, 2020.

Chávez, Karma R. "The Body: An Abstract and Actual Rhetorical Concept." *Rhetoric Society Quarterly* 48, no. 3 (2018): 242–50. https://doi.org/10.1080/02773945.2018.1454182.

Cisneros, J. David. "Contaminated Communities: The Metaphor of 'Immigrant as Pollutant' in Media Representations of Immigration." *Rhetoric and Public Affairs* 11, no. 4 (Winter 2008): 569–601. https://doi.org/10.1353/rap.0.0068.

Clare, Eli. "Stolen Bodies, Reclaimed Bodies: Disability and Queerness." *Public Culture* 13, no. 3 (Fall 2001): 359–65. https://muse.jhu.edu/article/26252.

Cultural Rhetorics Theory Lab. "Our Story Begins Here: Constellating Cultural Rhetorics." *Enculturation: A Journal of Rhetoric, Writing, and Culture* 25 (2014). http://enculturation.net/our-story-begins-here.

Darder, Antonia, and Luis F. Mirón. "Critical Pedagogy in a Time of Uncertainty: A Call to Action." *Cultural Studies ↔ Critical Methodologies* 6, no. 1 (2006): 5–20. https://doi.org/10.1177%2F1532708605282814.

Dickson, Barbara. "Reading Maternity Materially: The Case of Demi Moore." In *Rhetorical Bodies*, edited by Jack Selzer and Sharon Crowley, 297–314. Madison: University of Wisconsin Press, 1999.

Dolmage, Jay, and Cynthia Lewiecki-Wilson. "Refiguring Rhetorica: Linking Feminist Rhetoric and Disability Studies." In *Rhetorica in Motion: Feminist Rhetorical Methods and Methodologies*, edited by Eileen E. Schell and K. J. Rawson, 23–38. Pittsburgh: University of Pittsburgh Press, 2010.

Ellsworth, Elizabeth. "Why Doesn't This Feel Empowering? Working through the Repressive Myths of Critical Pedagogy." *Harvard Educational Review* 59, no. 3 (1989): 297–325. https://doi.org/10.17763/haer.59.3.058342114k266250.

Escobar, Arturo. *Pluriversal Politics: The Real and the Possible*. Durham, NC: Duke University Press, 2020.

Fleckenstein, Kristie S. *Embodied Literacies: Imageword and a Poetics of Teaching*. Carbondale: Southern Illinois University Press, 2003.

Fleckenstein, Kristie S. "Writing Bodies: Somatic Mind in Composition Studies." *College English* 61, no. 3 (January 1999): 281–306. https://www.jstor.org/stable/379070.

Freire, Paulo, and Donaldo Macedo. *Literacy: Reading the Word and the World*. London: Routledge, 2005.

Giroux, Henry A. "When Schools Become Dead Zones of the Imagination: A Critical Pedagogy Manifesto." *Policy Futures in Education* 12, no. 4 (2014): 491–99. http://www.wwwords.co.uk/PFIE.

Hawhee, Debra. "Rhetorics, Bodies, and Everyday Life." *Rhetoric Society Quarterly* 36, no. 2 (2006): 155–64. https://doi.org/10.1080/02773940600605487.

Hokowhitu, Brendan. "Haka: Colonized Physicality, Body-Logic, and Embodied Sovereignty." In *Performing Indigeneity: Global Histories and Contemporary Experiences*, edited by Laura R. Graham and H. Glenn Penny, 273–304. Lincoln: University of Nebraska Press, 2014.

Hsu, V. Jo. "Containment and Interdependence: Epidemic Logics in Asian American Racialization." *QED: A Journal in GLBTQ Worldmaking* 7, no. 3 (2020): 126–27. https://doi.org/10.14321/qed.7.3.0125.

Justice, Daniel Heath. "'Go Away, Water!' Kinship Criticism and the Decolonization Imperative." In *Learn, Teach, Challenge: Approaching Indigenous Literatures*, edited by

Deanna Reder and Linda M. Morra, 349–71. Waterloo, ON: Wilfrid Laurier University Press, 2016.
King, Lisa, Rose Gubele, and Joyce Rain Anderson. "The Story That Follows: An Epilogue in Three Parts." In *Survivance, Sovereignty, and Story: Teaching American Indian Rhetorics*, edited by Lisa King, Rose Gubele, and Joyce Rain Anderson, 210–16. Boulder: University Press of Colorado, 2015.
Knoblauch, A. Abby. "Bodies of Knowledge: Definitions, Delineations, and Implications of Embodied Writing in the Academy." *Composition Studies* 40, no. 2 (Fall 2012): 50–65. https://www.jstor.org/stable/compstud.40.2.0050.
Martinez, Aja Y. *The Rhetoric and Writing of Critical Race Theory*. Champaign, IL: National Council of Teachers of English, 2020.
Mirabelli, Tony. "Learning to Serve: The Language and Literacy of Food Service Workers." In *What They Don't Learn in School: Literacy in the Lives of Urban Youth*, edited by Jabari Mahiri, 141–62. New York: Peter Lang, 2005.
Ore, Ersula. "Pushback: A Pedagogy of Care." *Pedagogy* 17, no. 1 (2017): 9–33. https://muse.jhu.edu/article/641266.
Puar, Jasbir K. "'I Would Rather Be a Cyborg than a Goddess': Becoming-Intersectional in Assemblage Theory." *PhiloSOPHIA* 2, no. 1 (2012): 49–66. https://www.pdcnet.org/sophia/content/sophia_2012_0002_0001_0049_0066.
Riley-Mukavetz, Andrea. "Developing a Relational Scholarly Practice: Snakes, Dreams, and Grandmothers." *College Composition and Communication* 71, no. 4 (June 2020): 545–65. https://library.ncte.org/journals/CCC/issues/v71-4.
Ríos, Gabriela Raquel. "Cultivating Land-Based Literacies and Rhetorics." *Literacy in Composition Studies* 3, no. 1 (March 2015): 60–70. https://doi.org/10.21623/1.3.1.5.
Royster, Jacqueline Jones, and Gesa E. Kirsch. *Feminist Rhetorical Practices: New Horizons for Rhetoric, Composition, and Literacy Studies*. Carbondale: Southern Illinois Press, 2012.
Selzer, Jack. "Habeas Corpus: An Introduction." In *Rhetorical Bodies*, edited by Jack Selzer and Sharon Crowley, 3–15. Madison: University of Wisconsin Press, 1999.
Smyth, John. *Critical Pedagogy for Social Justice*. New York: Continuum, 2011.
Solorzano, Daniel, Miguel Ceja, and Tara Yosso. "Critical Race Theory, Racial Microaggressions, and Campus Racial Climate: The Experiences of African American College Students." *Journal of Negro Education* 69, no. ½ (Winter–Spring 2000): 60–73. https://www.jstor.org/stable/2696265
Spoel, Philippa. "Re-inventing Rhetorical Epistemology: Donna Haraway's and Nicole Brossard's Embodied Visions." In *The Changing Tradition: Women in the History of Rhetoric*, edited by Christine Mason Sutherland and Rebecca Sutcliffe, 199–212. Calgary: University of Calgary Press, 1999.
Stromberg, Ernest. "Rhetoric and American Indians: An Introduction." In *American Indian Rhetorics of Survivance: Word Medicine, Word Magic*, edited by Ernest Stromberg, 1–12. Pittsburgh: University of Pittsburgh Press, 2006.
Taylor, Diana. *The Archive and the Repertoire: Performing Cultural Memory in the Americas*. Durham, NC: Duke University Press, 2003.
Villanueva, Victor. "Blind: Talking about the New Racism." *Writing Center Journal* 26, no. 1 (2006): 3–19. https://www.jstor.org/stable/43442234.
Villanueva, Victor. "*Memoria* Is a Friend of Ours: On the Discourse of Color." *College English* 67, no. 1 (September 2004): 9–19. https://www.jstor.org/stable/4140722.
Yergeau, M. Remi. *Authoring Autism*. Durham, NC: Duke University Press, 2018.
Yosso, Tara J. *Critical Race Counterstories along the Chicana/Chicano Educational Pipeline*. New York: Routledge, 2006.

SECTION TWO

Careful Leadership

4
CONTINUING WRITING ACROSS THE CURRICULUM PROGRAMS AMID THE CONTRACTION OF HIGHER EDUCATION
Vision, Mission, and Strategy

Christopher Basgier

Some of the most formative historical moments for rhetoric, composition, and writing studies have occurred during times of expansion in higher education in the United States.[1] Today, however, we are in the midst of not another expansion of higher education but a contraction, one that promises to disrupt rhetoric, composition, and writing studies once more. As I describe below, the current, ongoing contraction of higher education includes the rising costs of a college education, cuts to state appropriations for public institutions, college closures, and demographic changes in the United States generally and in higher education specifically. As a writing across the curriculum (WAC) administrator, I am keenly aware that WAC programs often have precarious institutional positions and funding, leaving them vulnerable to reduction or elimination amid decreased enrollments and budget cuts—especially in the wake of the collective trauma of the Covid-19 pandemic (see Khoury, Behm, and Rankins-Robertson, chapter 5, this volume). National data are unclear about how these changes have affected WAC programs, which exist at somewhere between a third and half of institutions nationwide.[2] To better understand how contraction might affect WAC programs, we need a more localized, institutional view of programmatic threats, one I provide through a narrative of recent contractions in University Writing at Auburn University. In response to our own local contraction, my program has invested time and resources into reimagining our vision, mission, and strategy.[3] With my program as an example-in-progress, I illustrate how WAC leaders can respond intentionally, not reactively, to contraction. If we are to survive the contraction of higher education, WAC programs will need to ensure that faculty and administrators alike see the value of the program's vision, recognize how the program's mission aligns with the university's mission, and understand how strategies work to realize the mission in support of the long-term vision.

THE CONTRACTION OF HIGHER EDUCATION

Most of us are probably familiar with the rising costs of a college education and the austerity measures put in place in the wake of the 2008 financial crisis and the Great Recession. However, additional changes in the ensuing decade and a half signal an ongoing contraction of higher education in the United States.

On the face of it, higher education may not look like it is contracting, especially when we consider the continued increase in expenditures. According to the National Center for Education Statistics (NCES),[4] higher education expenditures rose 23.2 percent between 2010–11 and 2017–18. Although commentators like to point to administrative bloat and pricey amenities as the causes of increasingly large budgets, the real culprits are macro-level economic and political factors. According to Robert B. Archibald and David H. Feldman, "Productivity in higher education has grown very slowly relative to the average rate of productivity growth for the economy as a whole," a phenomenon known as "cost disease."[5] Cost disease, the authors explain, affects most personal service industries that struggle to increase the number of people served—whether students in a classroom or customers in a barber shop—without significantly reducing quality or increasing expenditures. Because the number served tends to stay relatively constant, firms must raise prices to keep up with growth in the rest of the economy. Simply put, everything from health benefits to building materials has become more expensive because the US economy continues to grow. Archibald and Feldman also note that colleges' highly educated workforce is becoming more expensive (8), and institutions tend to be early adopters of new technologies, when they are most expensive (9)—both of which contribute to the growth in higher education expenditures.

While these changes explain increased expenditures, they do not necessarily explain increased tuition costs. According to the NCES, the average cost of tuition across all institution types rose from $19,019 in 2007–8 to $23,835 in 2017–18.[6] Archibald and Feldman place the burden of increased tuition squarely in the lap of the government.[7] While overall revenues increased 33 percent between 2007–8 and 2017–18, federal, state, and local appropriations increased only 15 percent.[8] Moreover, the proportion of revenue from appropriations has dropped substantially

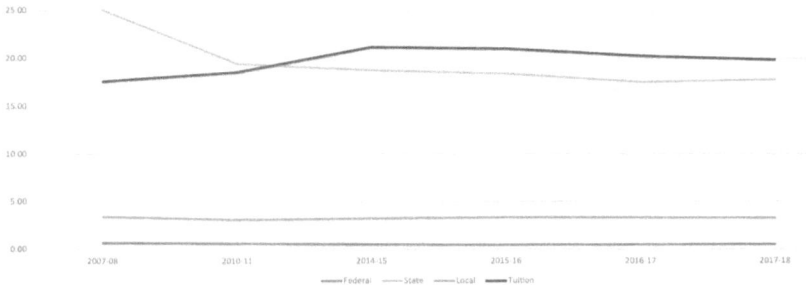

Figure 4.1. Percent revenues from tuition and appropriations, 2007–8 to 2017–18

compared with tuition. As illustrated in figure 4.1,[9] in 2007–8, public colleges and universities received 17.60 percent of revenues from tuition and fees ($5,782 per full-time equivalent [FTE] student) and 29.14 percent from appropriations ($9,568 per FTE). By 2017–18, public institutions received 19.88 percent of revenues from tuition and fees ($7,693 per FTE) and 21.61 percent from appropriations ($8,358 per FTE). The largest percentage reduction in appropriations occurred at the state level, which dropped from 25.05 percent of revenues to 17.83 percent over that decade. In short, appropriations have not kept up with a rise in costs due to cost disease, which has put an increased burden on students to bear the cost of college tuition, with many seeking and struggling to repay financial aid—a burden that has fallen disproportionately on the shoulders of women and Black, Indigenous, and people of color (BIPOC) students.[10] Preliminary data indicate that the Covid-19 pandemic exacerbated the economic precarity (see Khoury, Behm, and Rankins-Robertson, chapter 5, this volume) of women, BIPOC, genderqueer/gender-nonconforming, and international students and forced an estimated 4.4 percent of students to withdraw from college who might have been able to stay enrolled otherwise.[11]

Alongside public disinvestment in higher education, some colleges and universities have been closing or merging. After hitting a peak of 4,209 institutions in 2010–11, the number of institutions fell to 3,652 by 2018–19, a drop of about 13 percent.[12] As figure 4.2 illustrates,[13] most closures and mergers have affected public and private nonprofit two-year institutions and private for-profit institutions, with only public and private four-year institutions having modest growth in the number of institutions. Some analysts, including the late Clayton Christensen of the Harvard Business School, have predicted that up to 50 percent of all colleges and universities in the United States would be bankrupt by the end

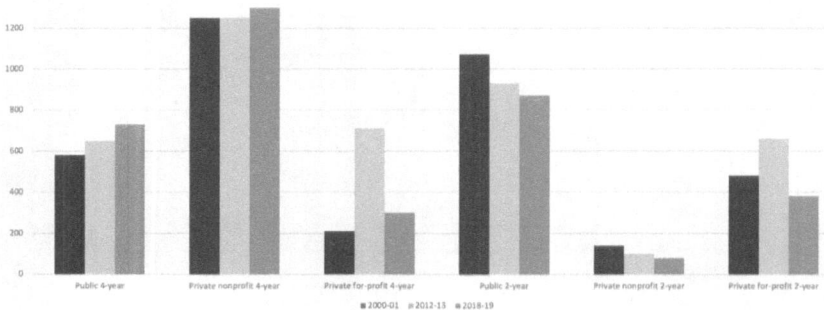

Figure 4.2. Number of US degree-granting institutions, select years

of the 2020s.[14] That said, such dire predictions appear to be overblown: according to the website *Higher Ed Dive*, which tracks college closures, 68 institutions had closed or merged since 2016 as of the time of this writing.[15] A significant acceleration in consolidation would have to happen to meet Christensen's prediction. Still, college closures do seem to be part of an overall pattern of contraction in the industry.

More pressing, perhaps, than college closures is a recent and ongoing reduction in enrollment. After a peak in 2010, undergraduate enrollment has dropped precipitously and is not likely to recover for many years.[16] In 2010, nearly 18.1 million undergraduates were enrolled in US colleges and universities. By 2019, that number had dropped 9.6 percent, to approximately 16.5 million, and is only expected to creep up to 17 million by 2029. As with college closures, two-year colleges have been hit the hardest. From their 2010 high of 7.6 million enrolled, two-year college enrollments have decreased 25 percent, to 5.5 million. Four-year institutions, meanwhile, have consistently increased their enrollments, although numbers are expected to remain essentially flat through 2029 (figure 4.3).[17] Some regions may be hit harder than others, even at four-year institutions. According to Paul Copley and Edward Douthett, the number of traditional college-age individuals is projected to decrease by 15 percent nationwide through 2029. Most drastically, the authors note, the midwestern states Ohio, Indiana, Illinois, Wisconsin, and Michigan are looking at a forecasted 22 percent drop in the number of college-age individuals. These declines are due in part to lower birth rates and a resulting reduction in the number of high school graduates.[18] Peace Bransberger, Colleen Falkenstern, and Patrick Lane predict that the number of high school graduates will rise to 3.85 million in 2027 and then fall through 2037 (see figure 4.4).[19]

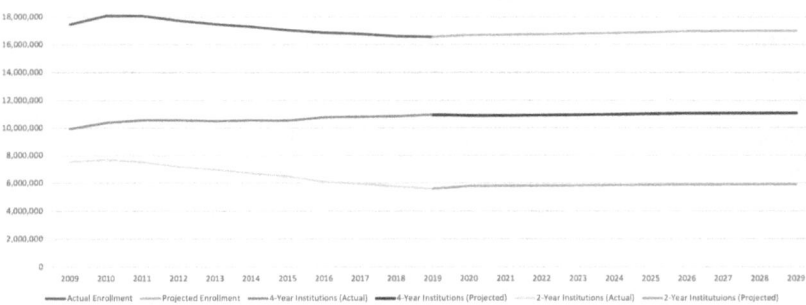

Figure 4.3. Actual and projected undergraduate enrollment in US colleges and universities, 2009–29

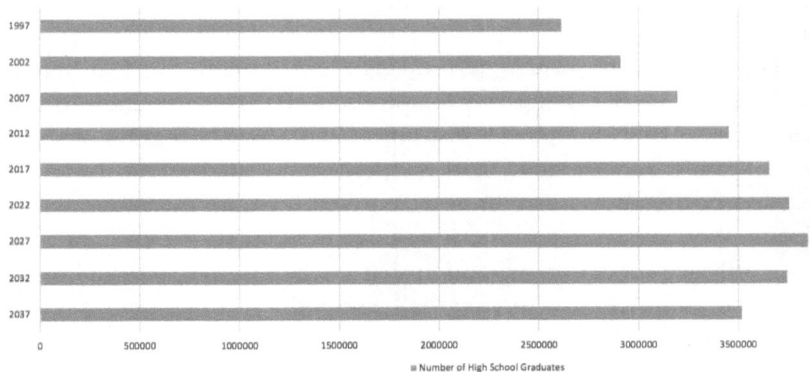

Figure 4.4. Actual and projected high school graduates, select years, 1997–2037

Taken together, these data suggest not so much a burst bubble, or "demographic cliff," as higher education media has called it,[20] but rather a depressurization within the bubble, a deflation—or, as I have characterized it, a contraction in higher education. In sum, we have, and will likely continue to see over the next decade and a half, (1) less state investment in higher education; (2) fewer institutions, as financially at-risk colleges and universities close their doors or merge; (3) fewer high school graduates; and (4) a decrease or at least flatlining of undergraduate enrollments, with some regions like the Midwest hit especially hard. The institutions that do remain will be left competing for a smaller pool of students whose tuition dollars will make up an increasing proportion of revenues, absent a substantial public reinvestment in higher education.

CONTRACTION AND WRITING ACROSS THE CURRICULUM

According to Michelle Cox, Jeffrey R. Galin, and Dan Melzer, WAC programs not built with sustainability in mind face "continuing vulnerability,"[21] a statement that seems doubly true amid the trends detailed above. National data are inconclusive about the current state of WAC in the United States; at best, we may be able to say that somewhere between a third and half of institutions have a WAC/WID program. According to the International WAC/WID Mapping Project, just over 50 percent of institutions reported having a WAC/WID program in 2008 (n = 566), versus 52 percent in 2020 (n = 261). Despite the modest increase in percentage, far more institutions responded to the survey in 2008 (n = 1,126) than in 2020 (n = 498).[22] Numerous explanations could account for the lower response rate, including a potential drop in the number of WAC programs nationwide, leading fewer individuals to respond in the first place.

The National Census of Writing data are similarly unclear, namely because the census changed questions between 2013 and 2017. In 2013, the survey asked whether the institution had a WAC program or upper-level writing requirement, and 53 percent of institutions (n = 341) replied in the affirmative. In 2017, it asked separate questions about a formal WAC program and a writing-intensive course requirement. That year, only 33 percent of respondents (n = 117) reported a formal writing program, while 52 percent (n = 182) reported a writing-intensive course requirement—a number more in line with the 2013 National Census of Writing and the 2008 and 2020 International WAC/WID Mapping Project findings.[23] These data suggest that many institutions with writing-intensive course requirements lack a dedicated, formal WAC program. Despite their shortcomings, the national data can help us imagine some potential effects of contraction on WAC.[24] Already, two-year institutions are less likely to have a WAC/WID program than are four-year institutions. The National Census of Writing reported WAC programs in just 23 percent (n = 7) of two-year institutions in 2017.[25] The data from the International WAC/WID Mapping Project are not much better, with WAC/WID programs in only 32 percent (n = 24) of community colleges in 2020. No doubt, WAC/WID programs are difficult to implement at institutions with high teaching and service expectations and little room for release time.[26] Given the fact that two-year institutions seem especially hard-hit by the contraction of higher education, WAC is likely to continue to languish at two-year colleges.

In general, WAC programs remain vulnerable to budget cuts that continue to afflict colleges and universities affected by the contraction of higher education. Those that are not sustainably embedded in the university infrastructure may morph into a small group of dedicated faculty without much agency to affect institutional culture—or else be unable to progress beyond that level toward a more established or integrated program characterized by features like permanent funding, dedicated space, and visibility in "larger institutional agendas."[27] They may settle for a boutique project like a week-long summer WAC seminar or a writing fellows' pilot for a specific college or department without growing into hubs for writing activity on campus. Alternatively, they may get folded into other programs, such as teaching and learning centers, which for some programs may provide independence and sustainable resources while for others may spell programmatic doom. As these examples illustrate, large, national datasets may not capture all the potential effects of the contraction of higher education on WAC. To fill in the picture, WAC will need local narratives and institutional data that illustrate threats and describe sustainable approaches to program development in the face of the contraction of higher education. To that end, the rest of this chapter will describe how my program, University Writing at Auburn, has responded to our own experiences of contraction by refocusing our vision, revising our mission, and building strategy that responds to recent and potential future cuts to our program.

EXPANSION AND CONTRACTION AT AUBURN UNIVERSITY

University Writing was formed in 2010 after a multi-year faculty-led task force on writing at Auburn University recommended (1) that the English Center become a university-wide writing center, (2) that a director of University Writing be hired who could implement an outcomes-based writing program for all undergraduate majors, and (3) that the Department of English reduce the size of its first-year composition courses. The first two recommendations led directly to the formation of the Office of University Writing (now called University Writing for short), which is housed in the Office of the Provost. The first director, Margaret Marshall, immediately set out to ensure that all undergraduate majors integrated significant writing experiences across the curriculum. Working with the University Writing Committee (UWC, a committee of the University Senate), Marshall developed a writing plan requirement that asked academic programs to describe five principles: multiple kinds of writing, multiple audiences and purposes for that writing, multiple opportunities to practice across the major, feedback and opportunities to revise, and a plan to assess writing for continued improvement. Numerous services and programs grew out of this writing plan requirement (as well as subsequent review cycles), including training for writing center consultants, workshops for students and faculty, and an annual celebration of teaching that included poster sessions on compelling writing assignments.

As Marshall and her colleagues reviewed writing plans, they also noticed that many academic programs required a portfolio, so she prepared a plan that allowed University Writing to house Auburn's 2013–23 Quality Enhancement Project (QEP) for Southern Association of Colleges and Schools Commission on Colleges (SACSCOC) accreditation: the ePortfolio Project. As leader of the QEP, Marshall was able to secure multiple additional full-time positions—seven at our largest—as well as a dedicated ePortfolio Studio adjacent to the Miller Writing Center in the campus library's Learning Commons. The ePortfolio Project included faculty development workshops, newsletters, a student workshop series, grants, and awards for faculty and students.

When I came onboard as associate director in 2017, I was asked to work across the writing- and ePortfolio-focused components of University Writing; by 2019, Marshall and I had set our sights squarely on building up support for high-impact practices (HIPs) across written, visual, and oral modes of communication. According to George D. Kuh, Ken O'Donnell, and Carol Geary Schneider, HIPs are "a demonstrably powerful set of interventions [that] foster student success," including "academic achievement, engagement in educationally purposeful activities, satisfaction, persistence, attainment of educational objectives, and acquisition of desired learning outcomes."[28] WAC is especially well-positioned to help scale HIPs' participation by integrating meaningful high-impact writing activities throughout the curriculum.[29] When assignments emphasize procedural knowledge, interactive writing process, meaning-making tasks, and clear expectations, writing can support students' learning and development.[30]

Although the Association for American Colleges and Universities (AAC&U) officially lists eleven HIPs, including writing-intensive courses and ePortfolios, many additional educationally purposeful activities can be high impact, assuming they are guided by eight key features:

1. Performance expectations set at appropriately high levels
2. Significant investment of concentrated effort by students over an extended period of time
3. Interactions with faculty and peers about substantive matters

4. Experiences with diversity, wherein students are exposed to and must contend with people and circumstances that differ from those with which students are familiar
5. Frequent, timely, and constructive feedback
6. Opportunities to discover relevance of learning through real-world application
7. Public demonstrations of competence
8. Periodic, structured opportunities to reflect and integrate learning.[31]

Marshall and I shared this framework widely on campus and began implementing faculty development efforts with these eight features in mind. We even designed our faculty development workshops to be high impact; for instance, we moved from one-off workshops to extended academies (feature 2) and built in regular reflective activities (feature 8).

In spring 2019, our program created a strategic plan centered on a vision "to be a nationally-recognized, and locally well-utilized, comprehensive program that works to enhance a culture of communication and the effective teaching of all forms of communication." As the emphasis on communication indicates, we believed we were poised to expand our scope and our services.

Instead, we began to feel the effects of contraction. First, after our communications and marketing specialist departed for a corporate job in the summer of 2019, the Office of the Provost decided to form a centralized communications and marketing team to save on costs and ensure continuity across the provost's reporting units. Then, Marshall stepped down as director of University Writing at the end of the 2019 calendar year. An immediate search for a permanent director was not forthcoming, so I stepped in as acting director of University Writing in January 2020 and then was named the permanent director in July 2021, becoming the steward of our program's many events and services.

Then the pandemic hit. Like everyone else in higher education, we had to spend substantial time figuring out how to shift to remote and eventually hybrid services, especially in the Miller Writing Center. There we especially felt the press of pandemic-fueled contraction, as our utilization by students across campus halved in 2020–21 compared with 2019–20. In January 2021, I also learned through our budget planning process that our operational costs would be cut by 5 percent and that funding for a third assistant/associate director–level position (ostensibly Marshall's replacement) had been pulled from our budget to support a new initiative focused on student recruitment and donor relations. I attribute both cuts directly to the contraction of higher education. The operational cuts were due to fears that the state would cut appropriations again in the wake of the pandemic, while the position reallocation was due to an awareness that Auburn would have to compete for a shrinking pool of traditional-age students in the coming years and would need to invest in recruitment initiatives and alumni engagement to ensure steady revenue streams.

RESPONDING TO CONTRACTION WITH VISION, MISSION, AND STRATEGY

As these signals of contraction affected University Writing, I recognized a need to respond not reactively but rather with vision, mission, and strategy. Even under normal conditions—in which programs are not imminently threatened by contraction—all three levels of planning have value. Vision emphasizes both the future state of the program and contextual factors that affect planning in the short term and the long term. Mission offers a clear statement of the primary objectives of the program, such as transforming curriculum, promoting a culture of writing, and improving students' writing abilities. Strategy names the concrete actions, policies, structures, projects, and services that serve the mission and vision. Successful WAC programs need all three—especially in the face of contraction.

Reimagining Vision

Vision entails both long-term thinking about the future and "peripheral vision," or an awareness of rhetorical, institutional, and interpersonal factors that may affect long-term vision.[32] Given the contraction we were facing, I knew the long-term vision could not be as expansive as it had been in our previous strategic plan: our operational and personnel cuts meant we would need to focus on a few core projects and services and do them well rather than create new projects and services that would require additional resources. We needed a vision that emphasized depth: to be a comprehensive WAC/WID program aiming for deep relationships with academic programs working on high-impact writing instruction and deepening our embeddedness in student culture. To me, a vision focused on depth meant focused outreach and sustained partnerships with academic programs, student support units, and student groups rather than expanding the number and kind of programs and services we offered, which would have been impossible given cuts to our staff and budget. The peripheral elements of rhetorical framing, institutional realities, and interpersonal relationships influenced how I sought to operationalize this vision.

Rhetorically, I recognized that too drastic a redirection might signal that the writing initiative heretofore had been unsuccessful, a waste of time. Many people invested time and labor in supporting Marshall's vision, and I wanted to honor her legacy even as I knew we needed change. Therefore, I sought to envision changes that were logical extensions of the program's success to that point. They needed to be highly visible, cultivate ongoing faculty involvement (both within and beyond the UWC), include ePortfolios and HIPs, and recognize the links among writing, thinking, and disciplinary or professional enculturation that had characterized much of the program's work over the decade.

Institutionally, the associate provost for academic effectiveness (my immediate supervisor) wanted me to work within the university's existing assessment infrastructure. Some of these assessments were compelling, such as graduation surveys focused on HIPs and post-graduate career placement, which have a nearly universal response rate with graduating seniors. Such data helped us understand students' experiences with HIPs and the relationship between their academic experiences—including writing and ePortfolios—and their success post-graduation. Less compelling was the menu of standardized assessments, taken by seniors, that rotated annually and which included a test of written communication with all the limitations of arguments against generic, university-wide assessment of writing.[33] I was also aware that in a few short years, the ePortfolio Project would no longer be the QEP: a new QEP focused on career placement was already in the works. Because of these institutional factors, I wanted to preserve University Writing's emphasis on HIPs and discipline-specific writing instruction even as I imagined a new approach to assessment that would utilize and supplement the university's assessment infrastructure.

Of course, interpersonal factors also influenced my work toward our new vision, such as the many faculty partners who had worked with Marshall during her tenure as director. However, two interpersonal relationships were most salient as I began planning the next phase of University Writing. First, I had to work closely with the associate provost, an accountancy scholar who took pains to understand University Writing and some of the disciplinary concepts informing our work even as he remained skeptical of some of the program's components, such as the writing plan mandate. At the same time, I had to work with a faculty co-chair of the University Writing Committee, who had served on that committee for many years and was invested in its work. Adding to the complexity, these two individuals had known each other for many decades, both inside and outside the workplace. As I began planning, I became not only a steward of the existing program but also a mediator between a skeptic and a champion, even as I sought to develop a new vision focused on programmatic depth over breadth.

Honing Mission

With a depth-focused vision in sight, I set about working with the associate provost, the UWC chair, and the University Writing team to craft a new mission. Unlike vision, which describes our aim for the future, mission describes our current objectives and activities. In the past, our mission had focused on promoting a culture of writing and writing instruction on campus, but I wanted to refocus our mission on students. As Elaine P. Maimon argues, "Students ought to be the primary beneficiaries of higher education funds and . . . the money should stay as close as possible to the students, rather than in support of bureaucracies at a far remove from the classroom."[34] Because we had seen a significant downturn in writing center utilization due to the pandemic, many fewer students were aware of and using our services. A student-focused mission would ensure that we were putting a significant portion of our remaining resources toward our most visible, most direct student support service. In addition, the associate provost wanted to ensure that the time we rightly spent on WAC faculty development had a clear and measurable impact on student learning. Taking this "invest in the students" approach to heart and working with the people named above, I composed our new mission:

1. To support students as thinkers and communicators by helping them become better writers through sustained and personalized services, especially the Miller Writing Center, and
2. To extend our contact with students by partnering with faculty who teach high-impact, discipline-specific, writing-focused courses and curricula.

This new mission put students at the center even as it recognized faculty as crucial partners in WAC work. It also dovetailed with the "first responsibility" named in the Auburn University mission: "to educate students and prepare them for life."[35] By linking thinking with communicating and writing, our mission recognizably connected with the university's mission "to expand [students'] minds, broaden their experiences, and hone their capabilities by imparting both theoretical knowledge and practical skills." Having established a new mission that aligns with that of the university, I was positioned to develop a new strategy by which we could invest resources in students and the faculty who teach them.

Building Strategy

Maimon warns academic leaders that "a vision without a strategy is a fantasy."[36] In WAC, we may know where we want to go, such as having more faculty utilizing research-based practices in teaching disciplinary writing or more students with the rhetorical flexibility to communicate across widely differing contexts. However, such visions will remain fantastical without a concrete strategy that includes actions, policies, structures, programming, and services that are meaningfully tied to the WAC program's mission. WAC scholars have named numerous potential strategies, including faculty development workshops,[37] interdepartmental partnerships,[38] writing-intensive courses,[39] writing plans,[40] and writing fellows programs. Knowing which kinds of programming to implement and what local adjustments to make to existing programming and services takes strategic thinking. According to Maimon, "Strategic thinking, like vision, requires sight and insight—seeing many pathways through a complexity of choices and discovering the best route to success."[41] The strategies the University Writing team and I developed are in various stages of implementation, with some already begun and others still in the planning phase.

The first strategic route I saw was through the Miller Writing Center, especially given our revised mission. I began by setting an ambitious strategic goal: to grow our reach with the student population from our 2 percent low during the pandemic, past our 4–5 percent historical mark, to reach 10 percent of the student population by 2026. We had two key strategies to achieve this goal. First, we increased our operating hours so we have more appointment slots available for students. In the future, we plan to hire more peer consultants by redirecting under-used financial resources traditionally devoted to faculty development, such as ePortfolio grants, and putting them toward recruitment and wages. Second, we have begun implementing a "touch-point plan" that includes every student organization and potential campus partner at Auburn, along with a plan for fostering partnership. Some of these points of contact have involved little effort, such as asking campus partners to update web copy. Others have involved creating ongoing, substantial partnerships, such as advanced registration for students who receive mentoring from our Office on Inclusion and Diversity (a strategy that has proven effective, with increased participation in workshops by those students). Still other points of contact have yet to be created, such as ensuring that every Greek organization lists the Miller Writing Center as eligible for study hours. All of these strategies will drive more traffic into the Miller Writing Center and position us to support students' thinking and communicating, in service of the first part of our revised mission.

The second strategic route builds on our faculty-focused work with HIPs and addresses the associate provost's desire for a new assessment strategy. Although I decided to respond to contraction by focusing on students, I did not want to forgo close work with faculty. After all, as Maimon writes, "Curriculum change depends on scholarly exchange among faculty members."[42] I also did not want to give up HIPs, both because of the university's investment in them and because they potentially mitigate some of the disparities in achievement experienced by low-income students and racialized minorities.[43] Therefore, with the help of the University Writing team, the associate provost, and the UWC chair, I created a new writing-enriched (WE) curriculum plan called WE Write. Like other writing-enriched curriculum programs,[44] WE Write engages faculty in long-term thinking and planning about their expectations and outcomes for student writing. WE Write also invites academic programs to identify writing-intensive courses—designated WE—to develop or redesign based on our faculty consultations. The UWC is in the process of developing and implementing criteria for WE courses, with the aim of increasing the visibility of writing on campus and incentivizing deep, high-impact faculty partnerships, in service of the second part of our revised mission statement.

The WE Write plan was crucial for helping me navigate the interpersonal dimension of my work with the UWC chair and the associate provost. In keeping with the UWC chair's desire to honor the original writing plan initiative, academic programs will be encouraged to integrate the five principles across multiple WE courses and to revise their writing plans while participating in the process. The UWC will have a new means for impacting writing at Auburn through the WE course designation, which is also crucial for meeting the associate provost's desire for a new assessment strategy. With the designation in place, WE courses will be folded into the HIPs graduation survey, giving us a measure of students' experiences in them according to the eight HIPs features. This affords us the ability to promote course-embedded HIPs, which is a key means of reaching underrepresented and minoritized students whose economic precarity often prevents them from participating in extracurricular HIPs such as unpaid internships or study abroad.[45] We can also understand how students who take WE courses perform on a range of different measures, including course grades, GPA, career placement, and even the standardized writing exam taken by seniors. At the same time, I also integrated locally owned, departmentally driven assessment into the WE Write plan to supplement the large, university-wide generic assessment of writing, with the goal of urging upper administration to think three-dimensionally about assessment.[46] I have begun piloting the WE Write consultation process with the biological and agricultural technology management and the physics majors. The consultation process will culminate in a summer WE Write Academy, where faculty from these programs will learn about the eight HIPs features and will learn to integrate those features into courses and assignments that are designed to promote and assess their programs' writing-focused learning outcomes.

Finally, to make way for expanded Miller Writing Center services and WE Write, I had to think strategically about how to reimagine our support for ePortfolios in University Writing. The ePortfolio Project was especially vulnerable to contraction and austerity measures. As a QEP, its funding was not guaranteed beyond the ten-year period required by the SACSCOC. At the same time, many of our ePortfolio programs decreased in popularity—with waning enrollment in our student workshop series, few or no grant applications, and lethargic attendance at faculty development workshops falling below the band of equilibrium for programmatic sustainability.[47] I attributed this decrease to saturation: simply put, the faculty and academic programs who wanted to use ePortfolio were already doing so, and they felt confident guiding students through the process of creating one. Still, I did not want to cut ePortfolios completely. To preserve our success with ePortfolios, my team and I began to integrate them more fully into our other services and programs.[48] For example, after cutting our ePortfolio student workshop series, we redesigned our professional development for Miller Writing Center peer consultants around an ePortfolio. Because they will have experience creating one, they will be in a better position to support other students and to articulate the impact of their professional experience working for us as well. In addition, courses that integrate significant ePortfolio experiences will be eligible for a WE designation. The ePortfolio Project funding will go more directly to support Miller Writing Center peer consultant training and WE Write faculty development, both of which may include ePortfolios. With this strategic integration of ePortfolios into other programs and services, I am now in a better position to argue for continuing our current funding levels beyond the QEP period.

As a by-product of our attention to mission, vision, and strategy and our resulting internal program cuts, we have also begun recognizing the extent to which we were, frankly, doing too much, spreading ourselves too thin. Nicole Khoury, Nicholas Behm, and Sherry Rankins-Robertson (chapter 5, this volume) critique higher education's culture of overwork in their chapter, in which they call on graduate programs to build an affective infrastructure to change that culture. For programs without a direct, instructional, and degree-granting function like most WAC programs, attention to vision, mission, and strategy can also afford a key opportunity to confront a "more is better" mentality and identify the most valuable activities that need sustained attention. As a result, WAC leaders can also experience a more "sustainable lifestyle" (Khoury, Behm, and Rankins-Robertson, chapter 5, this volume) in addition to structural sustainability.

CONCLUSION

Lest I paint myself as the lone hero of my own WAC narrative,[49] I want to reemphasize how much I relied on—and pressed on—the University Writing team, the University Writing Committee, the associate provost, and a host of colleagues and confidants with an investment of time and labor in University Writing. Vision, mission, and strategy should not be the province of solitary leaders but, rather, shared endeavors. When WAC leaders involve upper-level decision makers and supportive faculty in programmatic planning early and often, they are in a better position to withstand the effects of contraction because many people will have a deeper understanding of a shared vision and a clear mission that can be executed strategically.

Admittedly, some institutional leaders—deans, provosts, chancellors, and presidents—may have a bottom-line mentality that no amount of planning can shake. Some WAC leaders may find themselves in intractable situations with little or no control over their programmatic futures, especially when a college closure is on the table. Such situations are traumatic for everyone affected; as Khoury, Behm, and Rankins-Robertson (chapter 5, this volume) suggest, students, faculty, and staff facing deep cuts will need to own their collective vulnerability and work in solidarity to shore up one another's affective and economic well-being. On a smaller and less dire scale, I shared my own moments of vulnerability with colleagues during the most stressful moments of transition, and I was able to learn concrete steps WAC leaders can take to shore up their positions and even thrive in the future:

1. Identify or recommit to a programmatic vision with input from key stakeholders who can advocate for WAC, such as deans, provosts, and faculty governance leaders. A vision focused on one or two core values,

such as deep and abiding relationships with students and faculty, will be better suited to contexts characterized by contraction than an expansive vision that requires new resources.

2. Craft a coherent mission that aligns with institutional priorities and statements. While WAC has a long-standing emphasis on faculty development and curricular change, a student-focused mission will often be more compelling to administrators. Investing resources in students is a good bet, especially when faculty are partners in the endeavor. Even where they are organizationally separate from a writing center, WAC programs can still emphasize student success in disciplinary/professional communication, critical thinking, and community engagement.

3. Identify practical strategies that reallocate existing resources to achieve your program's mission. Look for opportunities to strategize at different levels of the WAC program, such as specific projects, personnel, curricular initiatives, and institutional structures. As always, key stakeholders should have input into cuts and reallocations. Whenever possible, rather than eliminating services that might benefit underrepresented and minority students, implement cuts or reallocations that ensure continued investment and support.

No WAC program is immune to the contraction of higher education. As I hope my narrative illustrates, WAC leaders need to be able to respond to institutional, political, and financial realities by naming our vision, honing our mission, and building a strategy for using what resources remain—even the scantest ones—to maximize impact on the faculty and students they teach.

Nationally, WAC leaders need more consistent data on programmatic health. Organizations like the Association for Writing across the Curriculum should devote resources to a national database of WAC programs that combines the best features of the International WAC/WID Mapping Project and the National Census of Writing, such as annual budgets, numbers of personnel, director status and release time (if faculty), a taxonomy of program components (e.g., faculty development or writing fellows), number of years the program has existed, and changes to program structure. WAC researchers, too, may wish to conduct studies of programmatic responses to contraction, using localized case studies of the sort I have shared here or else examining trends across various institution types (e.g., historically Black colleges and universities [HBCUs] or two-year colleges) or nationally. With more robust data and a richer picture of programmatic responses, WAC leaders will be in a better position to create and maintain healthy programs in the face of the contraction of higher education.

NOTES

1. In 1862, the Morrill Act established land grant universities, which enabled greater access to higher education for a growing middle class and for women and contributed to the formation of first-year composition, according to Connors, *Composition-Rhetoric*, 79–80. According to Russell in *Writing in the Academic Disciplines*, this period also saw the rise of disciplinary specialization, which replaced the generalized rhetorical curriculum of the early nineteenth century and would eventually spur the writing across the curriculum movement a century later. After World War II, the GI Bill once again opened higher education to more students. The Conference on College Composition and Communication was formed in 1949 in response to the need for writing instruction that could respond to this new, often lower middle-class student body (Connors, Composition-Rhetoric, 204–5). Then, between 1960 and 1980, the number of institutions exploded; many were open admissions institutions created to rectify inequities that became more visible during the Civil Rights movement. These changes, along with a Cold War-era emphasis on scientific and technical education, resulted in increased demand for writing instruction, both in the first year and in the disciplines (Russell, *Writing in the Academic Disciplines*, 273–76).
2. Zugnoni and Thaiss, "Survey of Programs in Writing across the Curriculum (WAC) and Writing in the Disciplines (WID)"; Gladstein and Fralix, *National Census of Writing*.
3. Maimon, *Leading Academic Change*; Cox, Galin, and Melzer, *Sustainable WAC*.
4. National Center for Education Statistics, "Total Expenditures."
5. Archibald and Feldman, "Drivers of the Rising Price of a College Education," 5.
6. National Center for Education Statistics, "2019–2020 National Postsecondary Student Aid Study."
7. Archibald and Feldman, "Drivers of the Rising Price of a College Education," 9.
8. National Center for Education Statistics. "Revenues"
9. National Center for Education Statistics, "Revenues."
10. National Center for Education Statistics, "Total Expenditures."
11. National Center for Education Statistics, "Characteristics"; National Center for Education Statistics, "Student Debt."
12. National Center for Education Statistics, "Characteristics."
13. National Center for Education Statistics, "Characteristics."
14. Nazeeri, "50% of Universities Will Be Bankrupt in 10–15 Years"; Natow, "Why Haven't More Colleges Closed?"
15. "How Many Colleges and Universities Have Closed since 2016?"
16. National Center for Education Statistics, "Total Undergraduate Fall Enrollment."
17. National Center for Education Statistics, "Characteristics."
18. Copley and Douthett, "The Enrollment Cliff."
19. Bransberger, Falkenstern, and Lane, "Knocking at the College Door."
20. Hoover, "The Demographic Cliff."
21. Cox, Galin, and Melzer, *Sustainable WAC*, 5
22. Zugnoni and Thaiss, "Survey of Programs in Writing across the Curriculum (WAC) and Writing in the Disciplines (WID)."
23. Gladstein and Fralix, *National Census of Writing*.
24. When surveys do not distinguish between the two, some respondents may conflate a course with a program. Therefore, WAC needs consistent, longitudinal, national data on the existence and persistence of dedicated WAC programs with budgets, personnel, and faculty governance, not just upper-level course requirements.
25. Gladstein and Fralix, *National Census of Writing*.
26. Kester et al., "Improving Success, Increasing Access."
27. Condon and Rutz, "A Taxonomy of Writing across the Curriculum Programs," 362.

28. Kuh, O'Donnell, and Schneider, "HIPs at Ten," 9; see also Brownwell and Swaner, "High-Impact Practices"; Finley and McNair, *Assessing Underserved Students' Engagement*; Kuh, O'Donnell, and Reed, *Ensuring Quality*.
29. Anderson et al., "How to Create High-Impact Writing Assignments"; Eodice, Geller, and Lerner, *The Meaningful Writing Project*.
30. Anderson et al., "How to Create High-Impact Writing Assignments," 10.
31. Kuh, O'Donnell, and Schneider, "HIPs at Ten," 11.
32. Maimon, *Leading Academic Change*, 12.
33. Anson et al., "Big Rubrics and Weird Genres."
34. Maimon, Leading Academic Change, 113.
35. Auburn University, "Vision and Mission Statement."
36. Maimon, *Leading Academic Change*, 11.
37. Fodrey and Mikovits, "Theorizing WAC Faculty Development in Multimodal Project Design."
38. Nowacek, *Agents of Integration*.
39. Farris and Smith, "Writing-Intensive Courses."
40. Anson et al., "Big Rubrics and Weird Genres."
41. Maimon, Leading Academic Change, 14.
42. Maimon, Leading Academic Change, 24.
43. Kuh, High-Impact Educational Practices; Maimon, Leading Academic Change; for conflicting evidence, see Zilvinskis, "Measuring Quality"
44. Flash, "From Apprised to Revised" and "Writing-Enriched Curriculum"; Fodrey et al., "Activity Theory"
45. Kuh, High-Impact Educational Practices; Kester et al., "Improving Success"
46. Anson et al., "Big Rubrics"
47. Cox, Galin, and Melzer, *Sustainable WAC*, 134–35.
48. Bartlett et al., "More than Assessment"; Haskins et al., "The Role of EPortfolio Workshops"; Marshall et al., "EPortfolio Assessment."
49. Cox, Galin, and Melzer, *Sustainable WAC*, 217.

REFERENCES

Anderson, Paul, Chris M. Anson, Robert M. Gonyea, and Charles Paine. "How to Create High-Impact Writing Assignments That Enhance Learning and Development and Reinvigorate WAC/WID Programs: What Almost 72,000 Undergraduates Taught Us." *Across the Disciplines* 13, no. 4 (2016): 1–18. https://doi.org/10.37514/ATD-J.2016.13.4.13.

Anson, Chris M., Deanna P. Dannels, Pamela Flash, and Amy L. Housley Gaffney. "Big Rubrics and Weird Genres: The Futility of Using Generic Assessment Tools across Diverse Instructional Contexts." *Journal of Writing Assessment* 5, no. 1 (2012). http://journalofwritingassessment.org/article.php?article=57.

Archibald, Robert B., and David H. Feldman. "Drivers of the Rising Price of a College Education." Minneapolis: Midwestern Higher Education Compact, 2018.

Auburn University. "Vision and Mission Statement." Auburn University, 2021. http://www.auburn.edu/main/welcome/visionandmission.php.

Bartlett, Lesley Erin, Heather C. W. Stuart, Justin K. Owensby, and Jordan R. Davis. "More than Assessment: What ePortfolios Make Possible for Students, Faculty, and Curricula." *Journal of Interactive Technology and Pedagogy* 10 (2016). https://jitp.commons.gc.cuny.edu/more-than-assessment/.

Bransberger, Peace, Colleen Falkenstern, and Patrick Lane. "Knocking at the College Door: Projections of High School Graduates." Boulder: Western States Interstate Commission for Higher Education, 2020.

Brownwell, Jayne E., and Lynn E. Swaner. "High-Impact Practices: Applying the Learning Outcomes Literature to the Development of Successful Campus Programs." *Peer Review* 11, no. 2 (Spring 2009): 26–30.

Condon, William, and Carol Rutz. "A Taxonomy of Writing across the Curriculum Programs: Evolving to Serve Broader Agendas." *College Composition and Communication* 64, no. 2 (2012): 357–82.

Connors, Robert J. *Composition-Rhetoric: Backgrounds, Theory, and Pedagogy.* Pittsburgh: University of Pittsburgh Press, 1997.

Copley, Paul, and Edward Douthett. "The Enrollment Cliff, Mega-Universities, COVID-19, and the Changing Landscape of US Colleges." *CPA Journal* (2020). https://www.cpajournal.com/2020/10/05/the-enrollment-cliff-mega-universities-covid-19-and-the-changing-landscape-of-u-s-colleges/.

Cox, Michelle, Jeffrey R. Galin, and Dan Melzer. *Sustainable WAC: A Whole Systems Approach to Launching and Developing Writing across the Curriculum Programs.* Urbana, IL: National Council of Teachers of English, 2018.

Elder, Cristyn L., and Karen Champine. "Designing High-Impact 'Writing-to-Learn' Math Assignments for Killer Courses." *Across the Disciplines* 13, no. 4 (2016): 1–31. https://doi.org/10.37514/ATD-J.2016.13.4.16.

Eodice, Michele, Anne Ellen Geller, and Neal Lerner. *The Meaningful Writing Project: Learning, Teaching, and Writing in Higher Education.* Logan: Utah State University Press, 2016.

Farris, Christine, and Raymond Smith. "Writing-Intensive Courses: Tools for Curricular Change." In *Writing across the Curriculum: A Guide to Development Programs*, edited by Susan H. McLeod and Margot Soven, 52–62. Newbury Park, CA: Sage, 1992.

Finley, Ashley, and Tia McNair. *Assessing Underserved Students' Engagement in High-Impact Practices, with an Assessing Equity in High-Impact Practices Toolkit.* Washington, DC: Association for American Colleges and Universities, 2013. https://eric.ed.gov/?id=ED582014.

Flash, Pamela. "From Apprised to Revised: Faculty in the Disciplines Change What They Never Knew They Knew." In *A Rhetoric of Reflection*, edited by Kathleen Blake Yancey, 227–49. Logan: Utah State University Press, 2016.

Flash, Pamela. "Writing-Enriched Curriculum: A Model for Making and Sustaining Change." In *Writing-Enriched Curricula: Models of Faculty-Driven and Departmental Transformation*, edited by Chris M. Anson and Pamela Flash, 17–44. Boulder: WAC Clearinghouse and University Press of Colorado, 2021. https://doi.org/10.37514/PER-B.2021.1299.2.01.

Fodrey, Crystal N., and Meg Mikovits. "Theorizing WAC Faculty Development in Multimodal Project Design." *Across the Disciplines* 17 (2020): 42–58.

Fodrey, Crystal N., Meg Mikovits, Chris Hassay, and Erica Yozell. "Activity Theory as Tool for WAC Program Development." *Composition Forum* 42 (2019). http://compositionforum.com/issue/42/moravian.php.

Gladstein, Jill, and Brandon Fralix. *National Census of Writing*, 2013/2017. https://writingcensus.ucsd.edu/.

Haskins, Megan, Parker Wade, Heather Stuart, and Ashlee Mills Duffy. "The Role of EPortfolio Workshops in Supporting Students and Faculty." *AAEEBL ePortfolio Review* 2, no. 2 (2018): 40–48.

Hoover, Eric. "The Demographic Cliff: 5 Findings from New Projections of High-School Graduates." *Chronicle of Higher Education* (2020). https://www.chronicle.com/article/the-demographic-cliff-5-findings-from-new-projections-of-high-school-graduates.

"How Many Colleges and Universities Have Closed since 2016?" *Higher Ed Dive*, 2021. https://www.highereddive.com/news/how-many-colleges-and-universities-have-closed-since-2016/539379/.

Kester, Jessica, Rebecca Block, Margaret Reinfeld Karda, and Harold Orndorff III. "Improving Success, Increasing Access: Bringing HIPs to Open Enrollment Institutions through WAC/WID." *Across the Disciplines* 13, no. 4 (2016): 1–17. https://doi.org/10.37514/ATD-J.2016.13.4.15.

Kuh, George D. *High-Impact Educational Practices: What They Are, Who Has Access to Them, and Why They Matter*. Washington, DC: Association for American Colleges and Universities, 2008.

Kuh, George D., Ken O'Donnell, and Sally Reed. *Ensuring Quality and Taking High-Impact Practices to Scale*. Washington, DC: Association for American Colleges and Universities, 2013.

Kuh, George D., Ken O'Donnell, and Carol Geary Schneider. "HIPs at Ten." *Change: The Magazine of Higher Learning* 49, no. 5 (2017): 8–16. https://doi.org/10.1080/00091383.2017.1366805.

Maimon, Elaine P. *Leading Academic Change: Vision, Strategy, Transformation*. Sterling, VA: Stylus, 2018.

Marshall, Margaret J., Ashlee Mills Duffy, Stephen Powell, and Lesley Erin Bartlett. "EPortfolio Assessment as Faculty Development: Gathering Reliable Data and Increasing Faculty Confidence." *International Journal of EPortfolio* 7, no. 2 (2017): 187–215.

National Center for Education Statistics. "Characteristics of Degree-Granting Postsecondary Institutions." National Center for Education Statistics, 2020. https://nces.ed.gov/programs/coe/indicator/csa#info.

National Center for Education Statistics. "Revenues of Public Degree-Granting Postsecondary Institutions, by Source of Revenue and Level of Institution: Selected Years, 2007–08 through 2017–18." National Center for Education Statistics, 2019. https://nces.ed.gov/programs/digest/d19/tables/dt19_333.10.asp.

National Center for Education Statistics. "Student Debt." National Center for Education Statistics, 2020. https://nces.ed.gov/fastfacts/display.asp?id=900.

National Center for Education Statistics. "Total Expenditures of Public Degree-Granting Postsecondary Institutions, by Purpose and Level of Institution: 2009–10 through 2018–19." National Center for Education Statistics, 2020. https://nces.ed.gov/programs/digest/d20/tables/dt20_334.10.asp.

National Center for Education Statistics. "Total Undergraduate Fall Enrollment in Degree-Granting Postsecondary Institutions, by Attendance Status, Sex of Student, and Control and Level of Institution: Selected Years, 1970 through 2029." National Center for Education Statistics, 2020. https://nces.ed.gov/programs/digest/d20/tables/dt20_303.70.asp.

National Center for Education Statistics. "Tuition Costs of Colleges and Universities." National Center for Education Statistics, 2021. https://nces.ed.gov/fastfacts/display.asp?id=76.

National Center for Education Statistics. "2019–2020 National Postsecondary Student Aid Study." National Center for Education Statistics, 2021. https://nces.ed.gov/pubsearch/pubsinfo.asp?pubid=2021456.

Natow, Rebecca S. "Why Haven't More Colleges Closed?" *Chronicle of Higher Education* 67, no. 14 (2021). https://www.chronicle.com/article/why-havent-more-colleges-closed.

Nazeeri, Furqan. "50% of Universities Will Be Bankrupt in 10–15 Years." *Extnsn Engine*, 2021. https://blog.extensionengine.com/50-of-universities-will-be-bankrupt-in-10-15-years/.

Nowacek, Rebecca S. *Agents of Integration: Understanding Transfer as a Rhetorical Act*. Carbondale: Southern Illinois University Press, 2011.

Russell, David R. *Writing in the Academic Disciplines: A Curricular History*. 2d ed. Carbondale: Southern Illinois University Press, 2002.

Zilvinskis, John. "Measuring Quality in High-Impact Practices." *Higher Education* 78, no. 4 (2019): 687–709. https://doi.org/10.1007/s10734-019-00365-9.

Zugnoni, Michele, and Christopher Thaiss. "Survey of Programs in Writing across the Curriculum (WAC) and Writing in the Disciplines (WID)." International WAC/WID Mapping Project, 2008/2020. https://mappingproject.ucdavis.edu/content/us-survey.

5
BUILDING AN AFFECTIVE INFRASTRUCTURE TO LEAD WRITING PROGRAMS

Nicole Khoury, Nicholas Behm, and Sherry Rankins-Robertson

Nearly twenty years ago, Shane Borrowman opened *Trauma and the Teaching of Writing* by reflecting on teaching in the wake of September 11: "I am left with an unshakeable feeling that I failed my students in some simple, fundamental way."[1] Throughout the Covid-19 global pandemic, the sentiment underlying Borrowman's words has likely echoed persistently in the minds of many educators who have struggled to process the disruption to their lives and profession caused by the pandemic. Frantically pivoting to emergency remote instruction in the middle of the academic year was extraordinarily overwhelming and disorienting, but it pales in comparison to the emotional and psychological burden of witnessing the indescribable loss of life. Our academic training didn't prepare us for the immensity of such a trauma and its concatenate relentless fear and despair. It didn't train us to identify, process, and respond productively to widely experienced precariousness—the decimation and elimination of the very necessities of life. Moreover, our academic training didn't teach us how vulnerability could be marshaled and mobilized as an expression and enactment of resistance.[2] Rather, our academic training, in ways subtle and explicit, stressed that vulnerability was something inherently negative, something that diminished academic standing and imperiled reputation.

Not surprisingly, then, like Borrowman, we have struggled with a gnawing realization that we have failed our students—not because we've lessened the academic rigor of our courses but rather because we've failed to respond emotionally in ways proportionate to the magnitude of the precarity and trauma caused by the pandemic. Instructors and students unremittingly anguished over the loss of livelihoods and loved ones, the loss of safety and security, and the loss of predictability and normalcy to daily lives during this time of "shared national trauma and tragedy."[3] We

https://doi.org/10.7330/9781646424665.c005

write to examine how to engage as a changed community and consider how our graduate courses and conversations (in both public and private spaces) can help graduate students grapple with ethical questions that probe them about their futures in a post-pandemic environment. Extending the scholarship of Judith Butler, we argue for the recognition of affective vulnerability and contend that enactments of affective vulnerability can powerfully resist dominant, unhealthy norms within graduate programs in rhetoric and composition.

Another purpose for writing this text is to suggest that doctoral programs in rhetoric and composition have socialized graduate students to ignore precarity, suppress vulnerability, conceal emotions, and ignore the psychological impact of matriculating through a doctoral program. As authors of this text, our commonality is that we share an academic lineage as former graduate students in the same doctoral program. While matriculating through our program, we understood the unspoken messaging of what it meant to be seeking a doctoral degree and what kinds of jobs were the "right" and "best" jobs for individuals who received a doctorate; we believe this experience is a trend that exists in many (if not most) doctoral programs located at institutions with high research activities. The pressures we placed on ourselves over the past decade by navigating what has traditionally been called an R1 institution (now an extensive research institution) and the expectations of securing tenure-track positions, achieving tenure, and climbing the administrative ladder have imposed a high price for each of us. However, let us say, by and large, that our graduate program adequately prepared each of us to secure jobs in the market, to thrive in the discipline, and to take on leadership roles. Each of us has mostly positive experiences from our program and deep, meaningful relationships with our faculty, so we call attention to the fact that we write based on our shared lived experiences, not out of criticism for the program we attended.

Over the past ten years, we have seen each other at conferences, and we have sat on telephone calls with each other interrogating how we have measured our own successes by unspoken norms and rising colleagues around us. To disrupt the cycle of self-doubt and negative comparison, we share our narratives to identify pitfalls and to speak directly to graduate students—especially those who are starting their doctoral journeys—about the approaches and mind-sets toward successes and failures that optimally would not come at the same costs of personal relationships, physical and mental health, and availability to our families that each of us has endured. In relaying our narratives, we urge directors of graduate programs to recalibrate their expectations of graduate students so that they help foster realistic and healthy ways to cultivate a more sustainable work/life balance in their programs and exert grace and patience with graduate students, colleagues, and themselves. Further, we call for department chairs to work with faculty to write realistic, rather than idealistic, job ads that acknowledge that graduate students are entering the field; they are not seasoned professionals with extensive publication records.

VULNERABILITY, PRECARITY, AND RESISTANCE

For more than two decades before the pandemic, scholarship in the discipline called attention to the work habits—often performed at "top speed, for high stakes, higher than just your own professional well-being"—of writing teachers and administrators.[4] These cautionary tales forewarned readers about how academic jobs required sacrifices that would come at the expense of personal lives;[5] if not sacrificed, the individual would decrease their likelihood of success in the academy.[6] Scholars shared where (and why) their jobs consumed their personal lives and identities; many acknowledged how their expectations were formed through the socialization received in graduate programs and from within professional organizations to get on and stay inside the metaphoric hamster wheel of academic success.[7]

Rhetoric and composition faculty and administrators, like much of the American population, grapple with mental health challenges; despite this fact, the silence in publication on this issue is profound. Though research in disability studies permeates rhetoric and composition scholarship, the scholarship on self-care for doctoral students in the field of rhetoric and composition is limited, and scholarship on emotional labor in higher education has only recently become available.[8] This emerging area of scholarship has yet to address the deleterious effects of academic work on the mental health of faculty and administrators. Current disciplinary scholarship has yet to name and identify the probable consequences of fulfilling the imposed expectations of the academy.

To help the discipline discern the affective dynamics circulating within graduate programs, writing programs, and writing classrooms and to understand the generative potential of vulnerability, we turn to Judith Butler. In extending Butler's reframing of vulnerability to graduate student experiences in rhetoric and composition programs and the discipline's evasion of discussions of emotional labor and mental illness, we acknowledge that we are applying Butler's conceptualization of vulnerability to a different and seemingly privileged context relative to sites and conditions of precarity than that which Butler and other scholars had intended. *Vulnerability in Resistance* troubles traditional, masculinist representations of vulnerability and resistance. To do so, Judith Butler, Zeynep Gambetti, and Leticia Sabsay critically consider how activists and historically marginalized groups and communities collectively marshal vulnerability and mobilize to resist inequitable power relations, police violence, voter suppression, environmental racism, systemic unemployment, and other manifestations of precarity. In the process, these communities expose themselves to state-sponsored violence, risking arrest and hazarding lives and limbs. Compared to social contexts in which physical violence is possible, the context of academic doctoral programs seems rather peaceful and subdued. Some scholars may criticize an extension of Butler's theory of vulnerability to an academic context as a result. However, although graduate students don't commensurately experience precarity in terms of physical violence relative to Black Lives Matter or pro-democracy activists, graduate students may and often do experience mental and emotional precarity: there is violence wrought on their emotional and mental wellness, particularly for students of color.

We believe, then, that an extension of Butler's theory of vulnerability to academic contexts, including doctoral programs in rhetoric and composition, is not only germane and warranted but also critical to complicating the traditional mind/body binary of vulnerability. We acknowledge graduate students' experiences and mediate disparate degrees of precarity depending on the intersectional socio-political formations that intersect their identities, as Anna Barritt and Kalyn Prince identify in chapter 8 of this collection. We acknowledge our own socioeconomically privileged positions as professors within the academy, and although we identify as and participate in disparate socio-political formations, we recognize that our identifications may reinforce the inequitable power dynamics that create and circulate mental and emotional precarity within our respective programs and departments. These facts acknowledged, we remain determined to make critical interventions into inequitable power relations and will look to Butler to help us do so.[9]

In *Vulnerability in Resistance*, Butler, Gambetti, and Sabsay reconceptualize vulnerability as inherently relational and generative, a force that can be galvanized as a powerful enactment of resistance to dominant, inequitable, and authoritarian power relations. Indeed, they argue that vulnerability serves as "one of the conditions of the very possibility of resistance."[10] Vulnerability is socially and politically fabricated and circulated (almost always inequitably) in specific sites that exist within, are constituted and informed by, and affect dynamic power relations in complex socio-historical contexts.[11] In situating vulnerability within socio-historical and socio-political contexts, Butler, Gambetti, and Sabsay move a discussion of vulnerability and resistance away from both a human rights framework, where communities are defined as victimized and in need of protection, and a traditional, masculinist framework, where vulnerability is equated with political impotence, dependency, and femininity.[12] Both frameworks are informed by paternalistic logics with probable negative ramifications: a human rights framework negates the collective agency of populations deemed vulnerable and dismisses collective enactments of resistance; a masculinist framework conflates vulnerability with femininity, oversimplifies it as an individual lived experience, and implicates it in "capitalist concepts of self-interest and masculinist fantasies of sovereign mastery."[13]

In re-conceptualizing vulnerability in ways that articulate vulnerability and resistance, however, Butler, Gambetti, and Sabsay demonstrate its generative power, particularly when it is marshaled collectively among traditionally marginalized groups to galvanize support for social justice and equity and to challenge inequitable power relations.[14] Distinctions between precarity and precariousness are critical to understand how Butler re-conceptualizes vulnerability and how it could be mobilized to resist inequitable power relations and effect positive change in communities. For Butler, precariousness signifies vulnerability to insecurity, instability, disease, and trauma concomitant with the human condition. By virtue of being interdependent, all humans are susceptible to disease, unforeseen tragedies, and inexplicable traumatic events.[15] The Covid-19 pandemic sharply exposed the precariousness of the human condition. It affected every community, although not equally. The unrelenting fear and sense of instability expressed by our colleagues, students, and staff during the pandemic conveyed our collective, pervasive precariousness to the disease and its physical, emotional, and mental damage.

Marginalized and disenfranchised communities experienced more acutely the suffering, despair, and death associated with the disease because of the extent of comorbidities, economic insecurity, displacement, lack of access to testing and affordable healthcare, and lack of access to effective treatments for the disease.[16] All of these lived inequities are rooted in inequitable power relations established to benefit dominant socio-political formations at the expense of and to the disadvantage of Black, Latino/a, and American Indigenous communities. Historically marginalized and disenfranchised communities, then, experience a more severe "condition of precarity," which made them more vulnerable to Covid-19 (and other medical conditions) and exacerbated the disease's negative outcomes. For Butler, then, a community's "condition of precarity" tracks with socio-political identifications and is the effect of structural inequities and pervasive exploitation wrought by neoliberal capitalism.[17]

Though not akin to socioeconomically challenged and chronically disinvested communities, graduate programs in rhetoric and composition function within the inequitable power relations of the academy. In many of these programs, a cadre of graduate students (and contingent faculty) experience significant precarity consisting of intellectual exploitation, labor insecurity, inequitable compensation, and untenable working conditions—to name just a few. These precarious material, emotional, and psychological circumstances only exacerbate the intensity and burden of the stress imposed on graduate students by their coursework, programmatic service, teaching, and scholarly activities. We suggest, then, that it is necessary to think critically and comprehensively about the emotional and psychological vulnerability of graduate students.

In her formulation of vulnerability, Butler delineates the contours of "bodily vulnerability"—as in a body's exposure to violence, want, pain, and suffering—and its relationship to social and political conditions. Here, we extend her conceptualization of bodily vulnerability to include affective vulnerability, which we define as mental and emotional distress, pain, suffering, and illness. We localize the context of our discussion to graduate programs and the affective vulnerability caused by the stress, trauma, and unhealthy norms and expectations internalized during one's matriculation through a program. Of course, neither bodily vulnerability nor affective vulnerability is mutually exclusive; they interrelate and interact, mutually constituting and constituted by each other in complex and dynamic ways. Graduate students experience significant precarity—economic instability and insecurity, for instance—intensifying their exposure to both bodily and affective vulnerability. Because of space constraints, our chapter will focus on the impacts of affective vulnerability.[18]

Butler argues for a political and social conceptualization of the body, one in which the body is individual and discrete but also informed by and existing within dynamic networks of relations constituted by discourse and social norms. As Christina V. Cedillo writes in chapter 3 of this collection, "Rhetoric establishes how bodies take on meaning in relation to each other; bodies determine how we engage in rhetorical activity; and affect informs this reciprocal process by guiding our uses of rhetoric to safeguard our humanity." Butler notes that "if we conceptualize the political meaning of the human body without understanding those relations in which it lives and thrives, we fail to make the best possible case for the various political ends we seek to achieve."[19] Seeing the body as both distinct and immersed in socio-political relations is critical for understanding the generative potential of vulnerability and how the networks in which one participates function as powerful "network[s] of support."[20] As in her previous scholarship on performativity and gender, bodily vulnerability is interrelated with "linguistic vulnerability" in which people are interpellated into particular gender, racial, and sexual socio-political norms: "We are treated, hailed, and formed by social norms that precede us and that form the constraining context for whatever forms of agency we ourselves take on in time."[21]

Akin to, though not commensurate with, norms of socio-political formations like gender, race, and sexuality are norms instituting, defining, categorizing, and naming interrelated performances. These norms impact success as a graduate student in graduate programs and can enforce powerfully proscribed ideals of what it means to act, perform, and live as a graduate student. Wading through the historical, social, and political milieu of programs as they matriculate, students are hailed and interpellated by particular performances that have been discursively constituted and reinforced year after year, generation after generation. This reinforcement comes in the forms of programmatic documents and expectations, in what mentors say and do, and by what actions are rewarded, chastened, or ignored altogether by faculty. As we discuss in the next section, our doctoral program, and we suspect other programs, idealized norms and created conditions where graduate students were expected to:

1. Labor excessively and relentlessly, without consideration for the negative effects on health, wellness, and family
2. Produce publishable research, without adjusting for students' inexperience with the academic publishing process
3. Commit to a multitude of programmatic or departmental projects, without acknowledging potential political and interpersonal dynamics contributing to graduate students' exploitation within programs

Moreover, in our graduate program we learned to suppress the strain, stress, and trauma that academic requirements and programmatic expectations induced. We suppressed our affective vulnerability and resisted empathizing with the experiences of other students. To identify and express affective vulnerability was to show weakness, inadequacy, and incompetence. To demonstrate empathy for other graduate students inhibited one's progress in a competitive programmatic environment where success was a zero-sum game, where a few were lauded and affirmed to the detriment of many. We were conditioned to disavow vulnerability altogether; there simply wasn't space for it, and there certainly were not opportunities for graduate students to coalesce around shared enactments of vulnerability.[22] Graduate students are expected to work through their vulnerabilities independently, as we are told that graduate programs should be rigorous and challenging. For Butler, the insistence on disavowing vulnerability reinforces masculinist notions of sovereignty and individualism where failure is not an option and a subject labors to master situational circumstances, environmental circumstances, and other subjects.[23] As we show below, conditioning graduate students to suppress affective vulnerability not only produces immediate negative outcomes but also causes long-term mental health consequences.

MODELING THE NORM WHILE IGNORING ITS EFFECTS: NICK'S NARRATIVE

I was a model graduate student—establishing an academic plan, presenting at the Conference on College Composition and Communication (CCCC) and the Council of Writing Program Administrators (CWPA), and fulfilling degree requirements expeditiously. As a result, I was praised by my mentors and portrayed as the model other graduate students should follow. That exhortation to follow my lead, though, never acknowledged the unsustainability and emotional toll of relentless work. It also never identified the intersectionality of racial, socioeconomic, gender, and ability privileges and advantages that enabled me to access, matriculate through, and succeed in graduate school. I failed to recognize the deleterious effects of my work habits on my mental and emotional health. I was lauded for my ambition, so I grasped at every opportunity to advance, accepted invitations to participate in national service organizations, and performed administrative duties. Although I felt inordinate stress and experienced what I now know were severe bouts of anxiety and depression, I ignored them, refusing to discuss my experiences with other students or medical professionals. Doing so imperiled my reputation as a model graduate student.

The obsession to succeed at all costs continued into my subsequent academic appointment. I labored relentlessly, dismissing signs that I was becoming increasingly unwell mentally and emotionally and striving for tenure and promotion. And I was successful: I earned tenure and promotion; I had a beautiful family with three kids and a strong, dedicated partner. Superficially, I was, again, a model to follow. My colleagues and former mentors stressed how polished and professional I was, even as I desperately hid the symptoms signaling that I was unwell. For years, this continued; for years, the stress, strain, and anxiety accumulated until my mind broke. Elsewhere,[24] I describe my iterative, fraught journey from breakdown to wellness. Working through a mental breakdown was the hardest and most painful event I have ever experienced. It took a full year, hundreds of pills, and dozens of hours of therapy; frankly, I am convinced it wasn't inevitable. If I had cultivated a healthier work/life balance, if I would have given myself space to recalibrate the expectations I was conditioned to fulfill, if I would have embraced vulnerability and shared challenges with colleagues and medical professionals, I certainly would have modeled healthier expectations for my students and probably avoided a mental breakdown.

DEMONSTRATING THE NEED FOR AFFECTIVE INFRASTRUCTURE: NICOLE'S NARRATIVE

Three months after giving birth to my first child, I accepted a rhetoric and composition lectureship in a traditional English department at a large research university in the Midwest, where my partner lived and worked. I incorrectly assumed a non-tenured position at the university would offer some flexibility, with lower expectations for research and service, which could allow me to attain some level of work/life balance with my growing family in a city where I had no family or support system. I was inadvertently "mommy tracked," a career decision made by women who give up their scholarship and professional trajectory to focus on caregiving.[25] The decision to remain in the academy directly affected my physical and mental health; I taught more classes while also continuing to work on my publication record to stay relevant in the job market. I often struggled with feelings of inadequacy and felt like I failed in both my profession and as a mother.

These emotions became more prevalent during my second pregnancy when I met resistance to my maternity leave request. I felt resentment toward academia for failing to offer viable options for junior faculty, lecturers, and graduate students to thrive within the academy unless they eschewed personal lives and responsibilities. The lack of institutional support for my family leave request also resulted in feelings of inadequacy, both as a professional and for my caretaking responsibilities. It was only when I relocated to a different state and a different university with leadership advocating on my behalf that I realized I was not alone in this struggle; the vulnerabilities I felt were common among faculty and new mothers in academia. I struggled at my previous institution because the support I needed, support required by many other academic mothers and faculty, was unavailable.

As we near the end of the third year of this pandemic, I believe caregiving is a non-negotiable necessity in our homes, our communities, and our institutions. The pandemic has provided us with a behind-the-scenes look at the care work involved in our daily lives, with the sights and sounds of our family members and pets in the background of our Zoom calls. The times in my life when I felt able to balance work and life happened because of community and institutional support. This support was then coupled with my ability to prioritize my caregiving responsibilities and successfully maintain my professional identity. My identity as an academic and a mother needs to come from my own definitions of success, and my ability to thrive in these roles is directly related to the support I receive from my institution, government, and community. In many cases, if we allow the institution or our field to define success for us, we have unequivocally failed. Work/life balance isn't possible if we don't offer people multiple viable options for thriving within the academy and fight to make these options available to them. These options are possible when leadership, institutional and otherwise, cares about us as people and gives space for our lives outside the academy.

ACKNOWLEDGING BROKEN ACADEMIC STRUCTURES: SHERRY'S NARRATIVE

Unlike Nick and Nicole, I came into the graduate program with a spouse and an eight-year-old daughter. In addition to being a wife and mother, I was a full-time, non-tenure track faculty member along with being a full-time graduate student. As I have written elsewhere, I entered my doctoral program knowing how to burn the candle at both ends.[26] One might think that being stretched between this many full-time roles might have allowed me to justify a low grade or a missed assignment, but it did not. Looking back, I can say that the lack of grace I extended to myself is painful. After finishing my doctoral degree, I accepted a position with dual roles as assistant professor and writing program administrator (WPA), which seemed to mean I'd need to perfect my candle-burning skills with surgical time and task management. While the time that had been spent being a full-time student was replaced with research and writing, there was not another bucket of time to borrow from to budget the labor of a full-time administrator, so I negotiated away time for myself. I minimized time with friends and family; I resorted to eating in front of the computer so I could work during that time. I stopped working out and began sleeping less so I would have more time to finish articles and projects or build initiatives to strengthen our writing program. I often told myself, "If you can get through this one week . . . ," which turned into one semester and then one academic year. The biggest mistake any of us makes is rationalizing away what's most valuable—our own well-being. We often cannot see it until it debilitates us.

After a decade on the tenure track, now as a full professor and department chair, I find myself with a new sense of responsibility to reexamine the "rest-when-you're-dead" mantra of graduate programming. I've carefully considered the responsibilities of leading and role modeling as I reflect on Christy I. Wenger's call to protect (and restore) emotional health and well-being.[27] Wegner writes that we are "socialized into performing emotional labor, often at the expense of [our] own self-care," and she acknowledges that "labor is a systematic and corporate issue."[28] Using the positionality of our leadership positions, we can recast the focus that is typically siloed through the lens of self-care to redirect collective action toward restructuring and revising a sustainable lifestyle and a healthier work environment for our colleagues and students. We can begin this labor by rethinking the expectations we write into job ads that drive graduate students to overperform and then burn out. The trauma wrought by Covid provides a kairotic opportunity to acknowledge the broken academic structures and examine how these structures are contributing to the impact on mental wellness of both current and incoming faculty, particularly female Black, Indigenous, and people of color (BIPOC) colleagues. Collectively, we must resist and disrupt the widely accepted meta-narrative of "the more we do, the more we are worth" and turn our gaze to building a community that cultivates and sustains care for its members.

BUILDING AN AFFECTIVE INFRASTRUCTURE OF SUPPORT

In sharing our narratives, in exposing ourselves to stigmatization, alienation, and shaming, we argue for the recognition of the affective vulnerability of graduate students. Our narratives not only demonstrate the lack of affective infrastructure in our graduate program but also suggest how a lack of affective infrastructure may have long-term negative consequences for graduate students. In this section, we contend that doctoral programs in rhetoric and composition need to cultivate an affective infrastructure that affords people—graduate students, faculty, staff—the opportunities, resources, and support to alter programmatic culture. These kinds of infrastructural changes would ensure that programs and perhaps institutions could convey healthy expectations to all members, cultivate mental and emotional well-being, and acknowledge, express, and enact vulnerability productively through outlets that empower and build coalitions among constituents in a program and diminish logics of competition and zero-sum expectations of success.

As noted above, Butler identifies a second function of a norm: its infrastructural purpose. An embodied subject is dependent not only on the social and material relations in which one participates and informs but also on the "infrastructural and environmental conditions" that determine the degrees or availability of support for performances of norms and enactments of vulnerability.[29] Support in the form of resources, traditional infrastructure, and opportunities for affective expression and processing, as well as public support for political movements, are necessary conditions for the enactments of bodily and affective vulnerability. In our doctoral program, there were material resources invested in graduate students, but there was no infrastructure for supporting mental and emotional wellness. Indeed, we were conditioned not to acknowledge vulnerability and failure; neither was to be named, as if naming them was instantiating their existence. There simply was no space for identifying and expressing affective vulnerability and therefore no space for the cultivation and performance of healthy norms of mental and emotional wellness.

In Butler's reframing of vulnerability and as Nicole's narrative vividly demonstrates, subjects are vulnerable to a lack of support and the decomposition or destruction of supports and systems that make life livable. The political and social actions of a subject cannot be sufficiently understood without critically considering a subject's relationship within and to particular structures: "We cannot talk about a body without knowing what supports that body and what its relation to that support—or lack of support—might be."[30] Critically, no action occurs in a vacuum, divorced from the social, historical, political, and infrastructural conditions that make it possible and inform it; moreover, all enactments of resistance, challenges to dominant power relations, and protests of inequity are troubled by the past, present, and future repercussions of such acts. Recognizing the existence and encouraging the expressions of affective vulnerability are essential components of an affective infrastructure. Here, in discussing our own experiences with failure and challenges with mental and emotional health, we risk the stigmatization, alienation, and shaming that predominantly characterize frequent backlash when subjects disclose diagnoses of mental and emotional health disorders and share their lived experiences of failing to meet dominant norms. In exposing ourselves to risk, however, we enact affective vulnerability to identify its existence and claim its agentic power in a deliberate attempt to reconstitute the norms of graduate programs.

The stigmatization of mental and emotional health still pervades and predominates in public discursive spaces such as graduate programs, departments, and institutions. That simply must change. Graduate programs and faculty must acknowledge the deleterious effects of the way graduate students are socialized to fulfill unreasonable and unhealthy norms and encouraged to contribute to a culture of competition that not only positions graduate students against each other but also very likely positions them against other ranks of contingent and exploited faculty. For far too long, people with power within the discipline have dismissed emotional labor and mental health challenges, cavalierly assuring graduate students that the affective vulnerability and trauma they feel is just part of the experience or encouraging graduate students to simply "work harder" or "be more disciplined." Worse yet, some faculty and mentors in graduate programs may have had or may be experiencing their own challenges with emotional labor and mental health but may possibly conceptualize those experiences as a kind of rite of passage or necessary ritual of disciplinarity. None of the trauma, affective vulnerability, and mental health challenges that graduate students or—for that matter—full- and part-time faculty experience are inevitable. As a discipline, we can and must change structures and the culture within our graduate programs and departments that produce so much angst, anxiety, and fear. Graduate programs should create and encourage constructive opportunities for graduate students to enact affective vulnerability to reconfigure dominant norms and revise the competitive culture within those programs. Collectively enacting affective vulnerability as a generative tool for revising norms, however, should not be conflated with the problematic politics of self-care or cavalier calls for emotional authenticity, both of which are derided by Butler because they reinforce the opposition of vulnerability to agency and discount the ways vulnerability can be powerfully mobilized as an act of resistance.[31] This resistance does not show up through social gatherings or listening sessions where directors, faculty, and mentors can perform the pretense of caring for the experiences of graduate students. We have a responsibility to take action within our professional organizations, on our campuses, in the scholarship, and with the campus leaders who write and approve job ads.

Another component of affective infrastructure relates to the material support of graduate students and how programs are structured to cultivate emotional and mental wellness and ensure equity across experiences and ranks. As Nick's and Nicole's narratives suggest, programs must make critical investments that are responsive to graduate students' material and economic realities and provide more strength and stability to their livelihoods and families. These investments include full tuition remission, health insurance, and a salary that equitably compensates graduate students for their expertise, experience, and labor and that is proportional to the cost of living in the areas where graduate programs are located. Graduate students need to be paid not just a livable wage but a salary indicative of the fact that programs respect and value their humanity and their invaluable contributions. Programs and institutions also need to provide paid parental and medical leave for graduate students, as well as for all faculty, so that people do not have to choose among their families, health, and work. As Nicole's narrative demonstrates, too often, faculty are forced to sacrifice time with family to the demands of their academic and work commitments because there is no alternative. Helping graduate students cultivate a healthy work/life balance and making the necessary material investment that ensures that balance may be the most important components of affective infrastructure.

Finally, faculty teaching in doctoral programs and serving on hiring committees must drastically change the expectations for what students must accomplish as they graduate from their programs and apply for various positions. As Sherry indicates, the expectations perpetuate fierce competition: we want graduate students who have published, who have facilitated multiple presentations at national conferences, who have served important roles in disciplinary organizations, and who have been exceptional teachers of a wide variety of courses. These were the expectations our doctoral program conditioned us to meet: publish and get/keep a job or fail to publish and perish. But, as detailed above, the emotional and mental costs of meeting those expectations are exponential and entail years of struggle, fear, pain, and trauma. Concomitant with these expectations is the threat of failure, the risk of humiliation, the exposure to exacting demands on lives and livelihoods. This isn't healthy. We can and must do better for our writing programs.

The pandemic has offered us a closer look at not only the ways our academic systems and university structures are broken but also the ways that brokenness affects the mental health of students, faculty, and staff.

Students have turned to us and to each other to maintain a sense of normalcy (as if there is ever such a thing) throughout the pandemic. As they have confided in us, reached out with stories of their struggles to complete their work in the face of hospital visits and illnesses, asked for extensions, and pleaded for our understanding, we have responded with care and empathy: shaping our assignments to best fit students' needs, whittling down our lessons to those that are of utmost importance to allow students room for managing their lives while managing their schoolwork, and so on. While we faced down the pandemic with partners and with children to care for, we have done so in between our lectures, office hours, department meetings, and what felt like endless amounts of grading, emailing, writing/reporting/assessing, and publishing.

As mentors, professors, and program directors, we need to stop pretending as if affective realities don't exist. We need to be willing to see and acknowledge how affective realities—whether the trauma of a pandemic, the trauma of unrealistic, unhealthy expectations, or both—impact our graduate students emotionally and mentally. In identifying, accounting for, and encouraging expressions of affective vulnerability, we can respond to our students in ways that affirm their lived experiences, foster empathy within a classroom as well as a program, and constitute healthy, productive norms of success in our graduate programs. We call for a community that fosters "ethics of care," as Jacob Babb and William Duffy discuss in chapter 1 of this collection. In doing so, instead of feeling as though we have failed our students as Borrowman laments, we can empower communities with our writing programs and fashion an affective infrastructure that constructs and supports healthy, egalitarian norms; this structure would create expectations that cultivate the health and wellness of our academic communities.

NOTES

1. Borrowman, *Trauma and the Teaching of Writing*, 1.
2. Butler, "Rethinking Vulnerability and Resistance."
3. Borrowman, *Trauma and the Teaching of Writing*, 4.
4. Bizzell, "Foreword," viii.
5. Hesse, "The WPA as Husband, Father, Ex."
6. Gillam, "Taking It Personally."
7. Bizzell, "Foreword"; Rhodes, "Mothers, Tell Your Children Not to Do What I Have Done."
8. Price, *Mad at School*; Driscoll, Leigh, and Zamin, "Self-Care as Professionalization"; Wooten et al. *The Things We Carry*.
9. Space constraints, however, prevent us from fully problematizing complex intercalations among race, gender, socioeconomics, sexual orientation, neurodiversity,

physical ability, and other socio-political formations. Such a project requires the delicate application and reticulation of feminist, critical race, postcolonial, Marxist, queer, and disability theories. This chapter does not intend to elide such critical work in identifying how vulnerability and precarity are inequitably experienced and imposed because of identifications with historically marginalized and disenfranchised sociopolitical formations; on the contrary, we hope this chapter provokes that needed critical engagement in the discipline around this topic.

10. Butler, Gambetti, and Sabsay, "Introduction," 1.
11. Butler, Gambetti, and Sabsay, "Introduction," 4.
12. Butler, Gambetti, and Sabsay, "Introduction," 5.
13. Butler, Gambetti, and Sabsay, "Introduction," 3.
14. Butler, Gambetti, and Sabsay, "Introduction," 7.
15. Kasmir, "Precarity."
16. Mude et al., "Racial Disparities in COVID-19 Pandemic Cases, Hospitalisations, and Deaths."
17. Butler, "Rethinking Vulnerability and Resistance," 12; Kasmir, "Precarity."
18. Neither type of vulnerability is sufficiently addressed in disciplinary scholarship. In focusing on affective vulnerability, we do not intend to minimize the impact of bodily vulnerability on the health and wellness of graduate students. Graduate students, particularly those who identify as BIPOC, experience bodily vulnerability, an effect of the inequitable power relations pervading the academy.
19. Butler, "Rethinking Vulnerability and Resistance," 16.
20. Butler, "Rethinking Vulnerability and Resistance," 20.
21. Butler, "Rethinking Vulnerability and Resistance," 18.
22. Also see Matzke, Rankins-Robertson, and Garrett, "Nevertheless, She Persisted."
23. Butler, "Rethinking Vulnerability and Resistance," 24.
24. Rankins-Robertson and Behm, "Performing Silence, Exhaustion, and Recovery."
25. Nadkarni, "Two Boards and a Passion," 67.
26. Rankins-Robertson and Behm, "Performing Silence, Exhaustion, and Recovery," 244–46.
27. Wegner, "Navigating WPA Emotional Labor with Mindfulness."
28. Wegner, "Navigating WPA Emotional Labor with Mindfulness," 252.
29. Butler, "Rethinking Vulnerability and Resistance," 19.
30. Butler, "Rethinking Vulnerability and Resistance," 19.
31. Butler, "Rethinking Vulnerability and Resistance," 25.

REFERENCES

Bizzell, Patricia. "Foreword: On Good Administrators." In *Kitchen Cooks, Plate Twirlers, and Troubadours: Writing Program Administrators Tell Their Stories*, edited by Diane George, vii–ix. Portsmouth, NH: Boynton/Cook, 1999.

Borrowman, Shane, ed. *Trauma and the Teaching of Writing*. New York: SUNY Press, 2006.

Butler, Judith. "Rethinking Vulnerability and Resistance." In *Vulnerability in Resistance*, edited by Judith Butler, Zeynep Gambetti, and Leticia Sabsay, 12–27. Durham, NC: Duke University Press, 2016.

Butler, Judith, Zeynep Gambetti, and Leticia Sabsay. "Introduction." In *Vulnerability in Resistance*, edited by Judith Butler, Zeynep Gambetti, and Leticia Sabsay, 1–11. Durham, NC: Duke University Press, 2016.

Driscoll, Dana Lynn, S. Rebecca Leigh, and Nadia Francine Zamin. "Self-Care as Professionalization: A Case for Ethical Doctoral Education in Composition Studies." *College Composition and Communication* 71, no. 3 (2020): 453–80.

Gillam, Alice. "Taking It Personally: Redefining the Role and Work of the WPA." In *Kitchen Cooks, Plate Twirlers, and Troubadours: Writing Program Administrators Tell Their Stories,* edited by Diane George, 65–72. Portsmouth, NH: Boynton/Cook, 1999.

Hesse, Doug. "The WPA as Husband, Father, Ex." In *Kitchen Cooks, Plate Twirlers, and Troubadours: Writing Program Administrators Tell Their Stories,* edited by Diane George, 44–55. Portsmouth, NH: Boynton/Cook, 1999.

Kasmir, Sharryn. "Precarity." *The Cambridge Encyclopedia of Anthropology,* March 13, 2018. http://doi.org/10.29164/18precarity.

Matzke, Aurora, Sherry Rankins-Robertson, and Bre Garrett. " 'Nevertheless, She Persisted': Strategies to Counteract the Time, Place, and Culture of Academic Bullying for WPAs." In *Defining, Locating, and Addressing Bullying in the WPA Workplace,* edited by Cristyn Elder and Bethany Davila, 49–68. Logan: Utah State University Press, 2018.

Mude, William, Victor M. Oguoma, Tafadzwa Nyanhanda, Lillian Mwanri, and Carolyne Njue. "Racial Disparities in COVID-19 Pandemic Cases, Hospitalisations, and Deaths: A Systematic Review and Meta-Analysis." *Journal of Global Health* 11, no. 05015 (2021). doi: 10.7189/jogh.11.05015.

Nadkarni, Anjalee Deshpande. "Two Boards and a Passion: On Theater, Academia, and the Art of Failure." In *Mama PhD: Women Write about Motherhood and Academic Life,* edited by Elrena Evans and Caroline Grant, 66–71. London: Rutgers University Press, 2009.

Price, Margaret. *Mad at School: Rhetorics of Mental Disability and Academic Life.* Ann Arbor: University of Michigan Press, 2011.

Rankins-Robertson, Sherry, and Nicholas Behm. "Performing Silence, Exhaustion, and Recovery: Articulating Faculty and Administrator Identity by Cultivating Mental Wellness." In *Preserving Emotion in Student Writing,* edited by Craig Wynne, 239–50. New York: Peter Lang, 2001.

Rhodes, Keith. "Mothers, Tell Your Children Not to Do What I Have Done: The Sin and Misery of Entering the Profession as a Composition Coordinator." In *Kitchen Cooks, Plate Twirlers, and Troubadours: Writing Program Administrators Tell Their Stories,* edited by Diane George, 86–94. Portsmouth, NH: Boynton/Cook, 1999.

Wegner, Christy. "Navigating WPA Emotional Labor with Mindfulness: Practical Strategies for Well-Being" In *The Things We Carry: Strategies for Recognizing and Negotiating Emotional Labor in Writing Program Administration,* edited by Courtney Adams Wooten, Jacob Babb, Kristi Murray Costello, and Kate Navickas Logan, 251–69. Logan: Utah State University Press, 2020.

Wooten, Courtney Adams, Jacob Babb, Kristi Murray Costello, and Kate Navickas, eds. *The Things We Carry: Strategies for Recognizing and Negotiating Emotional Labor in Writing Program Administration.* Logan: Utah State University Press, 2020.

6

ON NON-SCALABILITY AND TRANSFORMATIVE RELATIONSHIPS IN THE FIRST-YEAR COMPOSITION "JUMBO"

Laura Sparks and Kim Jaxon

From where we stand, the future of writing instruction, particularly in first-year composition courses, is not a fifteen–twenty person writing course staffed by a full-time writing instructor. We teach at a comprehensive state university, recently designated a Hispanic-serving institution, with a cap of thirty students in first-year composition courses. This cap is unlikely to decrease. So what structures can we create to support students' writing, research, and thinking practices while still valuing our own labor and mental health?[1] How might we proactively leverage large enrollments to make for productive, meaningful learning environments for students?

One such structure is what we call the first-year writing "Jumbo," a large-enrollment composition course taught with ninety students and nine embedded peer writing mentors. This course design is *not* simply a large writing class; rather, the Jumbo structure establishes a framework for relationships across participants, opening up an opportunity space for meaning making that potentially exceeds that of the traditional classroom model.[2]

This chapter first offers a brief overview of the Jumbo design, then takes up Anna Tsing's work on "non-scalability" to make the case for the Jumbo model's generative potential in first-year writing.[3] In particular, we conceptualize the Jumbo in terms of growth rather than expansion, arguing that it operates outside the logic of scalability. We further advocate for an imaginative, *active*, not reactionary, approach to course development. As Tsing aptly puts it, "Conceptualizing the world and making the world are wrapped up with each other—at least for those with the privilege to turn their dreams into action. The relationship goes both ways: new projects inspire new ways to think, which also inspire new projects."⁴ We contend that the large-enrollment Jumbo offers powerful possibilities for creating and sustaining vibrant, action-oriented communities—new projects for all of us.

JUMBO DESIGN

Kim Jaxon designed our English department's first "Jumbo" writing course in 2009, taking our mandated thirty-student cap and tripling it. As Jaxon explains, the large-enrollment Jumbo design was not a reaction to budgetary or staffing concerns; further, it was not imposed on our program by administrators. The structure "emerged from an 'entanglement' of the institutional environment and intentional innovation" rather than as a cost-saving measure.⁵ In a climate of higher education "contraction" rather than expansion, it is particularly important that we design proactively the kinds of learning environments we and our students need and value (see Basgier, chapter 4, this volume). The Jumbo was intentionally designed for the affordances of the size, including attention to practices that allow students to be seen and heard in a group substantially larger than those found in other writing classes. By building this peer-supported framework into our English curriculum, we also minimized "one-off" or "boutique" writing opportunities in favor of an established and institutionally endorsed design (Basgier, chapter 4, this volume). As noted by Jaxon and her colleagues, "Writing circulates across networks, platforms, readers, and critics: [with the Jumbo,] we are interested in the ways in which a large class can approximate complex systems of production and circulation and disrupt the primacy of the teacher-student dyad."⁶ The design called for the addition of nine embedded peer writing mentors, who would attend every Jumbo class and lead their own ten-person workshops each week. The Jumbo itself meets as a whole class twice weekly for one hour; peer writing mentors (first trained in our department's tutoring writing course) lead weekly workshops, and those workshop groups are maintained throughout the semester. The Jumbo design thus offers both large- and small-scale learning environments. The mentors see and respond to student writing frequently, with opportunities for more feedback and norming in weekly "mentor meetings." These weekly meetings between the mentors and the instructor allow for ongoing course design, feedback opportunities, class and activity planning, and so on.

For several decades, our program had been using a ten-person adjunct workshop model, developed by Judith Rodby and Tom Fox as a solution to "remediation" requirements.⁷ These writing workshops, led by peer writing mentors, had functioned separately from our first-year writing courses, providing a space for extensive peer review, revision, and so on.[8] The Jumbo model builds on this existing work by integrating writing workshops into the course structure, making them both a part of and running concurrently with the whole-class Jumbo meetings. No students are singled out by test scores or other factors into separate workshops; rather, everyone is part of a workshop, and the workshops' connections to the course itself are strengthened. By making the mentors part of the course itself, the workshops become a more central part of the writing ecology in which students, mentors, and the instructor participate.

Our Jumbo course, taught for over ten years with a range of foci—including human rights and digital culture—offers a "provocation to the field's focus on class size, including preferences for smaller student-teacher ratios and the assumption that only the writing instructor can give valuable feedback."[9] To imagine the space filled with 100 writers, start by picturing a large room furnished with flexible seating: movable tables, chairs, and whiteboards with large projection screens on three of the walls. On a typical Monday, visitors would see mentors checking in with their small cohort of 10 students before the official start of class. Mentors might ask students about weekend plans, inquire if work for the course was confusing, and invite students to get situated with laptops open and the reading for the day available. Nine groups spread out around their own large tables, talking animatedly with each other as the instructor fills the projection screens with plans for the day.

As the large class starts up, we typically begin by celebrating and acknowledging student writing. Our review board—a handful of students who rotate the responsibility of reading their small group's writing each week, highlighting class members' thoughtful work—shares the work of featured writers. The writing appears on the three large screens around the room. The peers talk about why they chose this writing and how it meets our goals for writing that week, and the review board members invite the authors (their selected peers) to talk about their writing process. Each week, 4–5 students are recognized; over a sixteen-week semester, another 60–65 will be noticed and their ideas will be amplified.

On some days we discuss reading, with small groups contributing reading passages to a class Google doc or Google slide deck that can be shared on the screens. The readings often serve as mentor texts; after a discussion, we might invite the class to try out some of the writerly moves we've uncovered in the reading in our own drafts. Other days we might share insights, writing, or other kinds of artifacts (multimodal texts) in a large gallery walk: students move about the large room engaging in each others' projects, much like a poster session at a conference. These sessions are lively with 100 people in the room, and students have a chance to meet and support students outside their small cohort.

In our community-based model, many more roles are available than those of student-novice and instructor-expert, a possibility space that we find enables more and different kinds of participation than might be experienced in a traditional classroom. We also find that this model invites a reconsideration of where expertise is located: the students, the mentors, and the instructor share the responsibilities for feedback and support for writers. The instructor does not have the capacity to respond regularly to all students' writing every week; the instructor's voice and feedback, then, is one among many. We intentionally attempt to disrupt the student-to-teacher one-way exchange of drafts to distribute expertise among participants. For example, in Kim's section, larger assignments might include a rubric for scoring. The rubric, however, is crowdsourced by the whole class *after* a first draft of a major assignment is written. Once students attempt a draft, they have a better idea of what might be included in the paper, and importantly, they know how their labor manifested in writing that first draft: did they spend more time on research and therefore want the research process to be heavily weighted in the rubric? Students score drafts, write memos that reflect on or explain their drafting and revision processes, and talk continually with each other, their mentor, and the instructor about drafts through both memos and marginal comments left on their drafts.

The Jumbo's distributed model makes the mentors and students important and valued interlocutors for peers' writing. The mentor-led workshop groups, for example, are crucial to creating participation structures for learning; students aren't simply continuing the work of the larger Jumbo space but rather extending it, with activities like composing blog posts, reading together, engaging in primary or secondary research, drafting major assignments or offering feedback, making group artifacts, designing portfolios, and so on. The workshop is an activity space that allows individual concerns and ideas to arise that might not have been brought up in the whole-class meeting. Because the peer mentors are full participants in the class, not adjacent or supplemental tutors, they try on a range of mentorship, leadership, facilitation, and co-learner roles within the Jumbo structure.

We identify several key affordances of this Jumbo class model. First, the large size means that students' participation can take many forms, from more typical verbal comments to curation and publication of peers' written work. The Jumbo, for example, may have its own social media hashtags that semester, and some students participate by sharing a play-by-play on social media platforms they choose. Second, the course structure helps students understand the ecology of their learning environments—and their own identities as learners—in ways beyond what may be available in traditional class settings. Third, the Jumbo provides professional development for students across the university, including future teachers. Interested mentors first enroll in our undergraduate course, Theories and Practices in Tutoring Writing, which offers a foundation in situated theories of learning, theories of literacy, and research in the teaching of writing. Once hired, mentors and the instructor meet weekly as a group to plan for the upcoming week, look at student writing together, design activities, share strategies and challenges, and so on; Jumbo teaching is necessarily collaborative between instructor and mentors. Finally, the built-in class community, with its wide and layered range of participants, affords extensive opportunities for students to enact meaningful, visible change—from designing support materials for first-generation students to promoting awareness about surveillance and student data privacy in learning management systems. The Jumbo has a built-in audience and, thanks to the sheer number of people involved, an expanded range of connections and affiliations beyond the classroom.

We also caution, however, that the Jumbo does not address the labor concerns frequent in higher education—especially writing programs—that may rely heavily on contingent, graduate, and adjunct labor to staff composition courses; offer insufficient notice for course assignments; and even underfund instructors and support staff. One of our concerns continues to be that the Jumbo might displace lecturers by occasioning fewer sections of traditional writing courses. As we argue in Jaxon, Sparks, and Fosen, institutional support for mentors and instructors—including course design, piloting, and assessment—is essential for developing and sustaining ethical learning environments of any kind.

SCALABILITY

We noted at the outset of this chapter that the Jumbo is not a *scaled-up* composition course. That is to say, participants' roles, responsibilities, and relationships to one another necessarily change in this shift from a traditional model to the Jumbo. We would further argue that the Jumbo itself is not scalable, insofar as we understand scalability to reduce or eliminate the possibility of change or variation. In her work on non-scalability, Tsing calls "scalability" "the ability to expand—and expand, and expand—without rethinking basic elements."[10] She further questions the possibility of diversity in scalable projects, writing that "transformative relationships are the medium for the emergence of diversity. Scalability projects banish meaningful diversity, which is to say, diversity that might change things."[11] Scalable design relies on consistency and precision; as the structure grows, its component parts remain fixed. The component parts of the Jumbo design are *not* scaled in relation to a traditional course. Rather, new elements have been added, along with room for new and not-yet-imagined relationships and connections. So when we insist that the Jumbo is not a scaled-up composition course, we mean to trouble the notion that the relationships among participants, tools, and activities can remain the same.

Indeed, in the shift from a thirty-person to a ninety-person cap, scalability remains counter to our aims. Our program has, from the start, understood both the workshops and the Jumbo meetings to be *unlike* traditional classroom experiences. Precision-nested scales would be not only impossible but undesirable—for example, writing mentors are not mini-teachers leading mini-classes in their workshops. Tsing is careful to caution against a celebration of non-scalability over scalability—non-scalable projects are not inherently better or worse—but she does imply that different outcomes and opportunities are possible in non-scalable projects, that relationships can be powerful in part because one is not always sure of the outcome. The Jumbo is imagined as a new possibility space, one in which the variety of participant roles, texts, digital activities, and possible collaborations can seed and change over time. Transformative social relations are really what it's all about. In what follows, we take up Tsing's theory to explore some of the Jumbo's non-scalable features and events.

ROLES AND RELATIONSHIPS

As suggested earlier, Tsing finds that "transformative relationships" by definition add new elements to the project or activity and thus characterize non-scalable projects. And these changes are not necessarily predictable. One of the crucial changes integrated into the Jumbo model is the addition of embedded writing mentors. Influenced by Jean Lave and Étienne Wenger's "community of practice" model,[12] the Jumbo relies on small learning communities and embedded mentor support;

knowledge is co-created through reciprocal processes of inquiry and revision. Students come to see their mentors as more capable peers who have learned to navigate not only the first-year writing classroom but also the university. Importantly, the mentors are full participants in the class, not a separate or supplemental source of support. They necessarily change the space by being part of it. In traditional classroom models, the instructor is often positioned as an expert, with the final word on class content, organization, and, of course, evaluation. Embedded writing mentors, typically undergraduates, bring a whole new set of experiences and expertise to the space.

By integrating more experienced students into the class, the Jumbo also amplifies possibilities for relationships among students within and alongside the large section. Mentors may help plan class activities and projects, facilitate discussions, serve as advanced peers, respond to student writing and compose their own texts, and lead workshops for their group of 10 students. Mentors attend each Jumbo meeting, bringing the total number of participants up to 100, but they also support their students in the smaller workshop space. Indeed, the role of writing mentors cannot be overstated here. Because they participate in myriad ways, they are also called to *relate* in myriad ways. The relationships possible between mentors and students can include everything from a supportive peer to a friend to a teacher to a writing coach. In describing his experiences with mentorship, Keaton Kirkpatrick notes, "The roles of mentors are overarching and extensive; but broadly, our role is to transition between peer, instructor, and tutor. A mentor's ability to move between multiple roles is what makes them an important resource in the classroom since they're able to serve the diverse needs of students."[13] The mutability of this mentor role is unmatched. "Relationships," Tsing argues, "are potential vectors of transformation," and including a third classroom role here both significantly impacts the class community and expands possibilities for the development of students' writerly and scholarly identity.[14]

Because the writing mentors work so closely with students, the relationships between students and the instructor can shift as well. The instructor-student relationship need not be the main vector; rather, the Jumbo invites teachers to rethink and redirect their own labor practices into potentially new arrangements. Instructors' labor is neither more nor less. It's simply different—interlaced with other participants in the community. The instructor becomes not the sole source of "answers" or the class rule gatekeeper but one option among many to discuss aspects of the course, projects, expectations, possibilities, and so on. Expertise gets located differently and in multiple places. As we discuss in Jaxon, Sparks, and Fosen, the Jumbo instructor's role is to "curate texts, classroom structures, discussions, and activities so students can choose from a range of options, and hopefully, find their own purposes for learning, reading, writing, and research. Students are not mucking around in the dark—the instructor still holds a disciplinary expertise that informs text selections and potential ideas for class consideration—but students have opportunities to use those texts as a way to solve problems and consider what use they might make of the content and ideas presented to them."[15]

Ideally, this role is not wildly different from the way thirty-person or smaller sections of first-year writing are taught. But consider, as an instructor, the difference in having nine interlocutors (the mentors) with whom to brainstorm and collaborate—more voices before, during, and after a class session; more eyes reading and responding to student work; more ears noticing concerns and cool ideas; more brains seeking out class materials, provocations, or examples. These ongoing relationships between instructor and mentors offer powerful possibilities for both supporting advanced students and inviting instructors to reimagine ways of working. As noted earlier, one of the Jumbo's key affordances is as a paid professionalization opportunity for future teachers and, with over ten years of the Jumbo under our belts, Jumbo alumni. Echoing Nicole Khoury, Nicholas Behm, and Sherry Rankins-Robertson's call for an "affective infrastructure" that values and supports vulnerable teachers and students (chapter 5, this volume), the Jumbo offers opportunities for coalition building across experiences and interests in first-year writing. Especially for first-generation college students and students from underserved communities, the Jumbo offers a space for mentors to grow into and model their expertise to new students. Writing students, in turn, may begin to imagine themselves as future mentors.

IMPRECISION

If we understand scalability in terms of precision-nested scales, then in refusing scalability, our project is potentially imprecise, fluid, even sometimes out of our immediate control. For example, students in the Jumbo spend twice as much time with mentors as with the instructor, and each mentor comes with their own approaches and preferences. The mentors themselves might be second-year students or graduate students, adding more expertise, experiences, and habits to the mix. And while an instructor may hold a class of twenty students in rapt attention, it is generally difficult to do so in a large-enrollment class; active, participatory structures are essential. We take up this notion of "imprecision" to consider that which does not easily fit: the excess and the play essential to non-scalable projects and good learning environments.

The Jumbo model, on its surface, has been attractive to other departments and universities because, similar to some administrators' desire for increased online course offerings and caps, it *sounds* more efficient. But in practice, it does not fit perfectly within most university spaces and support capabilities. We shared elsewhere that the Jumbo was not initially designed to solve a financial or labor problem. We emphasize this point again here because it has been our experience that the Jumbo is not less expensive or easier to house than our university's traditional class offerings. If one compensates instructors and writing mentors appropriately, it may even be more expensive. Too, it is not suitable for a standard lecture hall or in spaces where seating is fixed or tiered, electronic devices aren't supported with multiple outlets, and the instructor's or students' movement or visibility is limited. The Jumbo is not an extra-large composition class where more chairs and desks will suffice. Rather, the Jumbo invites classroom spaces that are fluid and changeable and where the materials available can be used in any number of ways.

As explained previously, the Jumbo is also not a typical lecture/discussion or TA model, however much it supports the mentors' professional development and can be a space for future TAs to gain experience. Further, the Jumbo's multiple learning environments are not tidy, efficient, or precise. For example, a large lecture course in which the instructor lectures/talks/presents and the students sit quietly and listen (perhaps taking notes or using clickers to participate) may lay claim to a certain tidiness or efficiency—if not efficiency of learning. There is one place to look (perhaps two if we count a screen) and one expert voice to listen to. But the Jumbo is, at all points, an activity space where students might write, read, talk, upload or download, share, or lead. The Jumbo meetings, from whole-class sessions to workshops, can be incredibly lively—with different mentors leading discussion, different activities happening simultaneously, and less centering overall on the instructor. Imprecision, messiness, and the addition of new elements and relationships all conspire to make the Jumbo a dynamic and highly student-centered learning environment.

Instructors may also find new levels of negotiation and collaboration in the Jumbo that require even experienced educators to rethink certain class policies or grading procedures, ways of evaluating student work, and so on. What role should mentors play in determining student grades?

Who offers feedback and at what stage? What should be the stakes of various assignments? Some of us have found, for example, that something akin to contract grading works better in the Jumbo.[16] Others have found that rules about technology use or social media use during class have become irrelevant. With nine mentors bringing their own ideas and student experiences to the table each week, it could not be otherwise. While we hesitate to use the term control here, in many ways that's what the Jumbo invites us to relinquish as instructors—even when that makes for moments of indecision or discomfort or requires more flexibility than we may be used to. In the Jumbo, we are called to trust our students.

MAKING

Trust, particularly tied to our desire to loosen instructor control, has roots in our field's claim to champion students' rights to their own language and in Jody Shipka's (among others) call for students' rights to control processes, methods, materials, and means of distribution of ideas.[17] This is not to pretend that instructors do not have power and authority in the classroom—indeed, claiming otherwise does a disservice to our students—but rather to emphasize the instructor's position as part of a wider and more complex ecology. First-year writing courses, designed as nested blocks in composition programs that call for multi-section uniformity, can sometimes leave little room for student-driven inquiries and products. The instructor-selected readings, prompts, sentence starters, and outlines and the emphasis on the paper—in the name of support for nascent writers—can shrink the world and the possibility space offered in our classrooms.[18]

Even when students are asked to make new meanings in school, they are often restricted to "schooled" modes of production, which look very different from the literacies they draw from outside of school. In a MacArthur Foundation report, Cathy Davidson and David Theo Goldberg point to a central division taking place between students' lived experiences in the world and their experiences in schools: the interactive, networked world made available through digital technologies versus the rigidly individualized world of personal assessment and achievement long emphasized in school.[19] Outside of school, students participate in open, collaborative, networked, production-centered environments where they blog, create films, write and share music, and even build robots. They are producers and designers in these environments, sharing their work through blogging and video platforms and other sites for digital communities. However, the literacy practices shaped by youth culture through these tools and platforms are not always familiar to the adults around them; in fact, the practices—ways of using these tools and the products that arise from them—are often not categorized *as* literacies. But as Mizuko Ito argues in the conclusion of *Hanging Out, Messing Around, and Geeking Out*, a volume of ethnographic studies focused on youth culture and their participation in new literacies, "As technical and media skills and practices become more mainstream, the kids who are associated with these more specialized groups will compete to differentiate themselves with even more specialized forms of expertise that test the boundaries of technical virtuosity. Because of this, a participation gap in relation to these practices is a structural inevitability, and in fact, drives motivation and aspirations. In this domain, we should value diversity rather than standardization to enable more kids to succeed and gain recognition in different communities of interest."[20]

The "technical and media skills" Ito points to represent a range of new literacies: remixing, composing, manipulating images—but, more important, the practices learned in these interest-driven spaces connect the participants to rich communities of practice, which leads to engagement and persistence in these spaces.[21] Ito asks us to consider how we might develop structures within more formal learning environments that value and connect students' literacies to systems of reward and achievement. Importantly, her study sheds light on the benefits of valuing a broad range of literate practices, particularly for students from low-income, underrepresented populations. Less privileged youth in her study, who were often skeptical of school and concerned that their literacies have no value in the literate economies of schooling, often found that their participation in interest-driven and production-centered networks outside of school was "a way out of alienating learning experiences in formal education."[22]

The Jumbo, where possible, places attention on the role of artifacts in meaning making and invites students to make their own writerly decisions.[23] Course designs that emphasize making invite "diversity rather than standardization" of the texts composed by students. In the construction of artifacts—from art to games to slam poetry to essays—students share cultural ways of knowing: we see traces of their homes, their heritages, and their languages. They weave Spanish, Hmong, and Black English into their creations as a means to "reconceptualize the world—and perhaps rebuild it."[24] We invite messy drafts, messy artifacts, knowing that learning is complex and that building communities where people thrive is often fraught, complex, and messy.

We argue that this project of non-scalability, this deliberate turn to meaningful social relations, to play, to imprecision, is also a world-making project. Following Elaine Scarry's theory of "making," we emphasize the significance of the generative relationships made possible in the Jumbo writing class. Making, Scarry argues, entails an extension of oneself into the world through the creation of artifacts; making is, in a sense, world making. She maintains that "the making of an artifact is a social act, for the object (whether an art work or instead an object of everyday use) is intended as something that will both enter into and itself elicit human responsiveness."[25] When one makes and uses artifacts, one also provides the means to enter into another's feelings and have one's subjectivity experienced in return. Making is a form of self-extension that can create social bonds, whether through the reciprocity inherent in making an object (someone is warm in the scarf I knitted) or the interactivity that characterizes the projective action (I knitted this scarf with the idea of making someone warm). The sociality ascribed to making exists in multiple senses: in the arc of creating that Scarry deftly theorizes, where there is always the desire that an artifact refer back to human sentience; and in the procedural act of making, the labored inventional process that generates or invokes before an artifact is actually shared.

What is a writing class but a space for making things? Making meaning; visual, written, and multimodal texts; artifacts; ideas . . . Because the Jumbo offers so many nodes for possible interactivity and artifact creation—so many possible points of connection—making's social and reciprocal aspects are amplified. Put another way, something "epic" can happen when a huge group of people get together, working side by side on similar tasks or toward connected goals. Jane McGonigal's notion of "epic scale," which she uses to describe gaming environments, suggests that people create strong bonds with one another and the projects they are engaged in when they feel a part of something bigger than themselves.[26] While McGonigal's concerns are not pedagogical, we find a similarly epic experience in the Jumbo. The Jumbo's size harnesses the vitality of a large, interconnected group—not unlike the crowd at a rock concert or a soccer match—to expand possibilities for students' participation, coalition building, community membership, and intervention in meaningful issues. There is a generative kind of making at work here, a particularly human kind of excitement, made possible in the Jumbo. Imagine a room with 100 people commenting on giant post-it notes with research project ideas. Or 100 people working together to find resources relating to a shared text. Pedagogical practices like students' curation and publication of their peers' work, team projects, student-led inquiry, and others increase opportunities for students to be enmeshed or caught up in one another's work. We call this epic element also a kind of world making.

CONCLUSION

As we hope is abundantly clear, the answer to creating environments for learning is *not* simply to add more people to the class. Expansion is not the same as growth (Tsing), and from the start, the Jumbo has been designed as a framework for growth and change—not replication or expansion. As Tsing observes, "The ease with which our computers zoom across magnifications lulls us into the false belief that both knowledge and things exist by nature in precision-nested scales. Scalability . . . is this ability to expand without distorting the framework"[27]—without changing. But what does that mean for the messy and mutable relationships between humans and even non-humans made possible in particular activities or environments? How can world building happen when we simply expand without growing or changing?

To propose that the Jumbo operates outside the logic of scalability is to recognize it as necessarily complicated and messy, as well as highly institutionally located. Our Jumbo's size—ninety students and nine writing mentors—functions well within the institutional ecology here, with our current student population, geographic location, material conditions, writing faculty's expertise, pedagogical leanings, and so on. We would not expect the Jumbo to look quite the same at another institution. When we reject scalability, we also reject the notion that the Jumbo is neatly replicable in other contexts. In her research on the matsutake mushroom, Tsing explains: "Most commercially collected matsutake grow in industrial forests or peasant forests. In these human-disturbed places, matsutake show us the forms of collaborative survival—the transformative social relations—that make life possible. The forests inhabited by matsutake are collaborations among many species, including humans."[28]

Tsing argues that growth and survival are heralded by "transformative social relations," and those relations are not separate from knowledge practices. If scalability projects attempt to block those relationships, we see the Jumbo as nurturing them by creating and sustaining opportunities for intimate learning environments even in larger groups. And these learning environments are not separable from their conditions of emergence. This human and non-human collaboration, this ecology of being, deserves the most careful attention we have to offer in our design of learning environments.

NOTES

1. For more on trauma, vulnerability, and mental health in the profession, see Khoury, Behm, and Rankins-Robertson, chapter 5, this volume.
2. At times we refer to a "traditional" classroom model. We recognize that there are significant differences in the ways courses are designed, staffed, and taught. By "traditional" we simply mean typical-size courses (15–30 students, approximately) led by a single instructor without embedded support. "Traditional" would thus encompass most of the writing courses taught at our university and in our state university system.
3. Tsing, "On Nonscalability."
4. Tsing, "On Nonscalability," 506.
5. Jaxon, "Epic Learning."
6. Jaxon, Sparks, and Fosen, "Epic Learning in a 'Jumbo' Writing Course," 119.
7. See Rodby and Fox, "Basic Work and Material Acts."
8. For a discussion of the Jumbo model's institutional history, see Jaxon, Sparks, and Fosen, "Epic Learning," 116–17.
9. Jaxon, Sparks, and Fosen, "Epic Learning," 116.
10. Tsing, "On Nonscalability," 505.
11. Tsing, "On Nonscalability," 507.
12. See Lave and Wenger, *Situated Learning*.
13. Jaxon, "Building Community with Peer Mentors."
14. Tsing, "On Nonscalability," 507.
15. Jaxon, Sparks, and Fosen, "Epic Learning," 121.
16. For example, see Inoue, *Labor-Based Grading Contracts*.
17. See NCTE / *College Composition and Communication* "Students Rights" policies from April 1974, November 2003, November 2014; Shipka, "Negotiating Rhetorical, Material, Methodological, and Technological Difference."
18. It is important to acknowledge here that instructors' attempts at "manageability" or "control" are in many ways a consequence of high course caps and teaching loads, for example, and not of a lack of interest in student-driven inquiry, for example.
19. Davidson and Goldberg, "The Future of Learning Institutions in a Digital Age."
20. Ito, *Hanging Out*, 348.
21. See also Lenhart et al., "Writing, Technology, and Teens."
22. Ito, Hanging Out, 351.
23. For more on the role of artifacts in learning, see Chaiklin and Lave, *Understanding Practice*; Engestrom, Miettinen, and Punamäki, *Perspectives on Activity Theory*; Piaget, *The Principles of Genetic Epistemology*; Salomon, *Distributed Cognitions*; Vygotsky, *Mind in Society*.
24. Tsing, "On Nonscalability," 524.
25. Scarry, *The Body in Pain*, 175.
26. McGonigal, *Reality Is Broken*, 98.
27. Tsing, "On Nonscalability," 523.
28. Tsing, "On Nonscalability," 523.

REFERENCES

Chaiklin, Seth, and Jean Lave. *Understanding Practice: Perspectives on Activity and Context*. Cambridge: Cambridge University Press, 1996.

Davidson, Cathy, and David Theo Goldberg. "The Future of Learning Institutions in a Digital Age." A MacArthur Foundation Report. Cambridge, MA: MIT Press, 2009.

Engestrom, Yrjo, Reijo Miettinen, and Raija-Leena Punamäki, eds. *Perspectives on Activity Theory*. Cambridge: Cambridge University Press, 1999.

Inoue, Asao B. *Labor-Based Grading Contracts: Building Equity and Inclusion in the Compassionate Writing Classroom.* Boulder: WAC Clearinghouse and University Press of Colorado, 2017.
Ito, Mizuko. *Hanging Out, Messing Around, and Geeking Out.* Cambridge, MA: MIT Press, 2010.
Jaxon, Kim. "Epic Learning: Large Class as Intentional Design." *Connected Learning Alliance,* February 23, 2017. clalliance.org/blog/epic-learning-large-class-intentional-design/.
Jaxon, Kim, and Keaton Kirkpatrick. "Building Community with Peer Mentors." *Connected Learning Alliance,* June 5, 2017. clalliance.org/blog/building-community-peer-mentors/.
Jaxon, Kim, Laura Sparks, and Chris Fosen. "Epic Learning in a 'Jumbo' Writing Course." *Composition Studies* 48, no. 2 (2020): 116–27.
Lave, Jean, and Etienne Wenger. *Situated Learning: Legitimate Peripheral Participation.* Cambridge: Cambridge University Press, 1991.
Lenhart, Amanda, Sousan Arafeh, Aaron Smith, and Alexandra Rankin Macgill. "Writing, Technology, and Teens." Washington, DC: Pew Internet and American Life Project, with the National Commission on Writing, 2008.
McGonigal, Jane. *Reality Is Broken: Why Games Make Us Better and How They Can Change the World.* New York: Penguin Books, 2011.
Piaget, Jean. *The Principles of Genetic Epistemology.* New York: Basic Books, 1972.
Rodby, Judith, and Tom Fox. "Basic Work and Material Acts: The Ironies, Discrepancies, and Disjunctures of Basic Writing and Mainstreaming." *Journal of Basic Writing* 19, no. 1 (2000): 84–99.
Salomon, Gavriel, ed. *Distributed Cognitions: Psychological and Educational Considerations.* Cambridge: Cambridge University Press, 1993.
Scarry, Elaine. *The Body in Pain: The Making and Unmaking of the World.* Oxford: Oxford University Press, 1985.
Shipka, Jody. "Negotiating Rhetorical, Material, Methodological, and Technological Difference: Evaluating Multimodal Designs." *College Composition and Communication* 61, no. 1 (2009): 343–66.
"To Readers of CCC: Resolution on Language." *College Composition and Communication* 25, no. 3 (1974): 1–18. Updated November 2003, November 2014.
Tsing, Anna. "On Nonscalability: The Living World Is Not Amenable to Precision-Nested Scales." *Common Knowledge* 18, no. 3 (2012): 505–24.
Vygotsky, Lev. *Mind in Society: The Development of Higher Psychological Processes.* Edited by Michael Cole, Vera John-Steiner, Sylvia Scribner, and Ellen Souberman. Cambridge, MA: Harvard University Press, 1978.

SECTION THREE

Drawing Together

7

ROOTING OUR TEACHING IN THE CHANGE AROUND US
Growing an Anti-Racist, Community-Interdependent Course Model

Zapoura Newton-Calvert

On March 30, 2020, I found myself drafting a welcome note to my university students that I had never imagined: "Welcome to our learning community for the Social Justice in K–12 Education Capstone course. We are on the cusp of a new season. We are invited to learn together at a crucial intersection of change: in the middle of a global pandemic, an environmental crisis, and a powerful local and national movement *for* racial justice and *against* white supremacy culture and violence." Portland State University (PSU), where I teach, is located in downtown Portland, Oregon, physically and metaphorically situated in an intersectional space where the campus, broader community, and city government converge. Even though we quickly transitioned into fully remote learning for the spring 2020 term due to Covid-19 restrictions, our awareness of our location was acute. We were participants in and/or witnesses to hundreds of days of protest for Black lives blocks from our campus; we were also spectators (and artists) of a massive creative and destructive response to the murders of Black folx by white police across the country and impacted by extreme air pollution from apocalyptic fires all across Oregon and California due to climate crisis. Even as an educator who has held learning space for exploring and enacting social justice for many years, this was the first time I'd seen such widespread pause and focus on where we were located and where we could proceed.

While we continue to live through this particular span of change, the conversation among educators has surprised me. Many talk about the 2020–21 academic year and beyond as a net loss in terms of learning and community building. As Nicole Khoury, Nicholas Behm, and Sherry Rankins-Robertson discuss in chapter 5 of this volume, so many educators and students lacked the tools and capacity to support each other through our collective trauma and to understand how it impacts our everyday teaching and learning. Despite this, what I participated in was something quite different. In fact, as a teacher/facilitator, I experienced an increasingly liberated educational space where our collective learning felt richer, more authentic, and more applicable than ever before. This writing serves as a way to document how change and disruption became catalysts for, rather than barriers to, our teaching and learning practices, to share an emerging model for anti-racist community-interdependent education space, and to explore how emergent strategy can help us vision ourselves forward into a more liberated future.

In *Teaching Community: A Pedagogy of Hope*, a book that has been my constant companion throughout my teaching years, bell hooks writes, "Our visions for tomorrow are most vital when they emerge from the concrete circumstances of change we are experiencing right now."[1] In this current time of change, what I've come to believe is that an increasingly disrupted world necessitates a breaking from more static teaching modes and a shift to a practice of what adrienne maree brown calls "intentional adaptation," a flexible relationship with and toward change as a guiding principle in our teaching.[2] What emerged from the concrete circumstances of change my community, my students, and I experienced? What did we vision and build together? The answer: an explicitly anti-racist, community-interdependent course model grounded in our relationships with each other and in the change around us. It is my hope that this model can be useful during and beyond the unsettling, fracturing, healing, and reparative work needed to create just relationships with our communities, the planet, and each other.

COURSE AND INSTRUCTOR BACKGROUND

The course described here is a "Capstone course," a required, senior-level community-based learning course that has been a long-standing part of the University Studies Program at PSU. While taught by many different instructors with varying community partner organizations and teaching approaches, these courses all "involve the integration of students' prior learning with an application of that learning, employing a student-centered pedagogy, and resulting in an individual or group final project."[3] I became part of the Capstone teaching community in 2008, four years after my start as a writing instructor. Over the years, I have developed and taught a host of sibling courses, but "Social Justice in K–12 Education" is the focus of this writing. Some defining aspects of this course are

- Alignment with critical community-based learning[4]
- Partnership with schools and education organizations
- Focus on racial justice and literacy justice in curriculum
- Writing-intensive pedagogy (writing as reflection, writing to process identity, writing for facilitation, writing a public-facing curriculum)
- Online and in-person teaching

In recent years, the University Studies Program has strengthened its commitment to critical approaches, adopting Tania Mitchell's framework of "critical service learning" and its focus on building authentic relationships, developing a social change orientation, and redistributing power.[5] In particular, I've found this model useful when partnered with identity and community-centered writing practices to go beyond "bridg[ing] the gap between the academy and surrounding communities" to understanding my teaching and learning groups as part of, rather than apart from, the community.[6]

Since teaching my first community-based learning course, I've become increasingly explicit about my role as a community member committed to racial justice in my teaching, parenting, and everyday practice. As a teacher, this process has required a deep dive into my own identity as a white-bodied teacher in an education system where white-bodied teachers are overrepresented and often reproduce (intentionally or not) racist ideas and policies in the classroom, harming the learning community in profound ways (see Edwards, chapter 13, this volume, to explore further the idea that students need better spaces in which to discuss and process race and racism). In his work around anti-racist assessment, Asao B. Inoue describes the importance of anti-racist educator identity work "in terms of how they set up their own relationship to the subject matter or the curriculum and the things they're asking students to do."[7] As an educator, this means I am committed to ongoing exploration of my relationships inside and outside my teaching, starting with my relationship to my identity and my ancestors and radiating out in larger circles to understand and work toward just relationships with curriculum, students, and community.

What I know about and how I understand my ancestral roots and my identity requires me to teach from a liminal space. I am white. I am from Swedish, Italian, and German immigrants who migrated at the turn of the twentieth century. I am from settler colonists in western Canada, French fur trading men. I grew up with the associated unearned and inequitable privileges of being white-bodied. And I am also Indigenous. I am from Anishinaabe women, from Lake Superior Ojiwbwe people. My great-grandmother Florence Vera was just five years old when she was taken from her mother to attend the Morris Industrial School for Indians in 1900. In 1910, my great-grandmother moved to Seattle, Washington, and started identifying as white on US Census documents. She was fifteen years old. As an adult, she rarely discussed her life before Seattle. The choices of my ancestors created a mixed matriarchal line that has both perpetuated in and survived assimilation and cultural genocide. I am also from a patriarchal line that, among other things, has invested and participated in systems of policing and harm.

What does this have to do with writing or teaching practices and the ways we can use emergent strategy to guide our pedagogies into the future? Everything. There is no one way to hold the capacity for the kind of intentional adaptation described as part of emergent strategy without first being rooted in anti-racist practices. And it is impossible to be rooted deeply in anti-racist practices without understanding one's multiple identities and the way they impact our languaging, ways of knowing, understanding of education, and more.

COURSE FRAMEWORK: EMERGENT STRATEGY, INTENTIONAL ADAPTATION, AND ANTI-RACIST TEACHING

Ongoing personal identity work should be understood as an essential component of emergent strategy practice: it is where we can see individual transformation reverberating to create pedagogical transformation and community change. Emergent strategy is a way of understanding and visioning movements that is grounded in life-sustaining patterns already occurring in nature. The definition of "emergent strategy," according to brown, is "the way complex systems and patterns arise out of a multiplicity of relatively simple interactions."[8] brown draws her examples from the natural world, noting, for instance, the way fractals "are infinitely complex patterns that are self-similar across different scales. They are created by repeating a simple process over and over in an ongoing feedback loop."[9] In nature, this looks like the way the Fibonacci sequence can be seen on a range of scales: from a simple sunflower to the spiral of an entire galaxy to our education spaces.[10] In these spaces, we can see emergent strategy in the way a seemingly simple set of teaching practices in a single course (for example, the one represented in the teaching model I discuss below) can help us build capacity for larger work in our community *as a community*.

The idea of scalable systems and patterns is often applied to social movements rather than to pedagogical methodologies; however, it can be extremely useful to educators as we navigate our ongoing relationships with and responses to inevitable change (from pandemics to decolonization). At the heart of applying emergent strategy is the practice of "intentional adaptation." "Adaptation" is defined as "a change in a plant or animal that makes it better able to live in a particular place or situation; the process of changing to fit some purpose or situation: the process of adapting," while "intention" is described as "the thing that you plan to do or achieve: an aim or purpose."[11] In my teaching during the 2020–21 academic year, to metaphorically sustain the life in our learning and to literally sustain life in our community, we were called to the practices of intentional adaptation. We adapted to Covid-19 protocols to protect our community's health and to develop more explicitly anti-racist learning spaces to push back against white supremacy systems and thus create a place where we could resist, grow, and heal.

Our intentional adaptation practice in the Social Justice in K–12 Education space was and continues to be oriented toward an explicit commitment to justice, in particular racial justice and anti-racist practice: "An antiracist approach elicits the understanding that the work of living and learning is about the solidarity created through shared struggle. Antiracist teaching is not just about acknowledging that racism exists but about consciously committing to the struggle of fighting for racial justice . . . All teachers, regardless of race or ethnicity, need to know that . . . resistance, in its various forms, is always an option."[12] The conscious commitment to the struggle Bettina Love describes is a sibling concept to what brown names "intentional adaptation," with attention to the patterns of movement and struggle of individual folx coming together for collective action. Of course, relationship building and joint struggle cannot happen unless we implement emergent strategies from the smallest pieces to the largest (across scale). In my learning community, intentional adaptation needed roots in my own living and facilitation practices to be authentically built and scaled up through my course and into my community.

While this is important for all teachers, it is particularly important for white educators whose ongoing anti-racist practice and unlearning of white supremacy culture require extensive internal and personal work: "We live, learn, and teach not simply in the racist ruins of bygone eras but in schools and disciplines firmly built and ever maintained by white supremacy . . . White supremacy is structured into the ways everyone reads and judges writing. We are all implicated, no matter how we identify ourselves or our political beliefs."[13] Holding a balance between personal and ancestral responsibility within multiple identities has been an important part of my work as an anti-racist educator.

To be clear, my Social Justice in K–12 Education learning communities had already experienced and taken part in disruption and elements of intentional adaptation throughout the years due to the course's anti-racist orientation, but the particular concurrent changes we experienced at this point in time proved to be significantly challenging and impactful. These changes included, but are not limited to, the following:

- We moved from in-person to online teaching.
- We could no longer partner with our community sites in person and, in most cases, at all. They did not have the capacity as they tended to the basic needs of students and families.
- Student and instructor rhythms were upended.
- Anxiety, stress, and rawness became increasingly prevalent states of being.
- The successive murders of Black people (Ahmaud Arbery, Breonna Taylor, George Floyd, and too many others) by white police officers and the surge in the Black Lives Matter racial justice movement and protests placed us all in a cycle of despair, anger, hope, fear, resilience, and fatigue.

These very real ruptures are at once specific to this particular moment in time and part of much larger ongoing patterns. Understanding this better equipped me as a facilitator in the learning space to hold our class community while also giving us the opportunity to "be like water," to ebb and flow and take the forms we needed to both solo and together as we navigated, survived, and rose up.[14] And in our responsive imaginations and actions, we formed a new way of learning together.

COURSE CONTENT: AN EMERGENT MODEL FOR ANTI-RACIST COMMUNITY-INTERDEPENDENT LEARNING

Informed by the practices of emergent strategy and the changes we were experiencing, the Social Justice in K–12 Education course continued to shift and grow within a loose structure with four main quadrants (see figure 7.1). This model held enough structure and space for us to process, grow, and even thrive in more robust ways in our learning community during widespread instability that was nearly immobilizing for many pieces of our school systems. In mapping out this particular emergent learning model, the shape of a sunflower's center, with its seed fractal face, functions metaphorically (the seeds, roots, and interaction with the sun can represent the ways we know and learn) and within emergent strategy principles. brown explains that the way fractals work in movements is that "what we practice at the small scale sets the patterns for the

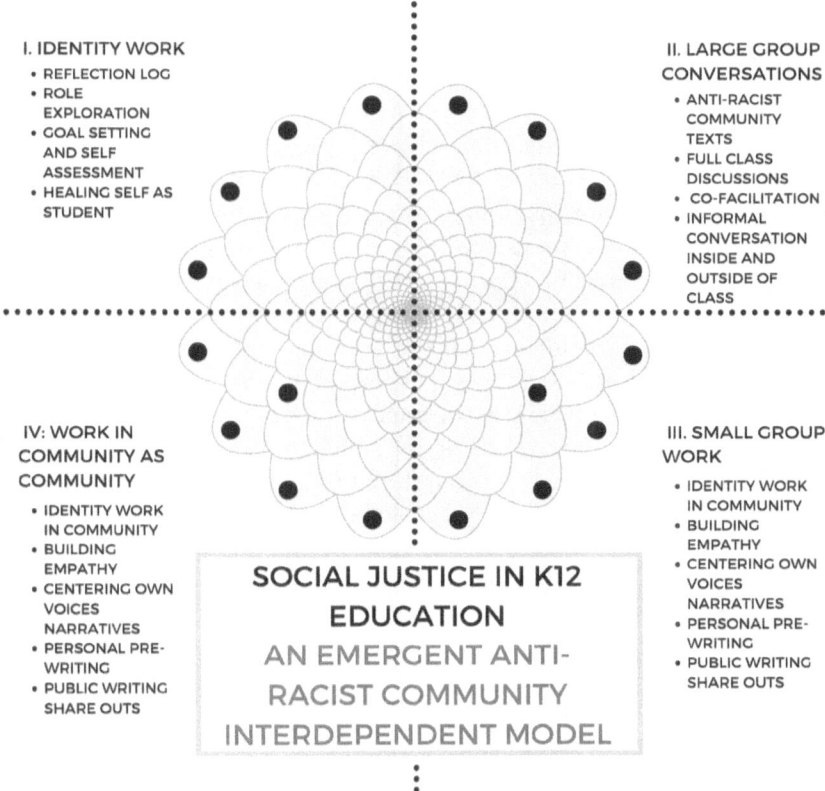

Figure 7.1. Social Justice in K–12 Education: an emergent anti-racist community-interdependent model. Course illustration metaphorically modeling, through the sunflower shape, the ongoing and interconnected nature of the course within the wider educational system.

whole system."[15] The teaching model in Social Justice in K–12 Education is also a fractal. Each piece of the work is ongoing (not limited by the course itself), and each also embodies small patterns that we would like to echo out into the entire education system and beyond.

Both writing and reading about racial justice play important parts in the root systems that hold the learning together. The impact of these practices and the way they are woven throughout suggest some larger structures/pedagogical moves for our teaching (in composition courses and beyond) now and into the future. The writing is by us and for us, as community in community; we are dependent on each other for the wholeness of our work and for our own continuing anti-racist practice. By dividing the teaching and learning model into four quadrants, we can take a closer look at how each major course component works as part of the whole while still noting that each section is not rigidly from but ultimately intertwined with the others.

BASIC COURSE PRINCIPLES AND AGREEMENTS

Before describing the four quadrants of this course model further, it is important to understand the basic principles and agreements that hold the entire course in alignment with our focus on social justice and explicitly anti-racist practice. In the first communication I have with students, it is clearly articulated that our learning community values each person's own unique identity set, experiences, and qualities and that each cohort of students makes an utterly unique learning collective. In fact, I directly quote the words of Taj James in his address to the environmental justice organization Building Equity and Alignment: "There is a conversation in the room that only these people at this moment can have. Find it."[16] Because our learning is not completely pre-set (in that it is designed to shape itself around what we can uniquely learn with a particular group of learners), it's vital to begin co-creating basic course principles from the moment students register for the term. The following are practices I have found useful in building the roots system of the course even before our term begins.

Initial Welcome Communication

As soon as students register for this course and well before the term begins, they receive a welcome email from me. The initial communication contains language specific to the philosophical framing of the course, alerting students to our anti-racist and community-interdependent model and giving them a host of role options for the community work they will self-select and participate in throughout the term.

Early Access to Course Guide and Learning Schedule

Once students have self-selected a community work role, I email a copy of the course guide and learning schedule to the group. Both of these documents very clearly state that we will be studying and dismantling the way white supremacy impacts the education system, our sense of self, and our collective anti-racist practice. These initial email interactions intentionally set the scene so that students are prepared for the radical work we will do together. In this way, they prepare the ground for a particular kind of anti-racist teaching and writing pedagogy, defined by Felicia Rose Chavez as nothing less than "aggressive activism. It's immediate, tangible action that disrupts the legacy of white supremacy by changing organizational structures, policies, practices, and attitudes, so that power is redistributed and shared equally."[17]

Agreements and Building Community

Our first full week of class is dedicated to laying more groundwork for cultivating our community. We use Glenn Singleton's *Courage Conversations about Race: A Field Guide for Achieving Equity in Schools* as a starting point and build on our own agreements and conditions.[18]

Pre-Course Video Meet-Ups

Optional pre-course video meet-ups take place before the course begins and during the first week of class. These are casual meetings with a loose agenda, including making introductions, sharing learning styles and needs, and brainstorming goals that will inform our time together. Pre-course procedures are necessitated by a short ten-week term system and also by the anti-racist and abolitionist teaching framework, which is "built on the cultural wealth of students' communities and creating classrooms in parallel with those communities aimed at facilitating interactions where people matter to each other, fight together in the pursuit of creating a homeplace that represents their hopes and dreams, and resist oppression all while building a new future."[19] From the very beginning, the students shape the learning and build relationships so that we can matter to each other. With these foundational relationships in place, we are able to move more easily within the four quadrants of our learning model. While all four quadrants are equally important, I will give an overview of Quadrants II and III while taking a much closer look at Quadrant I: Identity Work and Quadrant IV: Work in Community as Community, as they are most significant to understanding this particular kind of teaching and learning.

QUADRANT I: IDENTITY WORK

Creating consistent and ongoing identity work opportunities in the course demonstrates a high value placed on this aspect of our anti-racist commitment. In Ibram X. Kendi and Jason Reynolds's book *Stamped: Racism, Antiracism, and You*, Kendi talks about his own process of anti-racist practice as one in which he was "able to discover, self-critique, and shed the racist ideas I had consumed over my lifetime while I uncovered and exposed the racist ideas that others have produced over the lifetime of America."[20] This process looks different depending on each of our intersecting identities. When it comes to identity work connected to racial justice, using the emergent strategy principle of "never a failure, always a lesson" gives students an escape from binary thinking around the "rights and wrongs" of the work and instead allows a focus on an ongoing commitment to racial justice as central to our learning.[21] Love's work touches on this idea, saying that anti-racist work is "not just about acknowledging that racism exists but about consciously committing to the struggle of fighting for racial justice."[22] In this course, identity work takes place in reflection log writing, social justice ecosystem role exploration, goal setting, self-assessment, and healing opportunities.

Reflection Log

Weekly reflection logs are spaces for informal reflective writing and making connections among self, texts, and community work. Using texts like Tiffany Jewell and Aurélia Durand's *This Book Is Anti-Racist* and contemplative practices from Rev. Angel Kyodo Williams and colleagues, in addition to exercises like "Woke Wonderings" from Woke Kindergarten and poetic exercises like adrienne maree brown's "spell casting" for the new year, we are able to participate in a wide array of writing genres through which we can self-reflect.[23]

Social Justice Ecosystem Role Exploration

In course conversations (Quadrant II) and in the reflection log, we use Deepa Iyer's Social Justice Ecosystem, a "framework that can help individuals, networks, and organizations align and get in right relationship with social change values, individual roles, and the broader ecosystem."[24] Students use this model to recognize and commit to the social justice roles that are most natural for them. In the process, they challenge themselves to develop strength in roles they'd like to occupy in the future.

Goal Setting and Self-Assessment

Students in this course set their own learning goals and self-assess throughout the term. The self-assessment process culminates in a teaching or personal philosophy that articulates values and future visioning.

Healing Self as Student

One of the most interesting outcomes of this identity work process is the confrontation of school-induced trauma and the healing of that trauma through sharing school experiences, imagining and learning about anti-racist practice, and exploring liberatory education models. Opportunities for this kind of healing occur through the reflective writing process and in other quadrants of the learning model as well.

QUADRANT II: LARGE-GROUP CONVERSATION

"Large-Group Conversation" is the space for interacting with source materials and peers in discussion groups of ten–twelve students at a time. Our source material collections intentionally center anti-racist practice, with nearly all source materials written by people of the global majority and multiple modes of text equally represented (from peer-reviewed texts to personal activist writing and student story). Chavez writes about the importance of shifting from texts by "white literary 'masters'" to "a living archive of scanned print material and multimedia art by a range of writers, including people of color, differently abled writers, and people who are LGBTQIA2+."[25]

This web of varied sources provides ample room for us to travel back and forth between new thinking and lived experiences, in the process making connections and creating meaning. This can be described as anti-racist reading, "a practice of reading words and pausing to pose questions about the reader's relation to their material situation, their reality, and conceiving of those conditions as structures and systems, which are both outside and inside of them."[26] Personal reflection and discussion of questions such as "where am I in this" also encourage students to understand issues of racial justice in education as issues that involve all of us, are enacted by all of us, and are only broken down if we all participate in their dissolution.

QUADRANT III: SMALL-GROUP WORK

"Small-Group Work" takes place in the more intimate Anti-Bias Book Club setting, where students gather with a group of three–five people to read middle reader, or young adult (YA), books focused on issues of racial justice, school, and identity.[27] Based on many of the same principles and practices as the large-group conversation, this smaller setting gives space for more story sharing, deeper identity work in community, and the expanding of worldview by reading powerful children's literature from Black, Indigenous, and other authors of color, in addition to stories from white co-conspirators working toward collective liberation. The communal reading, reflection, and sharing process—nestled in the larger work around anti-racist practice and literacy justice—ends up being a contemplative and bonding act. In angel Kyodo williams, Rod Owens, and Jasmine Syedullah's work, they note that contemplative group experiences fortify us for community action: "That we stop checking out, check in and work together to try to do things in ways we might not yet know how to is more important than knowing the right thing to do . . . We must begin to practice sitting together to stand together."[28]

This is an anti-racist small-group model. While the traditional model "traps text on the page, asking workshop participants to impose their individual interpretations of the story's meaning, the anti-racist model pairs an assigned text with a conversation with the author, contextualizing their stories within a specific lived experience, making meaning relevant and real."[29] The goals of the anti-racist model are extended even further when layered with the identity work students do throughout the term to understand where they are positioned relative to these stories. The question we ask is: how are we each part of the story of racial injustice/justice in this country?

QUADRANT IV: WORK IN COMMUNITY AS COMMUNITY

"Work in Community as Community" describes the most significant intentional adaptation we embraced in Social Justice in K–12 Education—the shift to fully remote community-based work and a model I am calling "community-interdependent learning." In non-pandemic times, our community-based course has partnered with various local elementary, middle, and high schools to support the efforts of local public school teachers working in a social justice framework. This course typically partners with a variety of schools and educational organizations. However, due to Covid-19 restrictions and the chaos each school and organization was managing, starting in spring 2020, we quickly shifted to completely virtual community work, partnering with Reading Is Resistance. This organization, co-founded by my partner, Farnell Newton, and me, works to "support the efforts of parents and teachers to start or expand anti-racist, anti-bias home or classroom libraries and reading experiences for youth and children and for those libraries to seed deeper conversations and opportunities for action around racial equity in our community."[30]

Although the shift online was logistically challenging, our ability to continue community-based work was also freeing in various ways. With sudden changes to our ability to partner in school settings, we were liberated from our previous traditional model, which asked community-based learning students to move quickly into work directly onsite in community organizations with community members. Throughout the years, one of my concerns about community-based learning in partnership with schools has been the potential harm that takes place when university students—sometimes with no specific connection to the school communities we work with and with no prior experience—are plunged into classrooms without the deep identity and anti-racist work needed to build authentic relationships and imagine redistribution of power, among other components of critical and racial justice work. Because traditional "push-in volunteering" was impossible, we shifted the focus of our community work to rethink our model and develop our capabilities to serve community needs in new ways. In moving to completely remote work with Reading Is Resistance, the needs we served became multidimensional: we answered the community's call for more support for anti-racist teaching and learning through experiences with children's literature, but we also served our own learning community's needs and created space for the kinds of deeper identity and racial justice learning necessary for other kinds of activism and action.

Starting in the spring of 2020, community requests for resources from Reading Is Resistance increased rapidly. I received many requests from parents and teachers to support discussions and learning around police violence, anti-Blackness, the Black Lives Matter movement, and more. Reading Is Resistance already had an established framework and mode for sharing learning; after discussions with my spring cohort of students, we decided to move all our energy toward that work. So, we committed to creating, editing, testing, and revising resources for teachers and other caregivers, parents, and community members through an increased number of anti-bias/anti-racist reading guides to accompany picture book reading. With a focus on literacy justice, racial justice, and education justice, the work at Reading Is Resistance took on immediate depth, importance, audience, and authenticity as each student selected a role in the work.

Role 1: Content Creation of Anti-Racist Reading Guides for Picture Book Readers

Content creation entails writing anti-racist/anti-bias reading guides using the Learning for Justice "Social Justice Standards" to design discussion questions for grownups and young readers to use to ignite conversation while reading.[31] Each content creator generates material aligned with their own identities as well as those of the author and main protagonists of the selected book. This is not unlike Jessica Edwards's exploration of the significance of being able to tell our own stories as an integral part of the classroom (see chapter 13, this volume).

Role 2: Content Feedback on Student-Written Anti-Racist Reading Guides

Content editors are trained in the Learning for Justice "Social Justice Standards" and learn about anti-bias language practices and white language supremacy in an effort to undo the harmful lessons we have all been taught about language hierarchies. This is in alignment with what Chavez describes as moving toward empowerment of the author "to moderate their own workshop while participants rally in service of the author's vision."[32] This practice stresses that the author holds the deepest knowledge of the work. Editors, then, simply support the scaffolding of the reading guide and ask questions to support the revision process.

Role 3: Content Testing Using the Anti-Racist Reading Guides with Young Readers

Students who are parenting, teaching, nannying, or caregiving may select a content testing role. These students select picture books and reading guides from the Reading Is Resistance collection to read and discuss with their young readers. They then document the experience, giving us feedback on each guide and on the kind of anti-racist teaching and learning that happens when using these guides. Both grownup and young readers are learners and teachers here.

Role 4: Creating Content on Social Media to Share Anti-Racist Reading Guides

Students interested in design and communication build capacity for connection between the social justice reading and teaching communities through Instagram and Facebook. Training around captioning, the use of anti-racist language, and accessibility is part of the preparation for this work.

Through this work, students began to recognize the difference between writing for community as community and writing for community from outside community. The emphasis on their own voices writing, providing anti-bias feedback, sharing with teachers and parents, and reading with young readers in their own lives made the often separate realms of community and university come together. Centering the way our identities impact all our work in community, working together with each other's words and experiences, and sharing the impact made it clear that building real community with our own learning group rather than artificially helping others from an outside perspective is one of the most powerful and joy-giving types of education we can create.

CONCLUSION AND FORWARD VISIONING

While a Capstone is often defined as a culmination of learning experiences, I have always viewed the integrated, critical community-interdependent teaching and learning I do through a more roots-based metaphor grounded in the possibilities of our "radical imaginations." As political activist, educator, and philosopher Angela Davis is often quoted saying, "Radical simply means grasping things at the root."[33] Radical imagination is about becoming rooted in a new kind of present and future—one where we work creatively together for our collective liberation through racial justice and investment in community. For this reason, I think of this emergent anti-racist community-interdependent course model as a location of possibility, where more radical teaching—if nurtured and wildly imagined—has the possibility to grow.

Of course, I am also aware that this kind of course model and use of emergent strategy principles require a kind of flexibility, relationship building, and community connection that is not always centered in higher education, where concrete and pre-established learning objectives, the "teacher as expert" mentality, and "university apart from community" are still held as common norms. In addition, this particular setup of Social Justice in K–12 Education partnered with a program like Reading Is Resistance (with my roles as instructor and community partner coexisting in one person) may be rare. However, what can be more easily replicated is a model of community-interdependent learning that is responsive to change and that deeply embeds the students and instructor/facilitator in the community. When Linda Flower writes about community-engaged education, she describes it as making a "unique contribution . . . to the social significance of a college education more broadly. That is, it can give students an intellectually and experientially grounded preparation for a form of citizenship that works with and across cultural and social differences guided by ethical commitments."[34] But I argue that our next imagining of community-based writing and learning can take this in a slightly different direction. This direction, guided by emergent strategy principles, is one in which we challenge and expand the artificial boundaries of what Flower calls "citizenship" (I think of this as "belonging") and recognize that the university and the community are not separate but one and the same, that the changes and disruptions in one are experienced by the other.

Because our learning space in Social Justice in K–12 Education was already oriented to and prepared for responsiveness to change, the convergence of simultaneous and interwoven pandemics ultimately allowed our learning community to explore and reimagine what our education together could be and what impact it could have. We discussed decolonization, ethnic studies, and restorative justice from our kitchen tables and in our living rooms. We held quiet space as we awaited the verdict in the trial of Derek Chauvin and mourned the loss of George Floyd as we gathered in the break room at work and in the hallway at a local hospital. We shared what we knew when we heard about (or participated in) the toppling of the statue of Oregon pioneer Harvey Scott and when a bust of York, an enslaved Black man who was an integral participant in the Lewis and Clark Expedition, mysteriously appeared on the newly empty pedestal in the middle of the night in Mt. Tabor Park. Our kids or parents crossed back and forth behind us onscreen. Our pets or favorite blankets provided anxiety relief. While we were disembodied by our Zoom meetings, we were also somehow incredibly present, with many of our identities and contexts crashing together in the moment. Our dislocation from our campus-based classroom became, as bell hooks describes, "the perfect context for free-flowing thought that lets us move beyond the restricted confines of a familiar social order."[35] When so many of our school spaces coerce students into hiding bits and pieces of their identities for them to assimilate, to conform, and to behave, the impact is a fracturing: "Many of our students come to our classrooms believing that real brilliance is revealed by the will to disconnect and disassociate."[36] Being together, allowing our learning to emerge, was a lesson in finding wholeness even as our world was falling apart: "Education that serves to enhance our students' journey to wholeness stands as a challenge to the existing status quo."[37]

I am inspired by the fact that as we experienced so much sorrow, loss, and shift, my students and I also experienced some of the most profound learning and writing that we had ever done and that we continue to do together. Using ideas and frameworks from adrienne maree brown's emergent strategy and other justice movement–oriented practices, we become the embodiment of brown's notion that "small is good. Small is all. (the large is a reflection of the small)."[38] The smallest sunflower seed grows a plant that seeds hundreds of others. Our smaller teaching and learning spaces, rooted in the ancestral and present work of so many, shifted to become the space for students to be co-facilitators, authors, authorities, seekers, and creatives in ways that transcended the classroom. As we all work together to grapple with our future's inevitable disruptions, which can surely fracture and destroy us, we also have the potential to crack open the ground and find new places to plant seeds.

NOTES

1. hooks, Teaching Community, 12.
2. brown, *Emergent Strategy*, 67.
3. Smith-Arthur and Newton-Calvert, "Online Community-Based Learning."
4. While we use Tania Mitchell's "critical service learning" model, we use the wording "critical community-based learning" at Portland State University.
5. Mitchell, "Traditional vs. Critical Service-Learning," 54.
6. Iverson, "The Long-Term Effects of Service-Learning," 12.
7. Inoue, "Teaching Antiracist Reading."
8. brown cited in Obolensky, *Complex Adaptive Leadership*, 13.
9. brown, *Emergent Strategy*, 51.
10. brown, *Emergent Strategy*, 51.
11. brown, *Emergent Strategy*, 67.
12. Love, *I Want to Do More*, 54.
13. Inhoue and Pai, "Classroom Writing Assessment as an Anti-Racist Practice."
14. brown, *Emergent Strategy*, 41.
15. brown, *Emergent Strategy*, 53.
16. James quoted in brown, *Emergent Strategy*, 41.
17. Chavez, *The Anti-Racist Writing Workshop*, 14.
18. Singleton, *Courageous Conversations about Race*.
19. Love, *I Want to Do More*, 68.
20. Kendi and Reynolds, *Stamped*, xv.
21. brown, *Emergent Strategy*, 41.
22. Love, *I Want to Do More*, 54.
23. Jewell and Durand, *This Book Is Anti-Racist*; Williams, Owens, and Syedullah, *Radical Dharma*; Gross, "Woke Wonderings"; brown, *Emergent Strategy*, 191.
24. Iyer, "Social Change Ecosystem Map."
25. Chavez, *The Anti-Racist Writing Workshop*, 9.
26. Inoue, "Teaching Antiracist Reading."
27. Reading YA and middle-reader fiction with college students provides (1) a clear focus on the inner and outer experiences of school-age youth from their perspectives and (2) an opportunity to connect through storytelling and story receiving. Thus, the book club is focused on identity exploration, healing from school-based trauma, and reclaiming joy rather than on deciphering or critiquing the technical aspects or messaging of the literature.
28. Williams, Owens, and Syedullah, *Radical Dharma*, 85.
29. Chavez, *The Anti-Racist Writing Workshop*, 9.
30. Newton-Calvert and Newton, "Who We Are."
31. Learning for Justice, "Social Justice Standards."
32. Chavez, *The Anti-Racist Writing Workshop*, 10.
33. "Dream Defenders," Facebook.
34. Flower, "The Consequences of Engaged Education."
35. hooks, *Teaching Community*, 21.

36. hooks, *Teaching Community*, 180.
37. hooks, *Teaching Community*, 181.
38. brown, *Emergent Strategy*, 41.

REFERENCES

brown, adrienne maree. *Emergent Strategy: Shaping Change, Changing Worlds*. Chico, CA: AK Press, 2017.
Chavez, Felicia Rose. *The Anti-Racist Writing Workshop: How to Decolonize the Writing Classroom*. Chicago: Haymarket Books, 2021.
"Dream Defenders." Unlock Us, Abolition in Our Time—Featuring Dr. Angela Davis, Cherrell Brown, Dereka Purnell [Facebook]. n.d. https://www.facebook.com/watch/DreamDefenders/.
Flower, Linda. "The Consequences of Engaged Education: Building a Public Case." *Reflections* 20, no. 1 (Spring–Summer 2020): 52–67.
Gross, Akiea. "Woke Wonderings." Woke Kindergarten. March 15, 2021. https://www.wokekindergarten.org/wokewonderings.
hooks, bell. *Teaching Community: A Pedagogy of Hope*. Oxfordshire, UK: Routledge, 2003.
Inhoue, Asao B., and Minjung Pai. "Classroom Writing Assessment as an Anti-Racist Practice." Produced by Heinemann Press. Heinemann Podcast, Podcast MP3 audio 43:02. September 26, 2019. https://blog.heinemann.com/podcast-unlearning-supremacist-language-minjung-pai-dr-asao-inhoue.
Inoue, Asao B. "Teaching Antiracist Reading." *Journal of College Reading and Learning* 50, no. 3 (2020). doi: 10.1080/10790195.2020.1787079.
Iverson, Chris. "The Long-Term Effects of Service-Learning on Composition Students." *Reflections* (Baltimore, MD) 19, no. 2 (Spring 2020): 11–37.
Iyer, Deepa. "Social Change Ecosystem Map." Building Movement Project, 2022. https://buildingmovement.org/our-work/movement-building/social-change-ecosystem-map/.
Jewell, Tiffany, and Aurélia Durand. *This Book Is Anti-Racist: 20 Lessons on How to Wake Up, Take Action, and Do the Work*. London: Frances Lincoln Children's Books, 2020.
Kendi, Ibram X., and Jason Reynolds. *Stamped: Racism, Antiracism, and You*. New York: Little Brown Books for Young Readers, 2020.
Learning for Justice. "Social Justice Standards." 2018. https://www.learningforjustice.org/frameworks/social-justice-standards.
Love, Bettina. *I Want to Do More than Survive: Abolitionist Teaching and the Pursuit of Educational Freedom*. Boston: Beacon, 2020.
Mitchell, Tania. "Traditional vs. Critical Service-Learning: Engaging the Literature to Differentiate Two Models." *Michigan Journal of Community Service Learning* (Spring 2008): 50–65.
Newton-Calvert, Zapoura, and Farnell Newton. "Mission." Reading Is Resistance, 2020. https://www.readingisresistance.com/mission.
Obolensky, Nick. *Complex Adaptive Leadership: Embracing Paradox and Uncertainty*. Burlington, VT: Gower, 2014.
Singleton, Glenn. *Courageous Conversations about Race: A Field Guide for Achieving Equity in Schools*. Thousands Oaks, CA: Corwin, 2014.
Smith-Arthur, Deb, and Zapoura Newton-Calvert. "Online Community-Based Learning as the Practice of Freedom: The Online Capstone Experience at Portland State University." *Metropolitan Universities* 26, no. 2 (2015): 135–58.
williams, angel Kyodo, Rod Owens, and Jasmine Syedullah. *Radical Dharma: Talking Race, Love, and Liberation*. Sydney, Australia: Read How You Want, 2017.

8
WRITING WITH THE WORKING CLASS
The Future of Public Rhetoricians

Anna Barritt and Kalyn Prince

With an increase in workload and a decrease in funding across the humanities, it seems folly to consider the university as the site of our field's future. Despite the growing necessity for the field to spread its influence, there is still a disconnect between universities and the outside world. Surviving a global pandemic has made this dissonance painfully clear. In Oklahoma, scholars at the state universities took to social media to bemoan the red state's lack of interest in upholding masking policies, sometimes going so far as to say that Oklahomans are "stupid." To graduate students with Oklahoma roots—whose family members are those stupid Oklahomans—such complaints are concerning to say the least. While their frustration with the anti-masking movement is more than justified, labeling a group of people as stupid is also a dangerous oversimplification that highlights a major disconnect between the public work our field aspires to and the way we talk about certain communities. One of the most exciting draws of rhetoric and composition is its unique capacity to embrace "integrated, critical community-interdependent teaching and learning," as Zapoura Newton-Calvert argues in chapter 7 of this volume. In this field, we engage and intervene in public discourse, helping to solve communication issues that get in the way of productive civic life for the communities we've grown up in. Yet, that intervention too often stops at analysis and publication, enacting a kind of *trickle-down social justice* that does not address the rhetorical expertise and material realities of those communities. Moreover, to pursue life as an academic too often means distancing ourselves from the communities of our families.

Gary Tate, alongside John McMillan and Elizabeth Woodworth, argues that writing teachers must acknowledge the role of social class in our pedagogy.[1] Though class is a contested term, stratified by culture, identity, and job position, much work has been done to explore what it means to teach from a working-class ethos and to design working-class pedagogies in the writing classroom.² And yet, there is still a need to include our publics in the work of our field—building and disseminating knowledge *with* them rather than *for* them. How do we accomplish this goal inside the university? How do we take it outside? Who do we partner with? As a field, we must train our students to answer these questions so our work can live outside the academy and support community activism. This is critical for the survival of our field and for the health of the public more broadly as we fight against a neoliberal notion that education and work are separate, with one in service of the other. In this chapter, we share our hopes for how the field can survive an exciting yet contentious time within and without the university by taking its work home and partnering with the working class, including our own writing students from these communities. We share examples from our backgrounds—blue-collar workers and farmers in southwest Oklahoma—to demonstrate the ways our field is uniquely capable of partnering with our home communities.

To communicate these experiences throughout the chapter, we highlight personal narratives with a change of font for Anna and Kalyn. By blending the personal, the pedagogical, and the theoretical, we model how these facets of academic and public life do not occupy separate spheres but are, in fact, impossible to discuss in isolation. Finally, we present training areas for budding rhetorical scholars to best accomplish the work of a public humanitarian, from research methods to publication to partnership. If the field is to make critical interventions in the public sphere, as we are well poised to do, then we must care for the communities and students who are often left out of traditional academic conversations. The terms community and public are complicated, contested, and intertwined—encompassing competing political and philosophical orientations to community writing and engagement.³ By sharing our own experiences, we hope to offer insight into the boundaries we place around these terms and challenge the notion that certain communities cannot make meaningful public contributions. Rhetoricians must partner with blue-collar folks and become active in rural areas, not just in spaces we consider "public." For rhetoricians to change public discourse and promote civic engagement, we have to write with working-class publics too. In other words, *it's time for the field to roll up its sleeves and get to work.*

WHERE'S THE WORKING CLASS?

Anna: My father—a machinist—always told me to get myself an education so that I wouldn't have to work with my hands. He wasn't ashamed of his work, but his body had deteriorated from a lifetime of hard labor. Though I was not interested in working in a cubicle, I took his urgings to heart. I pursued a career in healthcare that would ensure both financial security and social respectability. I envisioned a future in which I could make tangible contributions to the greater good, all the while creating an economic safety net for my family—but then I became an English major. I finally admitted to myself that I did not want a life that required me to hone skills that did not come naturally to me when writing and critical thinking were my strengths.

Despite my desire for a stable career, I've wound up in the precarious life of a PhD candidate. I have been fortunate enough to enter a doctoral program close to my home community, but if I'm lucky enough to secure a tenure-track position, it will surely ask me to cut myself loose from my roots. Many mentors and internet fora tried to dissuade me from pursuing a PhD program in the same state I had received my bachelor's and master's degrees (both from a regional, open admissions university) and preached that if I wasn't committed to making sacrifices to pursue a top-tier program, then I had no business in grad school. Even so, I enrolled in the closest program and shoehorned my graduate studies into the life I had created. I'm proud of the work I've accomplished, but I live in fear of the next step—not only because of the likely possibility of physical separation from my home community but also of the increasing tension I feel between the values of my home community and those of the professoriate.

In the *Harvard Business Review*, Nicole Stephens and Sarah Townsend echo my feelings around my own social context and its clash with the professional environment I am pursuing.[4] They find that students from working-class backgrounds tend to see themselves as *interdependent* and highly adaptable to the needs of others. Common sayings include "you can't always get what you want" and "it's not all about you," engendering the spirit of solidarity, humility, and loyalty. Such has been my experience: my career aspirations have never overtaken my desire to stay near my family. In contrast, Stephens and Townsend find that folks from middle- and upper-class backgrounds value *independence*, manifesting in "the world is your oyster" and "your voice matters" and enacting the spirit of uniqueness, self-expression, and influence. To be clear, neither I nor these researchers would suggest that people so cleanly fit into either category. Students from upper social classes are not immune to struggles, and students from working-class backgrounds do not have uniform experiences. However, the cultural norm of *interdependence* appears to be a common factor that influences many working-class students' educational endeavors, often bolstered by the desire to give back to and/or return to their home communities. I exist in a strange space of being such a student while also occupying a position of limited power as an instructor and a junior administrator. Though I might never feel at home in academia, I have found meaning in knowing that I can make a difference in my own students' experiences, particularly if they are struggling to navigate the culture of higher education like I did and do.

Although I have always believed that rhetoric and composition needed to pay closer attention to writerly identities entrenched in working-class rhetoric, the context of 2020 fast-tracked its urgency. In the academic year following the emergence of the Covid-19 pandemic, several students enrolled in my Composition I course in the spring semester—a class most first-year students take in the fall—because they had delayed starting college. Many expressed that they were unsure if an education was worth it after seeing the economic devastation of worldwide closures and lockdowns. Most of my immediate family kept working without interruption—the physical labor did not stop. If anything, the work increased. Many students in this class came from similar environments and questioned whether the cost of tuition was worthwhile when they could work the kinds of jobs that were keeping their families afloat while so many college-educated folks found themselves without employment. Ultimately, they decided to enroll anyway, but these anxieties persisted. I share these stories to explain two things: (1) like any other identity marker, a student's social context is not left at the door of the classroom; and (2) the needs and interests of working-class students are becoming more prevalent as enrollment demographics slowly become more diversified, even while families question the worth of a college education.

To no one's surprise, the ancient origins of our field are not known for welcoming the non-elite to the fold. As William DeGenaro summarized, Aristotle viewed manual labor as a barrier to virtuousness, both morally and physically—it deteriorates the mind and body while precluding the laborer from participating in the activities necessary for civic life.[5] DeGenaro describes the ideology of the time: "If members of the banausic class—manual laborers—used their hands, they probably did not use their minds."[6] Furthermore, our origins have led us to conceive of formalized speech as the epitome of good communication worthy of rhetorical study. Political address and persuasive oratory are certainly cornerstones of our field's history, but we have since learned that rhetoric is not restricted to a podium. Since the 1960s revival of the study of rhetoric, scholars have posed challenges to the rhetorical tradition to (1) develop rhetorical theories that account for diverse perspectives and (2) unsettle common assumptions about the function of rhetoric.[7] Often catalyzed by social movements, these challenges have broadened not only *whom* and *what* is worthy of rhetorical study but also *how* researchers go about collecting and making sense of data. Women's rhetoric, for example, began by first recovering women's rhetorical contributions and integrating them into our canon. This destabilizing work led feminist researchers to begin adopting "radically new methods [that] violate some of the most cherished conventions of academic research."[8] Similar disruptions have occurred through other underrepresented discourses, and rhetoricians have taken up this momentum to understand how rhetoric functions in the mine, on the concrete pour, at the steel mill.

Julie Lindquist has demonstrated how rhetorical ethnographers may look to material sites—such as the working-class bar—as a location in which "people practice argument not only to identify themselves socially but also to participate in the invention of public belief."[9] In this case study and others, scholars have identified ways in which working-class publics, which can rarely be separated from the material conditions of their work or leisure, simultaneously uphold long-held beliefs about the *purposes* of rhetoric while subverting the views of its *functions.* DeGenaro argues that "the scope of rhetoric has too often consisted of elites concerned more with theorizing and less with doing."[10] Scholarship that has applied the principles of rhetorical analysis to doing has revealed to us the richness of "new" or "alternative" rhetorics and has contributed to the ongoing destabilization of what counts as rhetoric. Many of these cases, however, follow the traditional methods of ethnographies, case studies, and so on, by situating a particular working-class community as an object of study. In this chapter, we speculate as to what it might look like to *partner* with these communities rather than *study* them. If scholars hope to make meaningful interventions in the public sphere, we must expand our scope to account for communities that have been long overlooked, especially when members of those communities are showing up in our classrooms. To discuss how to do such work, we should first clarify what we mean by the working class.

Marx and Bourdieu are often referenced for their disagreements on the variables that constitute class more generally—namely, material versus symbolic conditions. Lindquist helpfully suggests that we commit to the belief that "class is a function of culture, and culture, a function of class."[11] This is especially true for working-class consciousness. Anna's experience attests to the reality that even if one now has access to increased social or economic power or both, a working-class worldview can remain deeply embedded. The checkboxes of being working class are also contested. Should an identity be based primarily on income level? Occupation title? Educational credentials? Furthermore, class—like most other sites of identity formation—overlaps and intersects with gender, sexuality, ethnicity, disability, and more. All this to say that a working-class consciousness is a category as much as it is an identity, one that cannot be easily pinpointed. The concise explanation provided by June Deery and Andrea Press is helpful in understanding class in general, which is that class "refers to one's position within a social structure of unequal access to available resources (material, social, political)."[12] The *working* class is marked by limited access to these resources and is largely composed of those "who must sell their labor, physical or mental, in exchange for a wage or salary *and* who as individuals have little say in the content and pace of their work or their rate of compensation," according to Nancy Welch.[13] Control over one's working conditions—or lack thereof—is a key variable in the working-class reality and is a factor in how students from working-class backgrounds adjust to the experience of higher education. Although we imagine working-class communities themselves as important sites of partnership for rhetoric and writing studies, we first imagine this work to occur in our own classrooms.

IN THE COMPOSITION CLASSROOM
Anna: I took a rhetoric course years ago in which Wal-Mart became a topic of discussion. We began to criticize the chain for driving out local businesses and perpetuating poverty by selling poorly made goods that require low-income customers to keep returning to replace broken items. It was a lively conversation, and the professor had highly articulate reasons for why Wal-Mart was bad, even down to the dirtiness of the stores. I had my purse stolen in a Wal-Mart once, so I also harbor negative feelings about the chain. In the next class session, though, the professor began by apologizing for their flippant remarks about the store; upon reflection, they felt themselves participating in elitist rhetoric that they found unacceptable. In response, a classmate, who had not engaged in the discussion, thanked the professor for this follow-up comment. They grew up in a rural, impoverished town, and Wal-Mart was all they had. Not only was the store a lifeline in what would otherwise have been a food desert, but it also employed many of the town's residents (including themself) and even served as a social space on Friday nights. I will never forget the shame I felt in participating in the grocery store slander. I had turned on one of my own. Working-class students are not a hypothetical student body that we should plan for; they are already here, although instructors may not always be aware of their unique social contexts.

Attention to working-class realities is not exclusive to rhetoric and writing studies, of course. Scholars in anthropology, history, cultural studies, and others are attuned to the complexities of how these communities function, especially as they relate to political and economic dynamics. But as specialists in rhetoric, what is our role as educators in engaging these communities in our classrooms and beyond? If Lynn Z. Bloom was right in arguing that first-year composition is inherently a middle-class enterprise, where students seem to be "disinfected" before being sent on to the "real business" of the university,[14] how can we recognize social class as a part of the rich fabric that is cultural diversity in higher education? We must consider the dynamics of the writing classroom, the topics we discuss, and how we encourage students to engage with them.

Reimagining Classroom Dynamics as Interdependent

In "Rhetoric on the Concrete Pour: The Dance of Decision Making," Dale Cyphert identifies three rhetorical norms of a working-class community: "*an accommodative rhetorical culture* in which a *wide distribution of knowledge* and *implicit techniques of meaning-sharing* are used to guide the community's collective action."[15] These key characteristics hark back to Stephens and Townsend's research that points to *interdependence* as integral to a working-class worldview, especially among students entering college. Cyphert found these norms emphasized on the concrete pour. The harsh material reality of the jobsite requires workers to adapt to the natural environment; weather cannot be controlled and cannot always be accurately predicted, leaving workers to develop an acceptance of constant uncertainty and an understanding that adaptability is key to success. Integral to this success is an understanding that each crew member plays an equal part in getting the job done, drawing on "information that is stored in the experiences, perceptions, and interpretations of several minds."[16] Most interesting, this knowledge, as well as the physical act of completing objectives, is largely communicated nonverbally; too much discussion can be a sign of a crew's dysfunction or of something gone wrong.[17] The features of the concrete pour jobsite can be translated to the writing classroom as its own community where students experience learning as a fluid and adaptable experience, diverse perspectives are valued, and knowledge is co-created through varied modalities.

Once again, interdependence is key. A classroom that is more welcoming to working-class students is one that values collaborative knowledge making. One way to foster an interdependent classroom is through collaborative note taking and group work, where students have multiple means of contributing to class discussions, assignments, and other activities. In daily work, we suggest moving away from assigning groups to work on the same questions or problems; instead, designate individual groups to tackle a particular feature or question of a larger topic, which can lead the class to weave together each group's findings. For whole-class discussions, we have found success creating cloud-based documents for class periods that we ask all students to take notes on. This gives students the benefit of a record of class meetings and opportunities to contribute in ways other than verbal discussion (which is a boon for accessibility purposes), and allows students to see themselves as an integral part of the learning community.

Topics That Matter

Beyond designing classroom dynamics in ways that uphold the value of interdependence, instructors can broach topics that matter to students and encourage them to engage in ways that feel meaningful. We will avoid providing a list of such topics, as working-class communities are obviously varied and unique. Rather, instructors can gauge students' interests through polling or assignments or investigate what public issues are being deliberated in local communities. We are fortunate enough to teach in a geographic area we are already familiar with, so we are attuned to the concerns and interests of the rural communities in which many of our students were raised. One such issue that created lively class discussions for Anna's class is deer hunting.

> Anna: I use deer hunting as a segue to practicing primary and secondary research skills and listening to perspectives that differ from one's own. I begin the conversation by explaining my investment in hunting, including some of my own moral questions. I grew up hearing stories of my father eating beans seven nights a week, with only the occasional helping of squirrel meat to supplement. Times were hard, but hunting was a way to provide. When I married into a family of avid deer hunters, my understanding of and respect for conservationist hunters grew, including the need to thin overpopulated herds of white-tailed deer that affect forestation and can cause dangerous wrecks on Oklahoma roads.
>
> My feelings about hunting are complicated, and I openly share this with my students. What often ensues is a rich discussion during which students from hunting contexts are able to share what the practice means to them (often, like me, it is a family tradition rooted in a deep love and respect for the land and its creatures rather than bloodlust), and students who are anti-hunting are able to provide counterpoints but leave the discussion with more understanding of the practice. I then send students into groups to conduct additional research on the topic; they discover the stakeholders involved and learn the intricacies of the issue that extend beyond the moral arguments surrounding taking animal life. Engaging a topic that I know will likely resonate with at least some students in my class, especially a practice they might assume they would be shamed for in a college classroom, increases students' sense of belonging and validates their own cultural experiences as worthy of rhetorical study. Furthermore, it helps students imagine rhetoric outside the classroom and into the field—or in this case, the woods.

Real-World Applicability

Kalyn: When was the last time you changed your mind?

I ask this question each time I teach composition courses that focus on argumentation. It takes students a long time to respond to the question because it's so challenging. Allowing ourselves to be persuaded is an action that is culturally discouraged, in working-class and academic groups alike. We value conviction, consistency, and being "right" above learning and growth. What's so important about this exercise for working-class students is that it prompts them to think of rhetoric—particularly deliberation—as a real and present force in their lives outside of formal educational contexts. Too often, students and professors think the home of rhetoric is in university classrooms where theoretical discussions and debates take place surrounding issues that do not materially affect anyone in the room. But that simply is not the case.

In many Composition II courses, students are asked to develop skills for research and argumentation, typically with the goal of eventually developing their own argument for a specific audience. In our Composition II curriculum, we encourage students to tailor their arguments to a stakeholder with whom they are already familiar, as opposed to a politician or organization that is not connected to their home or general sphere of influence. In doing so, we can encourage what Nicole Khoury, Nicholas Behm, and Sherry Rankins-Robertson (chapter 5, this volume) call "affective vulnerability," affirming students' lived experiences and fostering a healthy approach to argument. To borrow from William Keith, Roxanne Mountford, and Timothy Steffensmeier, argumentation is *relational*, and encouraging students to root their research and inquiry in relationality makes for more effective, productive discourse.[18]

FIELDWORK

As we affirm the working-class students in our classrooms, we cannot neglect the communities they come from. Our work as teachers and researchers in rhetoric and writing studies is thrilling when it intervenes in public issues, crafting productive responses to and solutions for the problems that affect material realities. As such, our scholarship requires us to operate beyond campus—to engage with public issues in the communities that grapple with them. Our work requires fieldwork. Maybe that fieldwork should take place in fields . . . literally.

Kalyn: At every family event I attended growing up, we would talk about the same subject: water. How full were the ponds? How was the wheat looking? Would harvest be on time? If we went too long without rain, the family was scared, and for good reason. For my family in a small farming community in southwest Oklahoma, there were unavoidable, undesirable material realities of water shortages. After I started college in 2011, the conversations I heard when I returned home at holidays and school breaks were much the same but had found a new face: hydraulic fracturing, or "fracking." Sitting at my grandma's kitchen table, I heard my aunts and uncles debating the costs and benefits of fracking, citing concerns over water pollution, loss of crops, and loss of land. Yet, they couldn't completely condemn the practice. To lease land to frackers was to guarantee profit in a livelihood with few guarantees; the "neoliberal economic structures" that conspired to normalize fracking practices and take advantage of "small-scale farmers' economic vulnerability" and "limited agency in dictating land use near their farms" was too strong a force to reckon with, creating dissonance between conflicting ideologies.[19] As I listened to my family negotiate these tensions, I felt the desire to help navigate this issue, but I also had no idea how to do it.

Part of my confusion was due to my uncertainty about who I was—either a budding academic or a member of my family's farming community. Neither felt totally right, but I also felt I couldn't turn back from the path I had chosen when I pursued a university degree in the humanities. Thus, I wanted to help "them," not me. A connected problem I faced was that I had already bought into a vertical approach to the public humanities. Robyn Schroeder describes a vertical public humanities project as one that "maintains traditional expertise and endeavors to extend it 'downward' to those otherwise lacking access to higher education."[20] I assumed that because I was seeking a degree, I should have wisdom to impart rather than assuming that I might be a collaborator as we worked together to solve the problem of fracking and water conservation in small farming communities. Rather than a trickle-down approach to public engagement, effective and ethical public work must take a horizontal approach. Such a tactic "valorizes participation, community leadership, and sharing or surrendering expert authority."[21] Horizontal community engagement is challenging for working-class and rural publics when we so often feel we must leave those communities behind to have a space in the world of academia. We need to stop thinking of our working-class communities as liabilities and start considering them as assets to our studies and to our broader public life.

Generalizations about the working class are problematic, so we note here that farmers do not all occupy the same social class. There are significant differences among migrant farm workers, small-scale farmers, and agribusiness owners. In addition, the economic "success" of small-scale farmers varies wildly from year to year, depending on a number of factors—rain, market values, equipment malfunctions, illness, and others. These are the tensions and shifting identities that, in a vertical approach to public humanities, make it challenging to know how to prescribe a fix for the public issues farming communities face. However, in a horizontal approach, fluid class and economic identities become tensions to explore in partnership with communities, bringing competing forces to the forefront as we work together to find solutions for public problems. The family farm Kalyn describes is increasingly rare, overwhelmed by more profitable, big-business farming. Thus, it becomes all the more important that we partner with rural communities such as these to fight the neoliberal forces that might reshape such communities and cause them to compromise their values for the sake of economic well-being. This is the work public rhetoricians can do alongside community partners.

So, what would this kind of public engagement look like with rural, working-class communities? How can rhetoricians participate with farmers to solve the problem of fracking in southwest Oklahoma? There are several public humanitarian programs in Oklahoma that might provide models that could be revamped to account for how our field can share its knowledge and learn from the expertise of working-class communities. The organization Oklahoma Humanities offers an example of how public humanitarian work is being done in the state. One of the organization's most successful programs is called "Let's Talk about It," which functions as a reading group with literary experts. Citizens discuss four or five pieces of literature with experts, fostering discussion and consideration of "timeless themes that resonate with readers."[22] Another organization, the Citizens' Institute on Rural Design, "empowers local citizens to use their unique artistic and cultural resources to guide local development and shape the future design of their communities."[23] The organization—which is run by a team of designers, architects, and policy experts—holds local design workshops that bring together residents, community organizations, local nonprofits, and government entities to solve rural design problems together. Both of these organizations model the kind of work that is possible in working-class communities. Our field must consider what its own version of such programs might look like.

Borrowing from both models, we envision a public rhetoric and writing program that engages in analysis and intervention. Much like Oklahoma Humanities's reading groups, rhetoric and writing scholars might work with community partners to facilitate discussion groups surrounding public issues. Just as meaningful writing takes place when students have the agency to take up subjects that hit close to home—figuratively and literally—so must our engagement with working-class and rural communities be on their terms and for the purpose of grappling with public issues the community actually cares about.[24] For Kalyn's rural farm town, this might mean a rhetorical public humanities project holding weekly discussions on fracking, prompting analysis of its history, environmental effects, and economic impacts as well as the town's ideological commitments, values, and beliefs. These groups could function like a discussion-based public forum, laying the groundwork for public intervention that might take after the Citizens' Institute on Rural Design model.

Rhetoricians have the unique capacity to run workshops alongside community leaders that allow citizens to explore the range of interventions possible in community issues. Following the structure of the Citizens' Institute on Rural Design's local design workshops, we can help facilitate public action workshops where we imagine how to implement necessary change. For the fracking issue, this could involve speaking to legal experts, setting up meetings with congressional staff, creating local environmental policies, and creating partnerships across local farms to resist the financial necessity of leasing land to frackers. At every step of the way, writing and rhetoric play a role in how the community meaningfully shapes itself. Such a prospect is exciting for our field as we continue to value public engagement and civic participation alongside communities that are too often neglected when considering issues facing the public sphere.

NEXT STEPS FOR THE FIELD

So, how does our field become better at partnering with working-class communities to find solutions for public problems like water conservation and other environmental issues? How do we address the needs of working-class writing students so they can bring their expertise into the composition classroom and take home newfound skills? We suggest four areas the field might develop to strengthen its utility in the public sphere.

Research from Home

As our discussion of the composition classroom notes, pedagogies for working-class students are by no means new. Donna LeCourt discusses the components of a pedagogy that attempts to ease the tension felt by working-class students as they navigate their two, ostensibly different worlds. Such a pedagogy (1) opens up paths for students to express excluded experiences and working-class discourse in the classroom, (2) allows students to communicate in their "home" language, (3) creates a "safe space" for negotiating class conflict, and (4) assigns projects that focus on class tensions and experience.[25] As LeCourt says, such steps are helpful in exposing issues of class in composition; she also acknowledges their potential to box students in to certain identities. Rather than encouraging students to speak authentically—a concept famously troubled by Jacqueline Jones Royster[26]—or to only view public issues in terms of class conflict, we suggest that a way forward is to encourage students to research the public issues and communities that they themselves care about—including their own.

Internships

Perhaps the most practical way to teach students how to engage meaningfully with traditionally neglected publics is to require internships for both undergraduate and graduate students in the field. Suggesting that internships might be helpful in fighting neoliberal educational structures to strengthen a partnership with working-class communities might seem ideologically incongruent on its face. After all, nearly all of the research currently conducted on internships for writing students emphasizes the benefit of students finding real-world jobs in which to use their English skills. This is especially true for graduate studies in the field as the outlook for university employment grows dimmer. Deborah Carlin argues, "We are . . . obligated to consider their [graduate students'] economic and professional welfare after they leave our institutions. Internship programs can lead to employment after graduate school and at the very least they provide real experience in a nonacademic field, experience that is a necessity in most job searches today."[27] Although it is certainly true that requiring internships for graduate students might put them in a better position to find non-academic jobs, we argue that internships also offer students the chance to begin their collaborative work in communities. Developing relationships with communities and community activists is no easy task, and working with local nonprofit organizations or government programs can allow students to initiate relationships and begin to understand more about a community's cares and concerns. Such work can help shape students' research questions, methodological commitments, and networks of accountability. A next step for composition and rhetoric graduate programs across the country is reevaluating programmatic requirements and finding spaces for students to work as interns within communities to fulfill course credits.

Publications

The field can also reconsider what constitutes a "good" publication when it comes to community work. Scholarship like Alan Tinkler and colleagues' article on community leaders' perspectives in service-learning partnerships reiterates the necessity of publishing alongside community partners, making sure their expertise is represented when knowledge is shared with the field.[28] This likely means reading—and encouraging our students to read—journals that aren't traditionally associated with composition and rhetoric and changing editorial review processes to better account for the skills and wisdom community partners bring to academic publications.

Conversely, thinking about the role of publication in bridging the gap between working-class or rural communities and universities requires that we consider non-scholarly venues through which to publish our ideas. If our writing is going to make an impact on a rural community, we would be better off publishing a column in the local newspaper than an article in one of the field's top journals. Such a move requires us to embrace rhetorical forms that are often discouraged in academic writing but that might ultimately improve our ability to translate and teach rhetorical concepts for the betterment of the public.

A Public Humanities Course

Finally, we need more courses in our writing programs and graduate programs designated to teach students how to engage in public humanities. Doing the work of a public humanitarian requires a number of skills many programs simply do not prepare their students for in our field. Such a course would require combining pieces of many classes already taught at the graduate level into one comprehensive course on community activism. For example, many of the skills currently taught in technical and business communications courses, such as writing grants and making popular translations, can be adapted for public work, serving the purpose of engaging with communities rather than achieving a job in a technical field. Similarly, research methods such as ethnography and archival research must be revisited in a public context, along with reconsiderations of ethical community research. A course on the public humanities should not only teach students the practical elements of engaging in community work but also prompt them to consider the larger questions surrounding such work, including what communities can and should I partner with? What public issues does a given community face? What interventions are possible? What does it mean to participate in the public sphere? Is public participation a goal that a community should even have?

CONCLUSION

To our families, the folks with the college diplomas and the bigger paychecks have little bearing on the hands-on work of making and doing. Mike Rose likens this tension to a larger conflict in American cultural history: "the tension between book learning and schooling versus practical experience and working in the world."[29] Students who have come up in environments with an emphasis on practical experience are likely to feel at odds in an environment that may appear to prioritize thinking over doing, which can be complicated by their families' feelings about the student leaving their home community to pursue a supposedly bigger and better life. Moreover, academia's failure to collaborate with and learn from blue-collar communities further sends a message to working-class students that their home communities cannot participate in meaningful, political progress on the public issues prioritized by the academy, that their communities are irrelevant or a hindrance to progress on issues of climate change, racial justice, disability justice, and gender and sexual equality. Tensions in the definitions of "communities" and "publics," as well as considerations of what groups are allowed to be progressive political actors, are made even more complex when we consider how groups may be written off as ideologically at odds with the values and aspirations of the academy and thus unworthy of possessing rhetorical and localized expertise. As we have outlined in this chapter, this is a tension rhetoricians can productively navigate in both the composition classroom and the working-class communities many of our students call home. By building these relationships with working-class communities—by taking our work home—we can offer a counter to neoliberal ideology that creates distinctions and hierarchies between jobs and education, between local communities and public activists. As instructors and administrators, we have the opportunity not only to make our classrooms more inclusive for students from working-class backgrounds, but we can also widen the reach of rhetorical study by partnering *with* the communities that have provided us with such students.

NOTES

1. Tate, McMillan, and Woodworth, "Class Talk," 15.
2. Hurst and Nenga, *Working in Class*; Carter and Thelin, *Class in the Composition Classroom*.
3. DeCamp and Cushman, "Intersectional Community Thinking," 96.
4. Stevens and Townsend, "Research."
5. DeGenaro, "Introduction."
6. DeGenaro, "Introduction," 2.
7. Foss, Foss, and Trapp, *Contemporary Perspectives on Rhetoric*, 273.
8. Bizzell, "Feminist Methods of Research in the History of Rhetoric," 204.
9. Lindquist, *A Place to Stand*, 4.
10. DeGenaro, "Introduction," 4.
11. Lindquist, "Conclusion," 6.
12. Deery and Press, "Introduction," 3.
13. Welch, "We're Here, and We're Not Going Anywhere," 225, original emphasis.
14. Bloom, "Freshman Composition as a Middle-Class Enterprise," 656.
15. Cyphert, "Rhetoric on the Concrete Pour," 146.
16. Cyphert, "Rhetoric on the Concrete Pour," 150, original emphasis.
17. Cyphert, "Rhetoric on the Concrete Pour," 153.
18. Keith, Mountford, and Steffensmeier, "Teaching Argument through Relationships," 355.
19. Malin, "There's No Real Choice But to Sign," 17.
20. Schroeder, "The Rise of the Public Humanists," 20.
21. Schroeder, "The Rise of the Public Humanists," 20.
22. "Let's Talk about It," Oklahoma Humanities.
23. "Strengthening Rural Communities by Design," Citizens' Institute on Rural Design.
24. Eodice, Geller, and Lerner, *The Meaningful Writing Project*, 33.
25. LeCourt, "Performing Working-Class Identity in Composition," 33.
26. Royster, "When the First Voice You Hear Is Not Your Own."
27. Carlin, "Graduate Internship Programs in the Humanities," 217.
28. Tinkler et al., "Key Elements of Effective Service-Learning Partnerships."
29. Rose, "Working with Working-Class Students," 14.

REFERENCES

Bizzell, Patricia. "Feminist Methods of Research in the History of Rhetoric: What Difference Do They Make?" In *Feminism in Composition: A Critical Sourcebook*, edited by Gesa E. Kirsch, Faye Spencer Maor, Lance Massey, Lee Nickoson-Massey, and Mary P. Sheridan-Rabideau, 194–205. Boston: Bedford/St. Martin's, 2003.

Bloom, Lynn Z. "Freshman Composition as a Middle-Class Enterprise." *College English* 58, no. 6 (October 1996): 654–75. https://doi.org/10.2307/378392.

Carlin, Deborah. "Graduate Internship Programs in the Humanities: A Report from One University." *Pedagogy* 2, no. 2 (2002): 213–28. muse.jhu.edu/article/26396.

Carter, Genesea M., and William H. Thelin, eds. *Class in the Composition Classroom: Pedagogy and the Working Class*. Boulder: University Press of Colorado, 2017.

Cyphert, Dale. "Rhetoric on the Concrete Pour: The Dance of Decision Making." In *Who Says? Working-Class Rhetoric, Class Consciousness, and Community*, edited by William DeGenaro, 144–63. Pittsburgh: University of Pittsburgh Press, 2007.

DeCamp, Abbie Levesque, and Ellen Cushman. "Intersectional Community Thinking: New Possibilities for Thinking about Community." *Reflections* 20, no. 1 (2020): 90–109. https://reflectionsjournal.net/2020/09/intersectional-community-thinking-new-possibilities-for-thinking-about-community-by-abbie-levesque-decamp-ellen-cushman/.

Deery, June, and Andrea Press. "Introduction: Studying Media and Class." In *Media and Class: TV, Film, and Digital Culture*, edited by June Deery and Andrea Press, 2–17. New York: Routledge, 2017.

DeGenaro, William. "Introduction: What Are Working-Class Rhetorics?" In *Who Says: Working-Class Rhetoric, Class Consciousness, and Community*, edited by William DeGenaro, 1–8. Pittsburgh: University of Pittsburgh Press, 2007.

Eodice, Michele, Anne Ellen Geller, and Neal Lerner. *The Meaningful Writing Project: Learning, Teaching, and Writing in Higher Education*. Boulder: University Press of Colorado, 2017.

Foss, Sonja K., Karen A. Foss, and Robert Trapp. *Contemporary Perspectives on Rhetoric*. Prospect Heights, IL: Waveland, 1991.

Hurst, Allison L., and Sandi Kawecka Nenga. *Working in Class: Recognizing How Social Class Shapes Our Academic Work*. Lanham, MD: Rowman and Littlefield, 2016.

Keith, William, Roxanne Mountford, and Timothy Steffensmeier. "Teaching Argument through Relationships." *Argumentation* 34, no. 3 (September 2020): 355–69. https://doi.org/10.1007/s10503-019-09506-x.

LeCourt, Donna. "Performing Working-Class Identity in Composition: Toward a Pedagogy of Textual Practice." *College English* 69, no. 1 (2006): 30–51. https://doi.org/10.2307/25472187.

"Let's Talk about It." Oklahoma Humanities. https://www.okhumanities.org/programs/lets-talk-about-it.

Lindquist, Julie. *A Place to Stand: Politics and Persuasion in a Working-Class Bar*. New York: Oxford University Press, 2002.

Malin, Stephanie. "There's No Real Choice But to Sign: Neoliberalization and Normalization of Hydraulic Fracturing on Pennsylvania Farmland." *Journal of Environmental Studies and Sciences* 4, no. 1 (2014): 17–27. https://doi.org/10.1007/s13412-013-0115-2.

Rose, Mike. "Working with Working-Class Students." *Diversity and Democracy* 13, no. 3 (Fall 2010): 13–14.

Royster, Jacqueline Jones. "When the First Voice You Hear Is Not Your Own." *College Composition and Communication* 47, no. 1 (1996): 29–40. https://doi.org/10.2307/358272.

Schroeder, Robyn. "The Rise of the Public Humanists." In *Doing Public Humanities*, edited by Susan Smulyan, 5–27. New York: Routledge, 2020.

Stephens, Nicole, and Sarah Townsend. "Research: How You Feel about Individualism Is Influenced by Your Social Class." *Harvard Business Review*, May 22, 2017. https://hbr.org/2017/05/research-how-you-feel-about-individualism-is-influenced-by-your-social-class.

"Strengthening Rural Communities by Design." Citizens' Institute on Rural Design. https://www.rural-design.org/overview.

Tate, Gary, John McMillan, and Elizabeth Woodworth. "Class Talk." *Journal of Basic Writing* 16, no. 1 (1997): 13–26.

Tinkler, Alan, Barri Tinkler, Ethan Hausman, and Gabe Tufo-Strouse. "Key Elements of Effective Service-Learning Partnerships from the Perspective of Community Partners." *Partnerships: A Journal of Service-Learning and Civic Engagement* 5, no. 2 (2014): 137–52. https://libjournal.uncg.edu/index.php/prt/article/view/944.

Welch, Nancy. " 'We're Here, and We're Not Going Anywhere': Why Working-Class Rhetorical Traditions 'Still' Matter." *College English* 73, no. 1 (January 2011): 221–42. https://www.jstor.org/stable/25790473.

9

GENERATIVE COMBINATION
A Guiding Principle for the Future of Composition

Matthew Overstreet

AN EMBARRASSMENT OF RICHES

We are now more than twenty years into what Gunther Kress labeled a "revolution in the constellation of modes and media."[1] Driven by relentless technological change, communication norms continue to evolve. Screens and networked connection are omnipresent, with new genres, rhetorical situations, and composing tools appearing almost daily. In response comes a steady push to expand the way writing teachers understand writing.[2] Although the extent to which Kathleen Blake Yancey's call for "composition in a new key" has been heeded remains a matter of debate,[3] it's fair to say that many if not most writing teachers now recognize the importance of introducing students to a variety of genres and writing tools, of teaching composition in a variety of modes and for a variety of audiences. This contingent will likely continue to expand, which in my opinion is an unqualified good. Writing teachers have an obligation, as Cynthia Selfe writes, to "provide students the opportunities of developing expertise with all available means of persuasion and expression."[4] As the available means multiply, writing instruction should keep pace.

Although the value of diversifying writing pedagogy is now recognized, the exact role of the non-textual and non-academic in writing class—and the relationship between old and new literacies—remains open for debate. As writing instruction's domain expands, choices must be made. What genres, tools, and modal skill sets do we foreground? What sorts of "writing" do we teach? You might say we face an embarrassment of riches. In the following pages I introduce a principle to simplify matters. I argue that in light of increasing communication options, writing teachers should best prioritize *generative combination*. To meet modern literacy challenges, writers need familiarity with a variety of genres and communicative modes. Integrally, though, they also need to be able to deploy literacy resources in combination to create wholes larger than the sum of their parts. Writing instruction can and should be informed by a similar dynamic.

How might we unlock synergistic relations? The first step, I argue, is to understand genres and other literacy forms as technologies, material objects with defining properties and logics that shape thought and behavior in semi-predictable ways.[5] In short, we need to recognize that different forms do different things. We then need to figure out what they do well and leverage complementary strengths. I suggest that we engage in material analysis to reveal the competencies, or materially grounded literacy skills, at the core of common forms. This can help us identify points of contact, thus simplifying a complex pedagogical landscape. It can also lay the groundwork for generative combination. After discussing some themes in the multimodal literature that I believe inhibit such work, this chapter examines two common, seemingly diametrically opposed literacy forms: the essay and the meme. I identify their core competencies and how these competencies might be combined. The chapter ends with examples of what generative combination might look like in the classroom.

GENERATIVE COMBINATION AND BARRIERS THERETO

The idea of generative combination is not entirely new to rhetoric and composition. Santosh Khadka, for instance, notes how different literacies—a facility with both text and sound or design and information search, say—"can lead to productive interactions and work dynamics."[6] "Productive interactions" can occur in a number of ways. Within the same document or communicative encounter, various forms might be deployed to heighten understanding or rhetorical impact. The ability to "layer" in this way is a powerful and increasingly important literacy skill.[7] Another important yet often overlooked literacy skill is the ability to productively sequence literacy activity, to combine work in various forms across time and space. As noted above, the old corporate buzzword synergy aptly describes the dynamic associated with generative combination. Synergy is when the interaction of two elements produces a combined effect greater than the sum of the elements' separate effects. Upon reflection, we can probably all identify times in our literate lives when we leveraged literacy activities in a synergistic manner. For example, I read Khadka's recent book and jot some marks in the margins. I attend a conference and give a presentation that responds to his claims, receiving feedback on my ideas. Later, I write an essay expanding on the same ideas. Here we have work in a variety of modes (visual, verbal, textual) and genres (annotation, presentation, essay), using a variety of tools (pencil, voice, laptop). The end result is a level of thought and rhetorical sophistication greater than that which could be achieved through any one literacy act alone. Diverse competencies supplement each other, creating a whole greater than the sum of the parts.

Although the opportunities for generative combination within writing pedagogy are undoubtedly many, it is perhaps best to center analysis around a familiar dichotomy: "old," primarily textual academic forms, on one hand, and "new," primarily multimodal non-academic forms, on the other. Advocates for multimodality in writing pedagogy have worked both with and against this dichotomy. J. Elizabeth Clark, for example, adopts the former stance, arguing that "traditional essayistic literacy" is "outmoded" and needs to be replaced by a pedagogy centering digital rhetoric.[8] Adam Banks agrees, arguing that the "individualistic focus of the essay"—the most traditional of academic forms—doesn't allow for the "communal approach to literacy" demanded in the networked era.[9] Thus, he claims, the essay should be promoted to "genre emeritus." Pamela Takayoshi and Cynthia Selfe, in contrast, challenge the textual/multimodal, academic/non-academic dichotomy. The processes and approaches students learn composing non-textual forms, they argue, can "serve to illuminate the more familiar composing processes associated with words and vice versa."[10]

Like Takayoshi and Selfe, I wish to dissolve any perceived dichotomy between textual and multimodal writing pedagogy. I worry, though, that certain themes within the multimodal literature hinder efforts to promote generative combination. Sketched broadly, these are (1) a tendency to dematerialize composing competency and thus under-theorize the specific affordances and constraints of individual literacy forms, and relatedly, (2) a sort of "new expressionism" when discussing multimodal affordances. The first, I believe, obscures the uniqueness of individual forms, depriving writers of a clear set of elements to be combined. The second frames writing as the expression of existing thoughts rather than the creation of new ones, thus limiting combinatory potential. To embrace generative combination as a guiding principle is to recognize and resist these tendencies. I will address each in turn.

Rematerializing Competency

Exploring the unique affordances of various semiotic resources has long been part of multimodal scholarship.[11] As Kress writes, different modes, genres, and tools "provide fundamentally distinct possibilities for engagement with the world."[12] They have different strengths and grant users different powers. For Kress, affordances and constraints denote "what any semiotic system makes possible or rules out."[13] Later formulations add nuance. Jenny Davis, for instance, suggests thinking of technologies—including literacy technologies—not in terms of *what* they afford but *how*. A frame that foregrounds *how*, Davis argues, can capture an object's impact on thought and behavior while simultaneously "accounting for creative and subversive human acts."[14] Applied to literacy, such a view means recognizing that context matters, that affordances and constraints are rarely absolute; semiotic resources are more likely to "encourage" or "discourage" to varying degrees rather than "demand" or "forbid."

Integrally, affordances and constraints are closely bound to the physical form of technologies. Therefore, Kress writes, "to understand the semiotic potentials of language, we need to engage with it as material . . . as substance."[15] When we do this work, he argues, we find that different semiotic resources have different physical properties and are defined by different logics, or principles of organization. The logic of any resource is grounded in its materiality and, along with that materiality, determines how a resource affords. Speech, for instance, grounded in the materiality of soundwaves—changes in air pressure that proceed one at a time, in succession—is defined by temporal and sequential logic. Speech thus privileges narrative, communications that identify salient entities and events, and the order in which "who did what."[16] The visual mode, in contrast, grounded in the materiality of spatial arrangement, is defined by spatial logic. Time and sequence are relatively more difficult to depict spatially. Instead, the visual mode privileges the representation of entities and their synchronic relations.[17] Kress and associates center their analysis on modes, but the same sort of work can be conducted on any semiotic resource. Genres, styles, and other literacy forms all have unique physical properties, giving rise to unique logics and granting each of those logics unique tendencies and capabilities.

The recognition that literacy forms have different properties and logics and are thus best used for different things is simple but powerful. Indeed, this principle underlies the entire idea of generative combination. Simply put, if writers are to layer forms or sequence composing tasks to build on and reinforce each other, they need a clear idea of the strengths and weaknesses of the resources involved. They need to know how to discern, categorize, and combine relative affordances. This work begins with recognition of and close attention to each form's unique materiality.

It is unclear to what degree practitioners of multimodal pedagogy currently recognize the importance of identifying and leveraging, and helping students leverage, diverse properties and logics. On one hand, familiarity with the affordances and constraints of various semiotic resources is a common goal of multimodal pedagogy. Students learn to compare modes, for instance, to "make informed and conscious choices about the most effective modality" in a particular situation, as Takayoshi and Selfe write.[18] On the other hand, meaning-making ability and rhetorical skill may be presented as attributes that transcend genre or mode. In multimodal pedagogy it is "the thinking, decision making, and creative problem solving involved in creating meaning through any modality," the same authors write, "that provide the long-lasting and useful lessons."[19] Per such a view, it is generalized rhetorical ability that transfers, that students take away from a multimodal composition course. It is not facility with a certain set of literacy forms, each unique and thus each requiring specialized skill.

In all fairness, Takayoshi and Selfe have good reason to suggest that composing skill transcends any particular resource. As Selfe writes elsewhere, she wishes to ensure "respect for . . . the various roles each modality can play in human expression."[20] Emphasizing generalized skill, capable of being honed through work in any mode, helps make a place for non-dominant forms. There are drawbacks, though. To dematerialize competency in this manner diverts attention from the unique affordances of individual modes and genres. It implies, intentionally or not, that literacy forms, rather than possessing unique traits, are simply undifferentiated raw material for human use.[21] This leveling tendency limits our ability to achieve generative combination. To layer or sequence, at the most basic, is to know and exploit the unique material tendencies of different forms. We can best help students do such work, I believe, by showing the upmost respect for those tendencies. This means thinking in terms of specific, materially grounded competencies, not generalized rhetorical skill.

Reconnecting with Writing to Learn
So far, I've suggested that to make generative combination a guiding principle of multimodal pedagogy is to reject the idea that literacy forms are functionally equal. It's also important to recognize that literacy forms can be used for purposes other than communication. Song, for instance, can be used to tell a story but can also facilitate relaxation and strengthen social bonds. In the same way, composing events often serve

purposes outside the communicative. Within writing studies, writing for the writer rather than the reader is often discussed in terms of writing to learn.[22] Proponents of academic discourse strike similar notes. David Bartholomae, for instance, argues for a writing pedagogy of "practical criticism" in which writers closely read their own texts to imagine and enact multiple revisions.[23] These revisions don't simply address rhetorical concerns. Indeed, the result is often writing that is *less* persuasive, *less* capable of effective communication. Instead, practical criticism is fundamentally a form of writing to learn; through close reading and multiple drafts, students reimagine their relationship to life and language.

Bartholomae's pedagogy, centered on the textual essay, stands in sharp contrast to contemporary multimodal approaches. His idea that composing is a way to know rather than just a way to communicate and connect also stands in contrast to those approaches. As we've seen, multimodal composition is often addressed through the lens of rhetoric, thus forwarding intersubjective concerns such as the ability to "[build] and [engage] with complex networks of people and information," as Banks writes.[24] A survey of the literature also reveals a heavy emphasis on self-expression. Clark, for instance, argues for multimodal production in writing class as a means for students to "reach large audiences" and "share their stories."[25] Selfe concurs, arguing that an embrace of multimodality is necessary to ensure that "all students have room to express themselves."[26] Student interviews reveal a similar emphasis on the expressive affordances of multimodality.[27]

The idea that multimodal forms allow for self-expression isn't a complaint. Quite the opposite: it provides another reason to engage multimodality in the classroom. At the same time, though, it's important not to let themes of self-expression, with connotations of externalizing something preexisting, supplant themes of intellectual and ethical transformation. Bartholomae's critique of the expressivist element of the writing process movement remains incisive. In expressivist classrooms, he writes, the "efficient production of text" became the paramount concern.[28] Rather than questioning their biases and beliefs, students simply learned to present them in more engaging form. Unfortunately, there are indications of a similar dynamic within some multimodal composition pedagogies.[29] We might, whatever our intentions, be teaching students that multimodal composition is primarily (or even solely) an act of expressing preexisting ideas rather than an inventive process of reworking ideas into more complex formulations.

Of course, learning new composing methods, often alongside new technologies, takes time and energy; students often don't have the mental bandwidth to simultaneously rethink default beliefs. In addition, writing teachers—often not formally trained in multimodality—might not be aware of the specific constraints and affordances of the forms they now teach. No literacy form completely rules out critical thought, of course, but some may make it more difficult. Others may have untapped inventive potential. This reality makes generative combination and the principles underlying it all the more important. Again, different forms have different properties and logics and are thus optimized for different functions. We need to figure out what does what and then find ways to sequence tasks to allow for both "practical criticism" and the "efficient production of text," in Bartholomae's terminology.

THE ESSAY AND THE MEME

So, how do we figure out what specific forms actually do? Such work, I suggest, requires viewing literacy forms as material objects. Analysis at the material level can reveal the competencies at the core of common forms. Identifying shared competencies can simplify an increasingly complex pedagogical landscape. It can also reveal potential combinatory elements.

To demonstrate how material analysis works, I'll turn to an example. As noted, an archetypal instructional dilemma involves choosing between text-heavy, traditional academic forms and multimodal, non-academic forms. Do we teach the essay or the meme? Advocates for the former point to the capacity of extended informational prose to help students develop the ability to formulate and support a claim, engage other voices, and experiment with style and structure.[30] Advocates for the latter point to the cultural and personal relevance of multimodal forms.[31] As is perhaps apparent, I believe there is a place for both the essay and the meme in the composition classroom. The competencies at the core of these forms shape writing in a variety of sites. They can also be combined in powerful ways.

The Logic of the Essay

To speak of the essay can be tricky, as the term actually denotes two different things. First, "essay" may be used as a "catch-all term for nonfictional prose works of limited length," as Robert Scholes and Carl Klaus observe.[32] Used this way, "essay" means something like "academic essay." The primary characteristics of this genre are well-known: a central claim or thesis supported by properly documented evidence, explicit signaling of logical relations, and an impersonal, objective tone.[33] While the academic essay can be found across campus, another type of essay often holds sway in English classrooms. This genre, what we might call the "literary essay," is less thesis-driven, less formal, and often more personal than the academic essay. Rooted in the erudite, exploratory prose of Montaigne, the literary essay is marked by a "self-revelatory stance, flexible style, and conversational tone," making space for the "wondering and question posing" that Hannah J. Rule (chapter 10, this volume) suggests writing teachers value.[34]

There is no shortage of proponents of both thesis-driven academic discourse[35] and exploratory prose.[36] In support of their preferred form, these scholars grapple with each other, as well as with those—like Adam Banks—who challenge the very place of the essay in writing pedagogy. I take an alternate view and suggest that in this case, the distinction between forms isn't as pertinent as many believe. While both academic and literary essays undoubtedly have their own unique affordances, we can identify a logic that animates both. Skilled manifestations of both these forms display what we might call the *logic of explication*.[37]

When discussing the defining features of the essay, scholars often reference the notion of the "autonomous text."[38] Essayistic prose, Marcia Farr writes, is marked by "explicitness and exactness, both in terms of content and in terms of connections between, and the ordering of, propositions."[39] This "explicitness and exactness" works to limit ambiguity, allowing an essayistic text to be understood across contexts. Such a text can thus function "autonomously"—at a remove from its author and circumstances of creation. Although the idea of "fully present meaning in a self-sufficient text" is often critiqued, the concept of explicitness provides a useful frame to understand the work of both the academic and the literary essay.[40] Whether dealing in claims and evidence or ideas and experience, the essay requires elaboration, the making connection explicit.

Explication could be achieved through any number of literacy technologies, but in the case of the essay, the form's logic is grounded in *elaborated prose*—written language that, via explanation and explication, seeks to "provide its own context."[41] As a technology, we can say that such prose requests its users to make their patterns of association visible. In turn, it allows its users to speak to those at a remove in time, space, and personal circumstance.

Apart from its communicative function, elaborated prose is a powerful means of cognitive enhancement. As Janet Emig noted more than forty years ago, the inherent logic of writing—its various "lexical, syntactic, and rhetorical devices"—acts to channel cognition into "explicit

Generative Combination   169

and systematic conceptual groupings."⁴² By encouraging explication, elaborated prose bolsters these organizational tendencies. Writing also stabilizes thought and makes it accessible to the senses; it turns ideas into physical objects, allowing for new forms of combination and manipulation.⁴³ Again, in this regard, elaborated prose, with its unique set of affordances and constraints, bolsters writing's inherent capacities—an idea at the core of writing-to-learn scholarship.⁴⁴

So, to summarize, the various permutations of the essay found in American academic culture share a logic of explication. This logic is grounded in elaborated prose, writing that makes visible otherwise obscure patterns of association. As with any technology, the utility of elaborated prose is intimately tied to its materiality. By converting thought into physical form, elaborated prose allows thought to be shared and reworked in unique ways. Non-textual forms—speech or gesture, say—simply do not offer the same advantages. The ability to construct and deploy elaborated prose is thus a core competency; by identifying it as such, we make it available for generative combination.⁴⁵

The Logic of the Meme

In the previous section, I studied the essay—an admittedly broad signifier—to reveal the material competency at the core of academic discourse. In this section, I will use the meme to do the same with popular multimodal forms. In its original formulation, a meme is an idea or representation capable of replicating itself and spreading throughout a human population.⁴⁶ Within the popular imagination, though, the term meme has come to signify fragments of media, often images combined with text, that circulate among internet users. As they circulate, memes are remixed, adapted, and altered—making them a key component of the internet's participatory culture.⁴⁷

What is the logic of the meme? What material properties define it? To find out, let's examine one. Figure 9.1 depicts a meme circulating on English-language social media circa mid-2021. As noted, a key feature of meme culture is the adaptation and alteration of shared templates. This particular template, known as the "these are rare events" or "ight who's the loser now" template, combines a space for insertion of text with a four-panel image of a male cartoon figure transforming into a more assertive and overtly masculine form.⁴⁸ In addition to the text depicted, another common version of the meme includes the text "when someone calls you handsome and it's not your mother."⁴⁹ In both cases, successful interpretation requires that the text and image be read in combination.

When your answer goes against the whole class and it turns out to be correct:

Figure 9.1. Meme displaying logic of juxtaposition

The rare events meme is a complex document. Of particular note is the way the image portion works against the prime affordances of the visual mode. As noted, speech and, by extension, writing are best suited for the depiction of action and event; the visual mode, in contrast, is best suited for depiction of synchronic relations.[50] Here, through skillful juxtaposition of two separate images, transformation (a sequential process) is depicted visually. These combined images are then further juxtaposed with the textual portion of the meme.

All told, we can say that the rare events meme is defined by the *logic of juxtaposition*. In this regard, the specimen is representative of both the meme genre and broader digital communication patterns.[51] Banks, for instance, in his pedagogy of "mix, remix and mixtape," leans heavily on juxtaposition, seeking to instill in his students respect for the ways "combining materials from many different sources can . . . lead to an entirely new creation."[52] The rare events meme, as enacted in figure 9.1, betrays just such a strategy, combining pop culture imagery and narrative drawn from everyday life experience to convey a message of broad relevance.

As with explication, juxtaposition could be achieved through work with a variety of semiotic resources. In the case of the meme, though, the form's logic is grounded in the *spatial arrangement of diverse modal elements*. The meme as a technology, we can say, encourages its user to express associative patterns through spatial arrangement of diverse elements. It discourages the explication of connection between elements. Facility in spatial arrangement is the form's core competency. Once again, the utility of this form (and associated competency) is tied to specific physical attributes. In the meme, use of image and arrangement reduces the need for text, allowing the form to be processed rapidly and all at once, like an image. Speed of processing thus allows for spreadability.

In addition to functioning as a means of communication, the meme, like other literacy forms, can supplement and thus enhance cognition. By allowing its user to participate in networked social space, the creation and circulation of memes may open up new learning opportunities. Also, the process of selecting and arranging elements might itself be generative. As the meme user, in the course of their communicative efforts, searches for semiotic resources and experiments with arrangements, new associative patterns may emerge. For instance, it is possible that the creator of the meme in figure 9.1 never previously considered (much less articulated) the feeling of transformation associated with offering an unpopular, yet correct, answer in the classroom. It perhaps wasn't until they observed the transformation of the cartoon figure that the necessary connections were made. Engagement with the meme thus allowed for novel thought.

So, like the essay, the meme can be a powerful tool. It's important to recognize the limitations of the properties and logics at play, though. As noted, the logic of explication, grounded in elaborated prose, defines the essay. By "providing its own context," elaborated prose allows communication across physical and social distance. It allows for what Lester Faigley calls "slow rhetoric," discourse defined by precision and rigor, as well as an unmatched ability to help users figure out what they (and their communication partners) think and why.[53] That said, even the strongest proponents of elaborated prose wouldn't suggest that it's of universal utility. If one's goal is to stand out in a crowded information landscape, for instance, elaborated prose is likely a poor choice.

A similar situation pertains in regard to the meme. The logic of juxtaposition, grounded in the spatial arrangement of diverse modal elements, defines this form. Per this logic, relationships between constituent elements are not expressly stated. The streamlined nature of the meme allows for efficient communication among the similarly situated but may hinder communication across boundaries. With communication through spatial arrangement, in other words, context is a relatively more important semiotic resource. If context is not shared, understanding may not be possible.

GENERATIVE COMBINATION AS PEDAGOGICAL PRINCIPAL

We've now identified the defining properties and logics of the essay and the meme. Our analysis reveals two core competencies: the ability to construct and deploy elaborated prose and the ability to spatially arrange diverse modal elements. Of course, this is not to say that these abilities are all that is required to compose a successful essay or meme. It is to say, though, that these competencies lie at the very heart of these forms. Facility with elaborated prose or multimodal arrangement is a necessary, if not sufficient, condition for successful creation of an essay or meme. Stripping the essay and the meme down to their core competencies is useful, first off, because it reveals that there's nothing magical about these forms. We can teach the literacy skills that define them using any number of genres, thus reducing the pressure posed by increasing communication options. As I'll show in this section, the identification of core competencies also sets the stage for generative combination.

So, how might the competencies at the core of the essay and the meme be combined? Earlier, I identified layering and sequencing as two possible types of combination. Thinking in terms of core competencies, we see that potential sites of combination are myriad. An assignment doesn't even need to involve an essay or a meme. For instance, the creation of a generic business proposal—a staple of the professional writing course—offers an opportunity to both layer and sequence elaborated prose and multimodal arrangement. Such a project might ask students to present a written proposal for a business idea—to make a claim, in other words—and support it with detailed reasoning. In their final draft, students would need to make explicit how their business will operate, why they believe it will succeed, and what evidence led them to this conclusion. They will need to explain rather than assume.

Integrally, in the same document, students might also be asked to supplement their textual analysis with a form defined by the logic of juxtaposition, that is, to layer. For instance, they might make a visual artifact that combines words, images, and symbols to express a claim or concept. As with the meme, in this form, associative patterns would need to be expressed through the juxtaposition of diverse modal elements. Logical

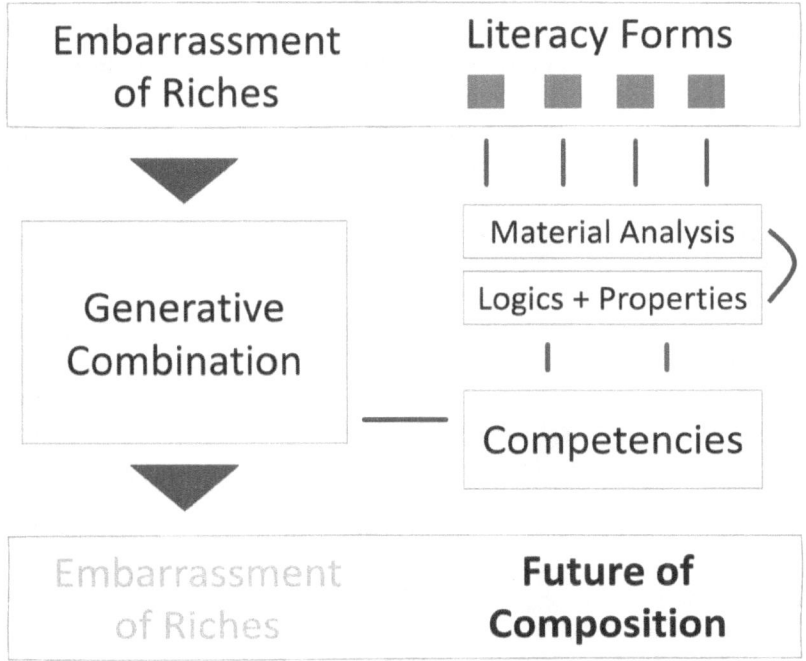

Figure 9.2. Visual artifact expressing the author's claim through arrangement of multimodal elements

relations would need to be implied rather than expressly stated. Figure 9.2, in combination with the text you're reading, provides an example of layering. Its inclusion means that this chapter displays the logics of explication and juxtaposition, elaborated prose, and multimodal arrangement. These diverse literacy forms supplement each other. On one hand, the explication-laden textual portion provides context for the streamlined multimodal portion. On the other hand, the multimodal portion presents the author's claim, which in the textual portion unfolds over many pages, as an immediately accessible whole. The resulting combination works to offer readers multiple ways to engage the underlying content, likely increasing comprehension.[54] In other words, diverse literacy forms are combined to achieve something more than either could achieve alone. To center generative combination as a pedagogical principle is to highlight and cultivate this dynamic.

In addition to layering, the composition of a business proposal offers an opportunity for generative sequencing. As we've seen, literacy forms are both communicative and cognitive devices. Different forms, in turn, offer different options for cognitive enhancement. In the case of the business proposal, working in elaborated prose offers writers the opportunity to make thought visible and examine ideas at a certain remove. It allows them to share ideas with peers and get feedback, thus helping them identify biases or blind spots in their thinking. Elaborated prose, in short, allows for acts of "practical criticism," as Bartholomae puts it. With proper support, these unique affordances can be leveraged to help writers rework their ideas into a more complex and generous form. It matters little whether the ideas reworked are contained in an exploratory essay, business document, or other genre.

Within the same project, engagement with streamlined, multimodal forms can open up different, yet equally exciting, opportunities for invention and revision. Suresh Canagarajah, in a recent article suggesting a "materialist orientation" toward language competency (an orientation I share), provides an example.[55] Canagarajah presents the case of Gunter, a graduate student who finds himself stuck while drafting an academic article. A breakthrough occurs when, with the assistance of a colleague, Gunter creates a visual artifact representing his claim. The visual artifact, similar to figure 9.2, combines words and symbols. Displaying a logic of juxtaposition, relationships are implied rather than explicated. The act of creating this visual—of abstracting away from the density of elaborated prose and thinking in streamlined, spatial logic—allows Gunter to reimagine the relationship between key elements. He then returns to his journal article and makes successful revisions. Thus, in his case, we see an example of the productive sequencing of literacy activity. Gunter uses work in different modes (visual and textual) and genres (artifact and article) to supplement each other, ultimately creating a whole greater than the sum of the parts. In other words, he engages in generative combination.

We can also imagine the above dynamic working in the opposite direction. Rather than using a streamlined multimodal arrangement as a site of invention, a writer might use such a form to share ideas previously worked out through elaborated prose. Santosh Khadka, in arguing for a pedagogy of multiliteracies, provides an example. In Khadka's classroom, students use the essay form (i.e., elaborated prose) to engage multiple perspectives, interrogate their own beliefs, and ultimately construct sophisticated and informed arguments. The same ideas are then remediated into streamlined and accessible forms, such as videos and websites, allowing students to communicate and connect about topics on which they've become expert. All told, Khadka's students practice a variety of material competencies. Tasks are sequenced, though, to leverage complementary strengths.

Khadka's model could well function as a template for pedagogies of generative combination more broadly. Such pedagogies, as I imagine them, would engage both conventional and emerging literacies. They would foreground the materiality of literacy forms and highlight connections among physical properties, affordances and constraints, and communicative impact. In terms of course outcomes, such pedagogies would ask that students display skill with core competencies, as well as a basic understanding of how and why forms might be combined. This insight into combinatory dynamics, I believe, could help students optimize their literate lives.[56]

THE FUTURE OF COMPOSITION

In this chapter, I've argued that writing teachers best teach in ways that allow for synergy between diverse literacy forms. To achieve synergy in the classroom and help our students achieve the same beyond it, we first need to recognize that modes, genres, registers, and other literacy resources possess different properties and logics, best used to achieve different ends. We then need to search for points of contact among diverse forms. I've offered the concept of core competencies—materially grounded literacy skills—as a means to sort and simplify our pedagogical options. The basic idea is that it doesn't matter if a writing pedagogy features essays or memes (or whatever else) as long as it helps students learn to create and deploy their chief components. In other words, it is student facility with common competencies that is of paramount import, not mastery of specific tools or genres. This insight does much, I believe, to ease the pressure posed by ever-increasing communication options. Whether a teacher is already committed to multimodal experimentation or engaging multimodality for the first time, the idea of core competencies makes clear that they don't have to teach (and learn) everything. The burden on instructors is thus substantially reduced.

Breaking forms down into core competencies also allows for generative combination among competencies. I've suggested two types of generative combination: layering and sequencing. The former involves presenting literacy resources informed by different competencies within the same document or communicative encounter. In constructing layered documents, students simultaneously engage multiple competencies. They can thus gain insight into how diverse properties and logics can work together to increase understanding and rhetorical impact. Sequencing is another type of generative combination. This is when literacy acts informed by different competencies are engaged in succession to leverage respective strengths. Multimodal arrangement, for instance, may be used to assist invention and organization in the composition of primarily textual forms. Conversely, work in elaborated prose may allow for the creation of sophisticated and informed multimodal arrangements.

In the end, the future of composition, like the future of everything, is uncertain. It's a fair guess, though, that communication technologies will continue to evolve, becoming ever more prolific and integrated into our lives. In turn, communication practices will become ever more varied. As many have argued, to maintain relevance and practical import, composition will need to adapt, using our stock of accumulated wisdom to help students tackle new literacy challenges involving new literacy forms. The underlying premise in these pages has been that no matter what path the field takes, there's little use in thinking in zero-sum terms. No matter what literacy forms the field comes to privilege, there will always be opportunities for synergy between different modes and genres. To center generative combination as a pedagogical principle is to be on the lookout for points of contact.

NOTES

1. Kress, "Gains and Losses," 6.
2. Clark, "The Digital Imperative"; Selfe, "The Movement of Air"; Yancey, "Made Not Only in Words."
3. Bearden, "Favorable Outcomes."
4. Selfe, "The Movement of Air," 617.
5. "Literacy form" denotes any conventionalized form literate activity might take. A genre (e.g., website) is a literacy form. Conventionalized patterns at the sub-genre level (e.g., a bullet-point list on a website) are also literacy forms, as are broader units such as registers and styles.
6. Khadka, *Multiliteracies*, 9.
7. Alexander, Powell, and Green, "Understanding Modal Affordances"; Dressman. "Multimodality."
8. Clark, "The Digital Imperative," 28.
9. Banks, "Dominant Genre Emeritus," 180
10. Takayoshi and Selfe, "Thinking about Multimodality," 4.
11. Cazden et al., "A Pedagogy of Multiliteracies"; Cope and Kalantzis, *Multiliteracies*.
12. Kress, "English at the Crossroads," 78.
13. Kress, "English at the Crossroads," 78.
14. Davis, *How Artifacts Afford*, 19.
15. Kress, "English at the Crossroads," 78.
16. To say that a resource "privileges" a certain type of content is to say that it makes that content relatively easier to create. In turn, that content becomes relatively more common in communications featuring that resource.
17. Jewitt, "Technology and Learning"; Kress, "Gains and Losses."
18. Takayoshi and Selfe, "Thinking about Multimodality," 9.
19. Takayoshi and Selfe, "Thinking about Multimodality," 4.

20. Selfe, "The Movement of Air," 626.
21. Alexander and Rhodes (On Multimodality) lodge a similar complaint.
22. Emig, "Writing as a Mode of Learning"; Klein, "Reopening Inquiry."
23. Bartholomae, "What Is Composition."
24. Banks, "Dominant Genre Emeritus," 181.
25. Clark, "The Digital Imperative," 32.
26. Selfe, "The Movement of Air," 644.
27. Alexander, Powell, and Green, "Understanding Modal Affordances"; DePalma, "Tracing Transfer across Media."
28. Bartholomae, "What Is Composition," 341.
29. Alexander, Powell, and Green, "Understanding Modal Affordances"; Scott and Welch, "One Train Can Hide Another."
30. Hesse, "Saving a Place for Essayistic Literacy"; Spellmeyer, "A Common Ground."
31. Banks, "Dominant Genre Emeritus"; Clark, "The Digital Imperative"; Selfe, "The Movement of Air."
32. Scholes and Klaus, *Elements of the Essay*, 46.
33. Faigley and Romano, "Going Electric."
34. Trimbur, "Essayist Literacy," 76.
35. Graff, *Clueless in Academe*.
36. Hesse, "Saving a Place for Essayistic Literacy"; Spellmeyer, "A Common Ground."
37. Both Marcia Farr ("Essayist Literacy") and Donald Lazere (Political Literacy) anticipate this claim.
38. Olson, "From Utterance to Text."
39. Farr, "Essayist Literacy," 9.
40. Trimbur, "Essayist Literacy," 76.
41. Emig, "Writing as a Mode of Learning," 122.
42. Emig, "Writing as a Mode of Learning," 128.
43. Clark, "Magic Words."
44. Elbow, *Writing without Teachers*; Emig, "Writing as a Mode of Learning;" Klein, "Reopening Inquiry."
45. Of course, there's no claim here that elaborated prose on its own is capable of anything; that's the kind of technological determinism that how-centered affordance analysis seeks to avoid. Context always matters.
46. Dawkins, *The Selfish Gene*.
47. Shifman, *Memes in Digital Culture*.
48. The first image is clearly Homer Simpson from an early episode of The Simpsons. It is claimed that the second image is also from The Simpsons, but I'm unable to verify.
49. Know Your Meme, "These Are Rare Events," https://knowyourmeme.com/photos/2035407.
50. Jewitt, "Technology and Learning"; Kress, "Gains and Losses."
51. Hesse; Yus, "Multimodality in Memes."
52. Banks, "Dominant Genre Emeritus," 185.
53. Faigley, "Rhetorics Fast and Slow."
54. Mayer, *Multimedia Learning*.
55. Canagarajah, "Materializing 'Competence,'" 5.
56. Some teachers may not feel adept at the sort of material analysis that underpins generative combination. This doesn't mean they can't deploy the pedagogy I propose. In my own experience, an attitude of productive noviceship often works quite well. For instance, teachers and students might engage literacy forms together and consider how form relates to function. Even without an answer key, the process of group inquiry, I've found, can generate actionable knowledge and hone the analytical abilities of all involved.

REFERENCES

Alexander, Jonathan, and Jacqueline Rhodes. *On Multimodality: New Media in Composition Studies*. Urbana, IL: National Council of Teachers of English, 2014.

Alexander, Kara, Beth Powell, and Sonya Green. "Understanding Modal Affordances: Student Perceptions of Potentials and Limitations in Multimodal Composition." *Basic Writing eJournal* 11, no. 1 (2011).

Banks, Adam. "Dominant Genre Emeritus: Why It's Time to Retire the Essay." *CLA Journal* 60, no. 2 (2016): 179–90.

Bartholomae, David. "What Is Composition and (If You Know What That Is) Why Do We Teach It?" In *Writing on the Margins* by Bartholomae, 327–42. New York: Palgrave Macmillan, 2005.

Bearden, Logan. "Favorable Outcomes: How Outcomes Can Make Space for Multimodal Composition Curricula." *Writing Program Administration* 43, no. 1 (2019): 139–61.

Canagarajah, Suresh. "Materializing 'Competence': Perspectives from International STEM Scholars." *Modern Language Journal* 102, no. 2 (2018): 1–24.

Cazden, Courtney, Bill Cope, Norman Fairclough, James Gee, Mary Kalantzis, Gunther Kress, Allan Luke, Carmen Luke, Sarah Michaels, and Martin Nakata. "A Pedagogy of Multiliteracies: Designing Social Futures." *Harvard Educational Review* 66, no. 1 (1996): 60–92.

Clark, Andy. "Magic Words: How Language Augments Human Computation." In *Language and Thought: Interdisciplinary Themes*, edited by Peter Carruthers and Jill Boucher, 162–83. Cambridge: Cambridge University Press, 1998.

Clark, J. Elizabeth. "The Digital Imperative: Making the Case for a Twenty-First-Century Pedagogy." *Computers and Composition* 27, no. 1 (2010): 27–35.

Cope, Bill, and Mary Kalantzis, eds. *Multiliteracies: Literacy Learning and the Design of Social Futures*. London: Taylor and Francis, 2010.

Davis, Jenny. *How Artifacts Afford: The Power and Politics of Everyday Things*. Cambridge, MA: MIT Press, 2020.

Dawkins, Richard. *The Selfish Gene*. New York: Oxford University Press, 1979.

DePalma, Michael. "Tracing Transfer across Media: Investigating Writers' Perceptions of Cross-Contextual and Rhetorical Reshaping in Processes of Remediation." *College Composition and Communication* 66, no. 4 (2015): 615–42.

Dressman, Mark. "Multimodality and Language Learning." In *The Handbook of Informal Language Learning*, edited by Mark Dressman and Randall Sadler, 39–55. New York: John Wiley and Sons, 2019.

Elbow, Peter. *Writing without Teachers*. Oxford: Oxford University Press, 1973.

Emig, Janet. "Writing as a Mode of Learning." *College Composition and Communication* 28, no. 2 (1977): 122–28.

Faigley, Lester. "Rhetorics Fast and Slow." In *Rhetorical Agendas: Political, Ethical, Spiritual*, edited by Patricia Bizzell, 3–9. Mahwah, NJ: Erlbaum, 2006.

Faigley, Lester, and Susan Romano. "Going Electric: Creating Multiple Sites for Innovation in a Writing Program." In *Resituating Writing: Constructing and Administering Writing Programs*, edited by Joseph Janangelo and Kristine Hansen, 46–58. Portsmouth, NH: Heinemann/Boynton-Cook, 1995.

Farr, Marcia. "Essayist Literacy and Other Verbal Performances." *Written Communication* 10, no. 1 (1993): 4–38.

Graff, Gerald. *Clueless in Academe: How Schooling Obscures the Life of the Mind*. New Haven, CT: Yale University Press, 2008.

Hesse, Doug. "Saving a Place for Essayistic Literacy." In *Passions, Pedagogies, and Twenty-First Century Technologies*, edited by Gail Hawisher and Cynthia Selfe, 34–48. Logan: Utah State University Press, 1999.

Jewitt, Carey. "Technology and Learning: A Multimodal Approach." In *International Handbook of Psychology in Education*, edited by Karen Littleton, Clare Wood, and Judith Kleine Staarman, 361–98. Bingley, UK: Emerald Publishing Group, 2010.
Khadka, Santosh. *Multiliteracies, Emerging Media, and College Writing Instruction*. New York: Routledge, 2019.
Klein, Perry. "Reopening Inquiry into Cognitive Processes in Writing-to-Learn." *Educational Psychology Review* 11, no. 3 (1999): 203–70.
Know Your Meme. "These Are Rare Events." https://knowyourmeme.com/photos/2035407.
Kress, Gunter. "English at the Crossroads." In *Passions, Pedagogies, and Twenty-First Century Technologies*, edited by Gail Hawisher and Cynthia Selfe, 66–88. Logan: Utah State University Press, 1999.
Kress, Gunter. "Gains and Losses: New Forms of Texts, Knowledge, and Learning." *Computers and Composition* 22, no. 1 (2005): 5–22.
Lazere, Donald. *Political Literacy in Composition and Rhetoric: Defending Academic Discourse against Postmodern Pluralism*. Carbondale: Southern Illinois University Press, 2015.
Mayer, Richard. *Multimedia Learning*. Cambridge: Cambridge University Press, 2009.
Olson, David. "From Utterance to Text: The Bias of Language in Speech and Writing." *Harvard Educational Review* 41 (1977): 257–81.
Scholes, Robert, and Carl Klaus. *Elements of the Essay*. New York: Oxford University Press, 1969.
Scott, Tony, and Nancy Welch. "One Train Can Hide Another: Critical Materialism for Public Composition." *College English* 76, no. 6 (2014): 562–79.
Selfe, Cynthia. "The Movement of Air, the Breath of Meaning: Aurality and Multimodal Composing." *College Composition and Communication* 60, no. 4 (2009): 616–63.
Shifman, Limor. *Memes in Digital Culture*. Cambridge, MA: MIT Press, 2014.
Spellmeyer, Kurt. "A Common Ground: The Essay in the Academy." *College English* 51, no. 3 (1989): 262–76.
Takayoshi, Pamela, and Cynthia Selfe. "Thinking about Multimodality." In *Multimodal Composition: Resources for Teachers*, edited by Cynthia Selfe, 1–12. Cresskill, NJ: Hampton, 2007.
Trimbur, John. "Essayist Literacy and the Rhetoric of Deproduction." *Rhetoric Review* 9 (1990): 72–86.
Yancey, Kathleen Blake. "Made Not Only in Words: Composition in a New Key." *College Composition and Communication* 56, no. 2 (2004): 297–328.
Yus, Francisco. 2019. "Multimodality in Memes: A Cyberpragmatic Approach." In *Analyzing Digital Discourse*, edited by Patrica Bou-Franch and Pilar Garcés-Conejos Blitvich, 105–31. Cham, Switzerland: Palgrave Macmillan, 2019.

SECTION FOUR

Writing Our Way Back

10
A FUTURE WITHOUT THESIS STATEMENTS

Hannah J. Rule

If we want our writing students to powerfully deploy their literacies to change the world, then one thing we must do is stop teaching thesis statements. We must imagine our pedagogical futures without them.

Thesis statements may feel far from an urgent ill to address. But, put simply, they are a highly visible instructional entity with too much baggage. Confronting that baggage can, if indirectly, move us toward a future for composition that is less trenchant and oversimplified and more open and connected to the worlds of the writers we work with. Instructional hyper-focus on the thesis statement blocks us from what we could be.

In my charge to dismiss the thesis statement, I follow the lead of Adam Banks, who in his 2015 Conference on College Composition and Communication (CCCC) address ceremonially retires the academic essay to the status of "Dominant Genre Emeritus."[1] Joking in a direct address to the essay that "we still love you," Banks allows that essays metaphorically keep their office, as they still have certain rhetorical affordances.[2] It's just that we must finally recognize that those affordances are far from all-encompassing. Banks knows that if we're going to "fly"—if we are going to enact cultural relevance and also attempt to match the pace of technological and writing change[3]—we must relinquish our default attachment to the essay as collective modus operandi. The essay, and so too the thesis statement, is far from the only option we have and need.

My call in this chapter is not a matter of nuance or qualification. It's more a deconstructive exercise, bordering on manifesto. It is also, though, not an accusation. Certainly, nuanced thesis statement instruction happens. And like most, I have at points surrendered to thesis statement teaching and occasionally to good end. I am also far from the first to question theses and their often associated ilk—the routine academic essay or its concentrated version, the five-paragraph theme.[4] In North

American instructional contexts, the "academic essay," the five-paragraph theme, and the thesis statement share territory. What we might critique about one, we could about all. But while most college writing teachers would likely espouse the limitations of the five-paragraph theme and while the "essay" can be deployed rhetorically and capaciously (even as it can also quickly become routine or formulaic), theses seem to endure uniquely in their formalistic certainty. They seem better at dodging scrutiny and maintaining rigid sameness. Their centrality and endurance beg the question: what if we imagined our work otherwise, and what if that work goes on without thesis statements taking center stage?

A CASE AGAINST THESIS STATEMENT LOGICS

Regardless of your current view of the thesis statement, I know one thing with near certainty: no one reading this book is wondering "what *is* a thesis statement?" Is there any other instructional entity that most every writing teacher and student in American classrooms at least knows about, is asked to practice, and maybe believes to be a cornerstone of writing? I struggle to think of one. Why are theses so enduringly represented in writing instruction in the United States?

No matter our stance, I'm sure we can each think of some reasons to put thesis statements down. Many have. For example, in a blog post that started as a footnote, Patricia Roberts-Miller appeals to published essayistic writing in the American tradition to confirm that impactful writers do not detail their argument up front and do not take only one concise sentence to do so, as textbook dictums insist. Doing so would be boring and circular, a "tell 'em what you're gonna tell 'em logic," in Roberts-Miller's words. A related problem is that thesis-forward writing isn't presented as one narrow form or a school genre. Rather, it's often trafficked as "good writing" in general. And as Roberts-Miller notes, "It isn't. No one would read the sample student introductions and think, 'Oh boy, I want to read this whole paper' unless we were being paid to read them. But we'd read King or Orwell. So, it isn't good writing—it's easy to grade writing. What I'm saying is that there is a genre ('student writing') that is not the same as writing we actually value. We're teaching students to write badly."[5]

Roberts-Miller sees thesis statements as a kind of manufactured fake. Theses don't exist in essayistic writing outside of classrooms. But they are, for some reason, nevertheless repped as key to "good" writing or at least an unavoidable "need" to succeed in college writing, such that students must spend an inordinate amount of time and focus on learning to write them. This kind of insistence serves no student writer and is especially damaging in the context of international composition, as it enforces conformity with a Euro-American discourse pattern (that perhaps none of us particularly values anyway) and creates a deficit relationship with various discourse patterns across cultures.[6] Hyper-focus on the thesis statement is out of step with the ranging strategies and styles that essayists—historical and contemporary, renowned and unknown, global and Western—deploy.

Like Roberts-Miller, I am disappointed by the priorities that thesis discourse sets. As she describes it, the tyranny of thesis statements makes a room of insightful English education students decry an essay—one that unknown to them was written by James Baldwin—because "it didn't have a summary introduction, it didn't start with a thesis, it didn't have paragraphs that began with main claims."[7] This scene alone shows us that something's terribly amiss. Thesis-focused instruction makes student writers miss the forest for the trees (or better, miss the forest due to the lack of a specific kind of tree they've been trained to look for and compose).

Other compositionists have similarly questioned the values the entrenched thesis statement enforces. For example, Virginia Perdue observed in 1992 that in light of increasing recognition of writing's sociality and meaning as negotiated rather than transmitted, composition scholarship had been questioning thesis statement instruction on the grounds of its limitations, hierarchical structuring, and commitment to provability and certainty.[8] However, such critique seemingly failed to penetrate the writing textbook. Closely reading three prominent textbooks as representative of current thesis guidance,[9] Perdue finds the doggedly traditional. For instance, she highlights Peter Elbow and Pat Belanoff's *A Community of Writers*, which overall "de-emphasizes thesis-oriented, argumentative writing."[10] Perdue observes that in spite of embodying a different paradigm, Elbow and Belanoff still include discussion of theses in a manner "that relies on our traditional understanding" without much question as to their nature or function, implying that the inclusion of theses was precipitated more by obligation to the expected than by their rhetorical fitness.[11] Overall, based on this and similar findings in other textbooks, Perdue undermines thesis instruction for its "rigidity," as well as its "powerful restrictions" on writers' subjects, stances, procedures, reader relationships, and critical thought.[12]

Similarly and more than a decade later, Anne Berggren details how thesis statements rocketed into her orbit only when she began to work in composition studies. While she says she does her best to ignore them—especially as she had never previously thought of them in her work in secondary education English and history, newspapers, publishing, medical writing, or law—she reports that about a third of students visiting the writing center where she works come in asking for help crafting a thesis statement, with most insisting that it must appear at the end of any essay's first paragraph.[13] This leads Berggren to wonder why we've committed ourselves to theses and from where such allegiance comes.

Berggren turns to the internet, which yields results that are not surprising but still illustrative: at her time of writing, *thesis statement* got almost 200,000 hits, with repetitious guidance geared to fifth graders on up to college students. The majority of first results, like today, are from university writing centers, where the advice on the thesis is unquestioningly treated "as the default mode in college writing."[14] In terms of an origin story, Berggren finds some connections dating back to Quintilian's theses as general questions or eighteenth-century textbooks' focus on "propositions."[15] Our modern sense of the thesis statement begins to appear in textbooks from the 1940s, she finds. Certain factors might have then encouraged the form's sedimentation: the GI Bill, a (still) mostly contingent teaching labor force without much rhetorical training, broad scientific orientations dominating the academy, or the rise of standardized testing in the 1980s.

Following Berggren's instincts, I too went online, where freely available instructional materials continue to garner allegiance to the thesis statement as a cornerstone of writing in college. To begin, my search for *thesis statement* now generates 9.78 million hits (which, granted, may say more about the growth of the internet than about the state of the thesis statement). Eager to find variation in this morass of advice, I began trying different search terms but found largely sameness and surety instead. When I search "stop writing thesis statements," results give me content such as "How to Make a Good Thesis Statement" or "Developing a Thesis Statement" or "Tips on Writing a Thesis Statement." When I search "thesis statements are bad," I get mostly pointers on bad thesis statements versus good ones. "Alternatives to thesis statements" similarly gets no on-target results. In other words, it's hard to locate any evidence of critique or awareness of the limitations of thesis statements even when you're looking for it.

I also engaged in some informal distanced reading methods to get a sense of the most recurring qualities and descriptions of thesis statements circulating today.[16] I collated the content of the first eight hits from a general search for "thesis statement" and, using a Wordle tool, generated the word cloud visualization shown in figure 10.1. This simple visualization strategy renders keyword repetition, which I compared and

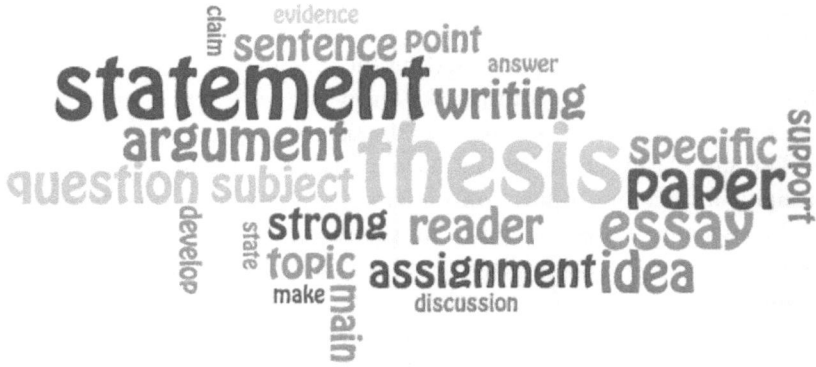

Figure 10.1. A word cloud visualization, created using Wordle.com, of text copied from eight websites related to thesis statements. Author photo.

contrasted to close reading across and beyond the set of resources on the thesis that I began with.

Beyond the most recurring terms (like paper, essay, argument, writing), I notice "sentence" standing out in the Wordle. Indeed, most every resource I encountered offers two bedrock qualities represented by this word: first, *a thesis is one sentence* (or, in very few cases, two). What this sentence is supposed to do varies, although all tasks described for it are tall orders (e.g., "state your point of view on the topic directly"). The second solidified characteristic is location. *Theses are delivered at the beginning*, either at the end of the essay's first paragraph or at the end of the introduction, which most often seems to be the exact same place.

Thesis sentences should also be "specific," a descriptor of near equivalent recurrence in the Wordle as "sentence." Specificity in part seems to convey what a thesis *shouldn't* be: it shouldn't be vague or general but specific. Specificity is also related to qualities of *control* and *connection*. For control, the thesis is to set limits on what the essay will say "without wandering," as one source put it. The thesis should enact control over the whole, summarize exactly what a reader should expect, provide a precise "roadmap," or limit the scope of the topic or relative size of the essay (or, said differently, present only one main idea, not multiple ideas). Specificity is also advised to promote seamless connections or confirming relationships between the controlling idea and its evidence. This baked-in control reflects Ian Barnard's description of the airtightness anticipated by thesis statements. Writing about deconstructing authorial intent, Barnard says: "A successful thesis statement is supposed to signal the writer's fully realized intent applied retroactively to a complete text, showing that the student writer has managed every detail of the text by marshalling it in the service of the thesis statement. Often the thesis statement is presented at the beginning of the text, even though it cannot be accounted for until after the text's end, thereby completing the ruse of pre-meditated mastery."[17]

The circularity described by Barnard is reflected in this seemingly straightforward, but in fact contradictory, description from one source: "A thesis statement is a sentence that sums up the central point of your paper or essay. It usually comes near the end of your introduction." A summary is, of course, a rehash, customarily delivered at the end of something. But the thesis-driven essay form makes writers start and end readers in the same place—a logic Paul Heilker calls "paradoxical," as it "begins with where is has already ended; it introduces the topic with its conclusion, it opens with airtight closure."[18]

Sometimes online resources do acknowledge that theses should respond to their rhetorical situations, but formalistic requirements often quickly override these concerns. For example, one source emphasizes that there are different kinds of theses depending on what an essay aims to do. But the same source then undermines those differences, extolling that "the thesis statement should always clearly state the main idea you want to get across. Everything else in your essay should relate back to this idea." Revision or development is also sometimes acknowledged, but most often in relation to taking the time to get the formula right or recognizing the long discovery and research process necessary to get to that controlled, one-sentence statement ("A thesis is the result of a lengthy thinking process"). Rhetorical purpose and process get flattened by the commitment to theses' formal, observable features.

Thesis-first instruction would seem to devalue, even ignore, the reader as a priority. So while the mention of readers in these thesis guides is somewhat surprising, how they are constructed isn't. In many of these resources, thesis statement readers are largely there to ensure that it's easy to glean the writer's "point." In other words, invoked readers in these guides are not complex or hard to engage. What they are said to want is precise and always already anticipatory of thesis logics. For example, "Readers need to be able to see that your paper has one main point" (do they?) or an essay needs a good thesis to "provide your reader with a 'guide' to your argument" (is that exactly what readers need? And is that even what theses do?). One sentence in particular stuck out to me for the ways it subs a blanket appeal to readers in general for a very specific kind of expectation for a specific breed of school writing: "Almost all of us—even if we don't do it consciously—look early in an essay for a one- or two-sentence condensation of the argument or analysis that is to follow." While I appreciate the modeling of imagining how readers read, I wonder: who is this "us" and why are we on this specific errand? Is reading an essay really about scanning for its one-sentence key?

To be sure, the meager scope of my distant and close reading can't guarantee I'm representing things accurately. Too, it's difficult and inadvisable to claim anything with rock-solid certainty—though, ironically, that is more or less what we ask thesis statement writers to do. Gary A. Olson has linked this repetitious request to declare and support with a composition's devotion to the "rhetoric of assertion." In more ways than one, he observes, "composing (at least the way it is often taught) has always seemed to be associated with asserting something to be true. Students are instructed to write an essay, which has usually meant to take a position on a subject (often stated in a 'strong,' 'clear' thesis statement, which is itself expressed in the form of an assertion), and to construct a piece of discourse that then 'supports' the position."[19] Olson finds the rhetoric of assertion to be "masculinist, phallogocentric, foundationalist, often essentialist, and, at the very least, limiting."[20] Allegiance to assertion, embodied by thesis statements, encourages all the wrong instincts. Perdue, for example, sees one such instinct as an overvaluation of authority and defense. We make the thesis the beginning and "endpoint of discussion, the central point which writers must defend and support with assertiveness and certainty."[21] Any complications, curiosity, qualifications, questions, or abandoned attempts all happen "offstage," if they happen at all. The only work for the writer to do in thesis-first writing is to stop questioning their statement and instead "argue for its truth or validity" by proffering support that confirms it.[22]

Alec R. Duxbury dramatizes this dynamic in a familiar way. He writes of the experience of "Charlie," a student taking up an assignment that asks for an interpretive reading of a literary character.[23] The prompt asks him to first craft a strong thesis statement, which will guide the selection of illustrative examples.[24] Charlie chooses to focus on Iago, believing the character to be obviously evil. But when Charlie goes looking for specific textual support, he begins to question his initial stance, finding contradiction and ambivalence in the text instead. Ultimately, Duxbury's story goes, Charlie flees this difficulty and enacts what's easiest (and to boot, what's asked for in the prompt): take and offer only the bits of text that support his initial read. Always better to change the examples than the thesis. The thesis, after all, must come first. The thesis game is a performance of controlled mastery secured by the deployment of tightly connected "support."[25]

You could well be thinking that Charlie will learn his lesson: he'll learn that a thesis doesn't stand unchanged, that good writers modify them given new information or research. But that doesn't get the prompt and the entire thesis-first enterprise off the hook. Why are we (over)valuing assertion in the first place? And why are we telling Charlie to do something so he'll learn not to do it like that?

Certainty, authority, unqualified connections between statement and support—when we pile these qualities into the admonition that writers hyper-focus on their thesis, for Duxbury it means "there is no room for curiosity and sense of self."[26] That's a problem, and it's just the beginning of the danger. Andrew C. Smith suggests that a focus on theses sends a misleading message about easy answers in general: "Overemphasizing the importance of a thesis to students can make plausible to them an idea that often turns out to be false: that it is sufficient to consider answers to difficult questions in terms of a single idea or a single sentence."[27] Those things we need writing to address, Smith says, including the "problems of our time—those of conflict and peace, international development, poverty, human rights and justice, energy and sustainable development"—simply cannot be addressed with "simple answers."[28] At my most skeptical, I know the warrant for commitments to say-and-support-only-one-idea is that we believe students' ideas must "start" simple before they can be complex or, worse, that students cannot possibly make a dent in complex issues. How cynical.

Too, overemphasizing the thesis statement encourages equivalent commitment to ideas that may or may not be interesting or even true. As Ed White satirically writes, you can ask whether God exists in a thesis-driven essay so long as you "say yes and give three reasons or no and give three different reasons."[29] Charlie did something like this: offer only confirming support and ignore the rest. Even more egregious, students are often asked to turn in a honed thesis statement before they've done any research, reconsideration, or learning and discovery.[30] I have often heard tell of frantic writing students asking librarians to help them find three pieces of support for the thesis they have already written. Pursuing the charade of always-already certainty, in all of these cases, the fundamental question driving thesis statement logics too easily becomes "what can I say that I can support."[31]

What might be worst of all is that thesis logics do not just control school writing. They seem to leak into practices that affect information literacy: airtight perspectives declared require just a little "evidence" to stay steadfast, immovable. Just look to social media. In a way, there, thesis statements pile on top of one another in comments. "Evidence" is demanded. Single links are provided. Repeat. Confirm what you've already asserted. Repeat. Berggren similarly wonders if generations trained on the thesis statement come to expect an obviousness in what they read, not just in what they write (for school). If the argument is implied or spreads in claims and suggestion across a work "rather than stated succinctly at the end of the first paragraph, students can't figure out what it is."[32] Berggren worries about a culture of preference for the simple over the nuanced, about the "course of history" when "a generation of citizens has internalized the school ideal that all good writing begins with a thesis statement."[33] It doesn't take much to realize that the consequences of such lessons are dangerous and counter to our values. So, how can writing instruction and its discourse stop encouraging this?

A FUTURE BEYOND THESIS STATEMENTS

After unpacking the ideology of authority baked into thesis statements and wondering why we routinely ask first-year college students to "be so certain so soon," Virginia Perdue asks, "Should we abandon the thesis altogether?"[34] Her answer is quick and somewhat surprising: "Obviously not."

It's interesting that Perdue poses this question as a precipice, a turning point, then retracts it. I think her response to her own question embodies the hold thesis statements have in composition. Although we can argue strongly against them, we probably still need them, Perdue relents. She does give one reason for rejecting their dismissal—namely, that a thesis statement is a "useful tool of argument" even if not as depicted in freshman rhetorics.[35] I'm skeptical of this defense. Are thesis statements key to effective argumentation? Although it may be good to practice forging connections between claims and evidence, does good argument reliably or even ever proceed from stating one's entire position in one sentence at the end of the first paragraph?

Instead of elaborating on why we can't abandon thesis statements (I guess obviousness doesn't need reasons), Perdue posits a quick alternative vision, a charge to "reassign value to writing which articulates the most thoughtful questions, not necessarily the most certain answers."[36] This call echoes almost exactly Gary Olson's call that compositionists finally "move away from a discourse of mastery and assertion toward a more dialogic, dynamic, open-ended, receptive, nonassertive stance."[37] Two decades since, and I believe most compositionists would cosign their vision. But have we collectively moved away from the assertion and support model? I'm afraid, not really. So, how do we finally get free of the rhetoric of assertion embodied in thesis statement routines?

Adam Banks offers one path to start. Uniting Black rhetorical traditions with the dynamics of digital communication, Banks raises the dynamic figure of Legba, "the ultimate linguist in Afrodiasporic oral traditions . . . presented as a guardian of mythic crossroads and skilled in all languages."[38] For Banks, Legba embodies active synthesis at intersections—those of past, present, and future; of tradition and transformation; of self/other; of multiple languages of people and of spaces. Banks imagines Legba as the contemporary DJ, engaging the praxes of mix, remix, and mixtape that serve as "tropes for critical writing practices."[39] To exercise mix, for one example, Banks details a Pecha Kucha–style presentation that serves as an end-of-course reflection. He asks students to present exactly twenty quotes from their course readings, a task that necessitates intensive consideration of arrangement as communicative and inventional. Banks asks, "How should they show the connections they have made across readings and class discussions? How should they demonstrate the shifts in their own thinking? How might they let other students know what was most compelling for them?"[40]

While Banks sometimes asks for an accompanying narrative of how and why students made the choices they did, more key to this exercise is whole class sharing. As one presentation after another is shared, repetition of similar quotes used differently becomes iteration, an embodied enaction of call and response that demonstrates the rhetorical power of collective, multiplied takes over any individual's alone (even as each individual presentation is, of course, in the first place built from others' words. It's remix all the way down). Banks writes, "The iterative playing of different elements of the course discussions and readings through different versions of slideshows helps a collective take on the ideas of the course come together, where students see multiple possibilities for playing within and without that collective take, and the signifying repetition, the repetition with differences, of many versions can make central ideas of a course more memorable."[41]

The sociality and rigor of this exercise exceed other tools we routinely deploy for reflection, like a written summary of takeaways at the start of a final portfolio or a "tired, retired, term paper type essay."[42] Such an activity is just one part of Banks's paradigm of contemporary (student) writers as "DJs with words and ideas,"[43] an approach that at once pre- and postdates the narrow college essayistic Euro-American tradition we remain steadfastly committed to. The writer-as-DJ exercises the creativity of arrangement, the flexible repurposing of discourses in order to connect with diverse communities and literate spaces, and the nimble navigation of information networks, cultures, and communicative spaces that are global and digital.[44]

Banks evidences what the entrenchment of the schooled essay routine occludes: otherwiseness. Other rich, long-standing (but in some spaces overlooked), and cutting-edge traditions and ways of being and doing composition. It doesn't feel crucial to me to have contemporary writers in our classrooms pretend to be hermetically sealed soliloquists, declaring their assertions while standing on a stage alone. But it does seem vital that they practice harnessing the kinetic energies of the dance floor, responding to the all-around-them "challenges of communication when anything can be copied, pasted, sampled, shared."[45]

My targeting of thesis statements also has to do with broader thinking about the entire enterprise of college writing pedagogy. The biggest problems in our practices of writing in school often come down to the *school* part. Just think of all the things school has made us do to writing. School has made us "test" writing in artificial conditions; assign letter grades to it; deem it proficient or not; "correct" it; deploy a single attempt at it as a placement tool predictive of general skills and instructional needs. It has made us pretend that "Standard English" is monolithic, stable, identifiable, and one thing; deem as less than certain language expression associated with cultural and racial identities in favor of enforcing that so-called standard; create a required class that promises to teach "how to write" for all of college and possibly life (as if that's possible. And as if learning to write—something we do anew to some extent each time—isn't happening all the time, everywhere, forever). The force of school has also made us insist that writers say their whole "argument" in one sentence upfront and that doing so is characteristic of (college) writing as a whole.

We should un-school writing. I'm not talking about writing without teachers per se but shifting the question of writing pedagogy itself. The question should no longer, if ever, be how we can best "teach writing." We should ask instead how we can help writers discover what writing is—what it does and how it does it in myriad ways. I'm talking about basing composition pedagogy not in school but in our worlds (including school), about approaching writing as a human phenomenon and technology that rolls on in different ways, fitting itself to differing rhetorical needs regardless of whether the writing teacher is there. I'm talking kind of about writing about writing or about rhetorical genre approaches.[46] I'm thinking of authentic writing instruction and what compels us to write anything at all. I'm talking about relinquishing narrowness and the charade that that narrowness is "writing" itself. As many have, I am troubling the notion that something called general "academic discourse" or isolated general writing skills even exists and that thesis statements are supposedly integral to them.[47] I'm talking about something like Matthew Overstreet's principle of "generative combination" (chapter 9, this volume), which positions writers to make the decisions about how best to deploy their literacy resources to meet a communicative situation. I am aligning with the many who have argued for helping writers discern among and approximate myriad academic discourses across the university (but more than just university discourse, let's shoot for the entire *universe*).[48] Recognizing writing's situatedness and differences—a focus on how writing works more than on how to do it "well" in some sort of general or universal way—is key to composition's futures.

I hope that someday schooled thesis statements are not our feature act, far from our greatest hit. My point has not really been that writing students never again write so-called thesis statements. My point is that they stop doing so mechanistically, automatically, routinely, each time with the same approach, or under the misleading sense that the thesis statement is forever "how college writing is." So, let's un-monolith the thesis statement. Let's finally put it in its place—as one kind of option among the infinity of options available in writing in the world.

NOTES

1. Banks, "2015 CCCC Chair's Address."
2. Banks, "2015 CCCC Chair's Address," 273.
3. Banks, "Dominant Genre Emeritus," 179.
4. For example, see Brannon et al., "The Five-Paragraph Essay"; Waite, "How (and Why) to Write Queer," 46; Xu, Huang, and You, "Reasoning Patterns of Undergraduate Theses," 69.
5. Roberts-Miller, "Thesis Statements."
6. See Mao, "Thinking through Difference," 105; You, Writing in the Devil's Tongue, 26.
7. Roberts-Miller, "Thesis Statements."
8. Perdue, "Authority and the Freshman Writer," 135.
9. Perdue, "Authority and the Freshman Writer," 136.
10. Perdue, "Authority and the Freshman Writer," 138.
11. Perdue, "Authority and the Freshman Writer," 138.
12. Perdue, "Authority and the Freshman Writer," 141, 138.
13. Berggren, "Do Thesis Statements Short-Circuit Originality," 55.
14. Berggren, "Do Thesis Statements Short-Circuit Originality," 55.
15. Berggren, "Do Thesis Statements Short-Circuit Originality," 57.
16. I elect to not cite or name specific sources from which the quotes and discussion come. I'm not interested in critiquing specific content related to theses but rather in confirming a sense of their advice as it recurs across freely available sources. Should readers wish to access the specific content from which I pull quotes, searching the quotes should suffice.
17. Barnard, "Authorial Intent in the Composition Classroom," n.p.

18. Heilker, *The Essay*, 4.
19. Olson, "Toward a Post-Process Composition," 9.
20. Olson, "Toward a Post-Process Composition," 9.
21. Perdue, "Authority and the Freshman Writer," 138.
22. Perdue, "Authority and the Freshman Writer," 139.
23. Duxbury, "Speaking My Mind," 16.
24. This promise of ease and order echoes exactly in an entirely different context: Wilson's "Aphorisms on Thesis Statements," the second of which is "Having a Good Thesis Makes Writing a Paper Easy: Everything else falls into place once you've got a well-thought-out, well-written thesis."
25. Olson, "Toward a Post-Process Composition," 9.
26. Duxbury, "Speaking My Mind," 18.
27. Smith, "Speaking My Mind," 97.
28. Smith, "Speaking My Mind," 99.
29. White, "My Five-Paragraph Theme Theme," 525.
30. Trenouth, "Speaking My Mind," 18.
31. Berggren, "Do Thesis Statements Short-Circuit Originality," 60.
32. Berggren, "Do Thesis Statements Short-Circuit Originality," 59.
33. Berggren, "Do Thesis Statements Short-Circuit Originality," 59.
34. Perdue, "Authority and the Freshman Writer," 140.
35. Perdue, "Authority and the Freshman Writer," 141.
36. Perdue, "Authority and the Freshman Writer," 141.
37. Olson, "Toward a Post-Process Composition," 14.
38. Banks, "Dominant Genre Emeritus," 183.
39. Banks, "Dominant Genre Emeritus," 184.
40. Banks, "Dominant Genre Emeritus," 186.
41. Banks, "Dominant Genre Emeritus," 186.
42. Banks, "Dominant Genre Emeritus," 186.
43. Banks, "Dominant Genre Emeritus," 184.
44. See Banks, "Dominant Genre Emeritus," 183.
45. Banks, "Dominant Genre Emeritus," 184.
46. See Downs and Wardle, "Teaching about Writing." I say "kind of" writing about writing (WAW) because I don't mean to emphasize introducing students to the discipline of writing studies and rhetoric but rather WAW's effort to help students see writing as a site of inquiry and situated practice.
47. See, for example, Crowley, *Composition in the University*, 28; Downs and Wardle, "Teaching about Writing"; Petraglia, *Reconceiving Writing*; Royster, "Academic Discourses."
48. See, for example, Lindemann, "Freshman Composition"; Russell, *Writing in the Academic Disciplines*.

REFERENCES

Banks, Adam. "Dominant Genre Emeritus: Why It's Time to Retire the Essay." *CLA Journal* 60, no. 2 (2016): 179–90.

Banks, Adam. "2015 CCCC Chair's Address: Ain't No Walls behind the Sky, Baby! Funk, Flight, Freedom." *CCC* 67, no. 2 (2015): 267–79.

Barnard, Ian. "Authorial Intent in the Composition Classroom." *Composition Forum* 24 (Fall 2011): n.p. https://compositionforum.com/issue/24/authorial-intent.php.

Berggren, Anne. "Do Thesis Statements Short-Circuit Originality in Students' Writing?" In *Originality, Imitation, and Plagiarism: Teaching Writing in the Digital Age*, edited by Caroline Eisner and Martha Vicinus, 53–63. Ann Arbor: University of Michigan Press, 2008.

Brannon, Lil, Jennifer Pooler Courtney, Cynthia P. Urbanski, Shana V. Woodward, Jeanie Marklin Reynolds, Anthony E. Iannone, Karen D. Haag, Karen Mach, Lacy Arnold Manship, and Mary Kendrick. "The Five-Paragraph Essay and the Deficit Model of Education." *English Journal* 98, no. 2 (2008): 16–21.

Crowley, Sharon. *Composition in the University: Historical and Polemical Essays*. Pittsburgh: University of Pittsburgh Press, 1998.

Downs, Doug, and Elizabeth Wardle. "Teaching about Writing, Righting Misconceptions: (Re)Envisioning First-Year Composition." *College Composition and Communication* 58, no. 4 (2007): 552–84.

Duxbury, Alec R. "Speaking My Mind: The Tyranny of the Thesis Statement." *English Journal* 97, no. 4 (2008): 16–18.

Heilker, Paul. *The Essay: Theory and Pedagogy for an Active Form*. Urbana, IL: National Council of Teachers of English, 1996.

Lindemann, Erica. "Freshman Composition: No Place for Literature." *College English* 55 (1993): 311–16.

Mao, LuMing. "Thinking through Difference and Facts of Nonusage: A Dialogue between Comparative Rhetoric and Translingualism." *Across the Disciplines* 15, no. 3 (2018): 103–13. https://doi.org/10.37514/ATD-J.2018.15.3.15.

Olson, Gary A. "Toward a Post-Process Composition: Abandoning the Rhetoric of Assertion." In *Post-Process Theory: Beyond the Writing-Process Paradigm*, edited by Thomas Kent, 7–15. Carbondale: Southern Illinois University Press, 1999.

Perdue, Virginia. "Authority and the Freshman Writer: The Ideology of the Thesis Statement." *Writing Instructor* 11, no. 3 (1992): 135–42.

Petraglia, Joseph. *Reconceiving Writing, Rethinking Writing Instruction*. New York: Routledge, 1995.

Roberts-Miller, Patricia. "Thesis Statements, Topic Sentences, and 'Good' Writing," April 2020. https://www.patriciarobertsmiller.com/2020/04/03/thesis-statements-topic-sentences-and-good-writing/.

Royster, Jacqueline Jones. "Academic Discourses or Small Boats on a Big Sea." In *ALT/DIS: Alternative Discourses and the Academy*, edited by Christopher Schroeder, Helen Fox, and Patricia Bizzell, 23–30. Portsmouth, NH: Heinemann, 2002.

Russell, David R. *Writing in the Academic Disciplines, 1870–1990: A Curricular History*. Carbondale: Southern Illinois University Press, 1991.

Smith, Andrew C. "Speaking My Mind: Going Beyond the Thesis." *English Journal* 99, no. 6 (2010): 97–99.

Trenouth, Peter. "Speaking My Mind: Heroic Teaching and Writing." *English Journal* 93, no. 1 (2003): 17–18.

Waite, Stacey. "How (and Why) to Write Queer: A Failing, Impossible, Contradictory Instruction Manual for Scholars of Writing Studies." In *Re/Orienting Writing Studies: Queer Methods, Queer Projects*, edited by William P. Banks, Matthew B. Cox, and Caroline Dadas, 42–53. Logan: Utah State University Press, 2019.

White, Ed. "My Five-Paragraph Theme Theme." *College Composition and Communication* 59, no. 3 (2008): 524–25.

Wilson, Jeffrey R. "Aphorisms on Thesis Statements," 2021. https://wilson.fas.harvard.edu/aphorisms/thesis-statements.

Xu, Mianjun, Chenchen Huang, and Xiaoye You. "Reasoning Patterns of Undergraduate Theses in Translation." *English for Specific Purposes* 41 (2016): 68–81.

You, Xiaoye. *Writing in the Devil's Tongue: A History of English Composition in China*. Carbondale: Southern Illinois University Press, 2010.

11
TEACHING TOWARD A MORE JUST CITATION PRACTICE

Elizabeth Kleinfeld

I recently noticed that my 2006 dissertation is nearly entirely white. I am white, all four of my case studies are white, and only three of the ninety-seven sources I cited are by authors I can readily identify as scholars of color. My committee was also entirely white. In 2006, none of my committee members or peers thought to bring the whiteness of my dissertation to my attention because it was simply typical. The very fact that someone who has been paying attention to the politics of citation for several years would not notice until 2021 that their dissertation was so white is an example of how normalized this level of whiteness is in composition and rhetoric scholarship, practice, and pedagogy. Another example of how normalized this level of whiteness is is the fact that a reader of a draft of this chapter gave me props for acknowledging my dissertation's whiteness. Sara Ahmed notes that documenting your own racism as evidence of your anti-racism is an example of "the non-performativity of anti-racism."[1] Note, too, that Ahmed's observation was published in 2004, my dissertation was completed in 2006, and here we are, seventeen years later, and I have yet to be held accountable for the whiteness of my dissertation or most of my subsequent scholarship or even had it remarked upon in any way by a peer reviewer, editor, colleague, or conference session attendee.

I begin with the whiteness of my dissertation, first, to illustrate what an unjust citation practice looks like and, second, to demonstrate just how normalized this practice is. I want to juxtapose my own unjust citation practice with Eric Darnell Pritchard's citation practice in his 2016 book *Fashioning Lives: Black Queers and the Politics of Literacy*.[2] The book begins with eight pages of acknowledgments, thanking everyone who contributed in some way to the ideas in the book, from librarians to colleagues to friends and mentors. To meticulously identify every single person who has impacted one's thinking at the level Pritchard has indicates a profound understanding of the social and collaborative nature of scholarship and knowledge construction. The lengthy acknowledgments are demonstrative of an argument Pritchard makes in a post on Carmen Kynard's blog: giving meaningful credit goes beyond simple citation; it entails engaging deeply with source material and respecting the power and privilege differences cited scholars experience.[3] In the book, Pritchard articulates the concept of literacy normativity as "the creation of discourses that marginalize, ostracize, and condemn people for their identities and other ways of being."[4] It is this literacy normativity that enabled the whiteness of my dissertation and subsequent scholarship to go unremarked upon.

The availability of people of color in the pool of potential dissertation committee members, potential case studies in my classes, and potential scholars to write articles and books I might cite is impacted by systems in place that work to maintain whiteness in academia. I mention this not to defend the whiteness of my dissertation, which is indefensible, but to point out the systemic nature of racism and other forms of oppression that make it appear that its whiteness is a result of a lack of available case studies, committee members, and sources by people of color. In fact, it is a result of a complex set of pedagogies and normalized practices embedded in a racist institution.

In this chapter, I examine source citation practices and pedagogy through the lens of Pritchard's concept of literacy normativity. I argue that traditional citation practice and pedagogy are ableist, racist, and patriarchal—not only presenting sources as being about ideas that are separate from the embodiment of the authors who articulate them but, through their reliance on the cloak of neutrality, actually rendering invisible the work and intellectual labor of marginalized authors. Building on work by Eve Tuck, K. Wayne Yang, and Ruben Gaztambide-Fernandez, Brittany Williams and Joan Collier, and Kate Marston,[5] this chapter challenges the idea that source citation can ever be neutral and aims to disrupt existing practices and pedagogies, exposing assumptions that inform current citation pedagogies and make them appear "natural" or "commonsensical."[6] I argue that we must as a field move away from presenting source citation as a matter of replicating formats and established voices and toward a practice of source citation that allows writers to further their own purposes and be accountable for them. As an example and model, I describe an assignment that asks students to formulate a citation policy for their final research project and reflect upon the implementation of that policy.

To highlight the normative hegemony this chapter aims to resist, I want to make my citation practice for the chapter explicit. While I explain here the intention of my citation practice, I also acknowledge that there will likely be unintended consequences of my practice, and I take responsibility for those unintended consequences—regardless of whether they are aligned with my intentions—and seek to repair harm done by any inadequate acknowledgment of sources and influences. Throughout this chapter, I use full names of authors the first time I mention them. The practice of naming authors by only their last name obscures gender and ethnicity, gives a false sense of neutrality, and ultimately contributes to a hierarchy in which white, male authors are referred to by last name only and their female or minoritized peers are referred to by their full names. In a piece for the online magazine *Slate*, Chris White explains how the practice of identifying famous music composers by last name only creates a hierarchy in which the composers who are identified that way are understood to be the really important ones and composers identified by full name are understood to be lesser ones.[7] White's point is that the way we refer to composers (and others) can entrench or resist hierarchies of valuing humans and their contributions that are built into our systems. I have deliberately cited scholars of color, scholars who identify as women or queer, and disabled scholars where I can. I acknowledge that I likely missed many opportunities to cite these scholars, and I welcome critiques of my citation practice in this chapter.

Many before me have argued for a more ethical citation practice. In fact, Pritchard notes exactly this when he reflects on a conversation with scholar Carmen Kynard about how "the imperative to develop an ethical and dogged practice of honoring the intellectual and emotional labor of people of color in rhetoric and composition and beyond" is not a new conversation and that he and others have called for it before.[8] Kynard reminded Pritchard that he has "been writing this critique for a LONG TIME because this bullshit is so constant and unrelenting." If we are serious as a discipline in upending systemic oppression, we need to do more than nod our heads in agreement when Pritchard, Kynard, and others say this and examine our own citation practices and pedagogies, be accountable for the harm they have done, and commit to changing them.

CITATION AS A SITE OF OPPRESSION

Unless we make this commitment and undertake the arduous work it entails, the way citation is currently taught will continue because the apparatus around citation pedagogy—our own citation practices, textbook treatment of citation, and online resources for citation—does not support change. Citation hegemony is well embedded in higher education, leading to inherited pedagogies. Until very recently, I taught source citation the way it was taught to me. I cited sources in my dissertation the way my mentors cited sources in their work. This is the normative literacy hegemony Pritchard discusses.

Jaqueline Jones Royster points out that the status quo always reinforces itself, remarking that "disciplinary practices have built up a high intolerance to the assigning of value and credibility to any site, focal point, theory, or practice other than those whose contours are already sanctioned historically within the circle of understanding."[9] Royster reminds us that knowledge is always interpretation.[10] We teach our students this when it comes to the knowledge claims of the sources they use, but we do not teach them this about their citations. We selectively apply the concept that knowledge is always interpretation, emphasizing that students should understand their sources as making knowledge claims rather than stating facts but then ignoring the mechanisms through which some authors are deemed more cite-worthy than others, as if there is no interpretation and thus no bias involved in creating knowledge about who the "big names" to be cited are. Royster notes that for change to happen, a discourse community must be convinced (1) "to notice," (2) "to incorporate" what they noticed, and (3) "to use [the knowledge] meaningfully."[11]

A barrier to simply taking that first step of noticing is the status quo itself, which normalizes itself again and again through repetition. We don't tend to notice citation practices as political because in college and graduate school, we inherit knowledge about who to cite. In first-year writing classes, we focus our attention on the mechanics of citation: the formatting of the works cited list, the punctuation of quotations, the crafting of a decent paraphrase. Those of us who teach composition have internalized these practices of knowledge production, and we pass them on to our students.

Several scholars have called for an examination of how source citations actively reproduce inequality. Paula Chakravartty, Rachel Kuo, Victoria Grubbs, and Charlton McIlwain's study of citational patterns in communication, "#CommunicationSoWhite," was motivated by noticing—Royster's first step in working toward change—a lack of BIPOC voices in communications scholarship.[12] The authors found that communication scholarship was, as the hashtag in their title makes clear, "so white," with longtime entrenched citation practices "produc[ing] a hierarchy of visibility and value." Because authority, expertise, and other qualities that lead to publication are associated with whiteness, work by white scholars is more likely to demonstrate these attributes. They further note that because white scholars are more likely to be cited, they are more likely to publish, leading inevitably to more citations of white scholars.[13] It is a self-reinforcing mechanism: the higher citation rates for white authors lead to even higher citation rates for white authors. Harry G. Rolf elaborates: "The number of citations that a publication receives is often used as a proxy for measuring its importance, so the practice of citing another's work can affect how certain groups are represented and included or excluded from a scholarly community."[14] This impact on the perception of groups of scholars is an example of Pritchard's literacy normativity, which he notes is used by "institutions and individuals . . . to construct historical narratives that exclude Black queer life and contributions," as well as those of other marginalized identities.[15]

Matthew Houdek describes white supremacy as being "upheld by a taken-for-granted system that protects its own interests and beneficiaries through everyday habits and routines, most of which seem benign and unintentional to those who carry them out."[16] This taken-for-granted system skews our perceptions so we miss intentional source use and misunderstand it as error. An excellent example is taken from Malea Powell's Conference on College Composition and Communication (CCCC) address.[17] She shares Kendall Leon's story about being scolded by a scholar during a job interview for citing Chicana theorists rather than Foucault. Leon explains:

> The organization that I studied made intentional choices about what to include or omit in their archives, and he wanted me to be critical of their choices and actions, to question their intentionality.
>
> As a researcher, I was more interested in what *was* there, what those Chicanas had decided was important to include in the making of their organizational memory. And I didn't cite Foucault, whom I adore, because instead I cited Chicanas precisely because their writing, their theory, comes from a place that, as Cherrie Moraga writes, is emergent from the "physical realities of our lives."
>
> What was lost on this scholar was the intentionality of my practice, the intentionality in citation, in making a lineage worth building upon.[18]

White supremacy makes it so the possibility that Leon did this deliberately and intentionally is not even considered and the "lack" of Foucault citations is assumed to be evidence of her unfamiliarity with the presumed necessary body of scholarship.

White hegemony is so baked into academic knowledge creation that when the Association of College and Research Libraries (ACRL) adopted revised Information Literacy Standards for Higher Education in 2016 that recognize information literacy (IL) as socially constructed, it omitted any mention of race.[19] Marcia Rapchak points out how the new standards are infused with white supremacy, in part by their refusal to name race as a bias even while explicitly naming worldviews, gender, sexual orientation, and cultural orientations.[20] Rapchak argues that the standards "emphasize neutrality, civility, and intellectual freedom" over "social justice and anti-racism," which ultimately means maintaining an understanding of IL and source citation that is "not racist"; as Ibram X. Kendi explains, "not racist" is equal to not pushing back against racism or upholding the status quo, which is racism.[21] Rapchak—and I—would prefer pedagogies that are anti-racist, actively working to dismantle racism.

Citation campaigns and policies directly challenge the idea that citation is unbiased and that oft-cited sources are the "best" ones. Citation campaigns call attention to the political aspects of citation and how our citation practices contribute to normalizing the idea that authority is white. Three prominent scholarly citation campaigns—Tuck, Yang, and Gaztambide-Fernandez's Citation Practices Challenge, Williams and Collier's CiteASista campaign, and Christina A. Smith's Cite Black Women campaign—invite scholars to reflect on whose work gets amplified and whose gets erased through their citation practices.[22] Citation policies make explicit the choices an author makes about who they cite. Sara Ahmed, for example, deliberately and explicitly cited only women in *Living a Feminist Life*.[23] Similarly, I articulated my own citation policy for this chapter in its opening. Were I to have stated a citation policy for my dissertation, it might have looked something like this: In this dissertation, I cite primarily white authors because through systemic racism, that's who has historically been able to attain the mantle of "authority." I have not paid the least bit of attention to the gender, sexual orientation, or able-bodiedness of my sources because although I understand patriarchy and ableism to some extent, I have not reflected meaningfully on how those forms of oppression impact who gets published and cited.

WHO'S TALKING ABOUT THE POLITICS OF CITATION—AND WHO ISN'T

The political nature and ramifications of citation practices and pedagogies are being discussed in other fields, but ironically, one of the very fields that teaches and studies the teaching of citation remains mostly quiet. I say mostly quiet because scholars of color—such as those I have already cited, Royster, Kynard, and Pritchard—have been making these points in our field and adjacent fields for years.

Other fields are way ahead of us in this reckoning. Writing about geography, Carrie Mott and Daniel Cockayne powerfully articulate that citation matters because it impacts who gets published, hired, tenured, and promoted.[24] Further, they connect a discipline's citation practices to knowledge production, noting that only citing established scholars does a disservice not only to researchers and writers who are othered by white heteromasculinism but also to the prevailing impression of geography on those who may be less familiar with the discipline—most notably, our students. Paying attention to the impact of our citation practices on our students matters because they fill the pipeline that creates new scholars. Looking at citation in geography through an anti-racist feminist lens, Mott and Cockayne note that "citation is equally a technology for reproducing sameness and excluding difference," echoing Royster's comments about the status quo reproducing itself.[25] They further push back against neoliberal ideologies that understand citation as measures of "influence and impact" and instead view citation as "a technology of power."[26] They use Butler's performance theory and the rhetorical concept of identification to elucidate how the repetition of the citation of the same sources over and over "accumulates the force of authority."[27] This is significant for classroom practice because when students learn over and over again that certain voices are more important than others, that repetition takes on "the force of authority."

When the same people with the same ideas are the ones who repeatedly get cited, it is that much harder for different people with different ideas to be cited. Margath A. Walker and Emmanuel Frimpong Boamah use network graphs to show how a small number of scholars dominate citations in critical urban studies, leading to a homogeneity of thought.[28] Similarly, in the field of communication, Andrea Press, Deb Verhoeven, Jonathan Sterne, and Vicki Mayer identify "who is cited in canonical summaries of the discipline" as a mechanism of power, maintaining as dominant the loudest voices.[29] In critical ethnic studies, Tuck and Yang call on authors to consider the politics of their citation practices, noting that "our practices of citation make and remake our fields, making some forms of knowledge peripheral. We often cite those who are more famous, even if their contributions appropriate subaltern ways of knowing."[30] Connie Russell makes a similar call in environmental education, advocating for what she calls "generous scholarship," which is similar to Pritchard's support for engagement and "give[s] credit to those who have inspired our work rather than appropriating ideas."[31] Noting the whiteness of the field of music theory, Philip A. Ewell describes the depth and breadth of white hegemony, identifying the vast majority of members of the Society for Music Theory and tenured professors of music as white, which in turn infuses music theory with white values.³²

The clear and cogent arguments presented in other disciplines have not yet created a sea change in academia, which is why the ways we in composition and rhetoric approach and teach citation matters. Beyond Royster, Kynard, Pritchard, and Houdek, few in our field seem to have noticed that citation practices are not neutral. Composition scholars Drew M. Loewe, Elizabeth Wardle, and others have publicly discussed on Twitter the need to move citation pedagogy away from a fixation on formats and toward an emphasis on the knowledge relationships they represent.³³ Darrel Wanzer-Serrano suggests that we as a field examine all of our practices, including who and how we cite, to notice "how we value certain sources of knowledge and erase or Otherize the rest."³⁴ This sweeping self-reflection as a field has not happened, but change is afoot. For example, Asao B. Inoue very publicly resigned from the Council of Writing Program Administrators over the organization's resistance to examining how white supremacy suffused its processes.³⁵

Acknowledging the weight citation holds over careers and reputations, Kelly Blewett, Christina M. LaVecchia, Laura R. Micciche, and Janine Morris describe steps they have taken as editors of the journal *Composition Studies* to resist structural inequality, including moving beyond the traditional genre of scholarly article and working closely with authors who receive revise-and-resubmit requests to increase the likelihood of publication.³⁶ In the same vein, a collective of technical communication scholars composed "Anti-Racist Scholarly Reviewing Practices: A Heuristic for Editors, Reviewers, and Authors," outlining how those involved in the peer review process can use anti-racist practices to diversify the voices and ways of knowing that are featured in scholarship; the University Press of Colorado published on its website "Our Publication Processes and Timelines," which aims to make explicit publication processes that are often shrouded in a secrecy that functions to maintain the dominance of the established voices who have already made it through the system and thus understand it.³⁷

HOW CITATION IS TAUGHT

Historically, first-year composition has been the site where students learn how to cite sources. The Citation Project, led by Sandra Jamieson and Rebecca Moore Howard, was significant in identifying what first-year writing students actually do when they cite sources; Vicki Tolar Burton and Scott A. Chadwick, Randall McClure and Kellian Clink, and others provided insight into how students go about finding sources.[38] The course syllabi and handouts I studied demonstrate that the standard way of teaching source citation is to present it as neutral, existing outside of social contexts and power relations.[39] Source citation is typically framed in terms of formatting technicalities and neoliberal ideas about idea ownership. Sources are presented as being about ideas that are separate from the embodiment of the authors who articulate them.

Those ideas are echoed in the many popular online resources students turn to for help with citing sources. The Purdue Online Writing Lab includes multiple examples of presuming neutral source citation, such as this description of scholarly journals: "Academic and trade journals contain the most up-to-date information and research in industry, business, and academia. Journal articles come in several forms, including literature reviews that overview current and past research, articles on theories and history, and articles on specific processes or research . . . [A] well-regarded journal represents the cutting-edge knowledge of experts in a particular field."[40] The concept of "a well-regarded journal" is left unexamined, with no explanation of whose regard for the journal matters or what metrics those people might use to measure the journal's worthiness. The concept of "a well-regarded journal" is assumed to be unaffected by identities, perspectives, biases, or the hegemonic values of the institutions where journals are embedded.

Other popular online materials similarly focus on helping students identify types of sources and components of citations without getting into the political nature of citations. For example, the Fraser Hall Library's website (SUNY Geneseo) has a rich section on ways to "Engage First-Year Students through Creative Citation Instruction" but never mentions the ideological or political nature of citation.[41] Similarly, the University of Michigan's Sweetland Center for Writing's student-facing material steers clear of the ideological nature of citation, focusing on the conventionally accepted idea that "authority" is a neutral concept.[42]

The Sweetland Center for Writing's faculty-facing material is more promising, stating "you might use a discussion of citation norms as an opportunity to help students become more aware of how those norms function rhetorically within your scholarly community."[43] Unfortunately, the classroom activity suggestions that follow focus on helping students identify citation conventions without unpacking the politics of citation. For example, one activity invites faculty to share their own "academic genealogy" with students, explaining "the scholars to whom you are indebted. How do you fit into a larger picture of scholarly exchange? How do you acknowledge your academic debts in your own writing?"

These questions are a great starting point for talking about the politics of citation—but failing to bring racism, sexism, and other structurally embedded systems of oppression explicitly into the discussion allows the illusion that scholarly exchange and academic debts are based purely on the merit of ideas.

WHAT CITATION REALLY DOES (WHAT CITATION PEDAGOGY SHOULD TALK ABOUT)

Citation does not merely offer credit to others who have influenced a writer's thinking. I find Amy Robillard's taxonomy of citation functions helpful because of its careful movement beyond the limiting trope of economics—giving credit and acknowledging debt—and into the realm of relationship signaling and building.[44] Building on work by Robert Connors, Shirley Rose, and Rebecca Moore Howard, Robillard identifies fourteen different functions of citations—breaking them down into two that serve the reader, five that serve the citing author, and seven that serve the author of the cited work. Of the functions Robillard explicates, several are aligned with the traditional ways citation is taught; for example, one function of citation for readers is to "provide access to source material."[45] I want to call attention to some of the functions of citation Robillard identifies that are particularly relevant to normalized whiteness of authority.

One function of citation for readers that Robillard describes is to "establish relationships among texts," borrowing from Rose that citations indicate whether sources build on, exemplify, set the ground for, or argue against other sources.[46] Looking at this function of citation through the lens of white hegemony, we can start to notice that perhaps all the sources that seem to lean in one direction are by authors who are white or male. Or we might notice that the relationships signaled by the citations indicate a very small network, which could call attention to a need to broaden the source base.

I want to elaborate on two functions of citation for the author doing the citing that Robillard identifies. "Affirm the citing author's membership and participation in a particular discourse community," when understood in the context of normalized whiteness of authority, is particularly sticky for authors of color. Think about Kendall Leon, who was quoted in Powell's Cs address, being questioned about her choice to not cite Foucault. Leon deliberately positioned herself as a member of a discourse community that values Chicanas over Foucault. At the same time, the scholar who questioned her choice did so assuming she would want to be associated with the discourse community that values Foucault over Chicanas.

Remembering that being cited leads to more citations for an author while not being cited leads to fewer citations, the impact of simply being cited becomes clear. When thinking about the function of "align[ing] a citing author with a particular school of thought,"[47] we can see that the range of schools of thought one can align themselves with will be limited by citation moves that erase scholars of color and scholars from other marginalized groups.

Robillard[48] identifies three functions of citation for authors of cited work that I think are particularly important when we consider the politics of citation: "identify and legitimate contributions to a discipline's economy,"[49] "call attention to the work of a little-known or an up-and-coming scholar," and "indicate the citing author's respect for the cited author's work." These all get at the power of a citation. When an author is cited, their work gets attention; the more attention an author's work gets, the more influence they have, the more credible they appear, and the more likely they are to be cited again in the future. The reverse is also true: the less an author is cited, the less attention their work has, the less influence they have, and the less likely they are to be cited again in the future. Powell used her own position of power to call attention to Leon's work. When we tell students that they should cite the "big names" without calling into question why those names are "big" and other names are not, we abdicate the responsibility these three functions of citation imply: building up the influence and power someone has or doesn't have. Being cited confers opportunities; not being cited deprives one of opportunities.

REMEDIES

I offer several suggestions for a citation pedagogy that pushes back against the normalized, taken-for-granted approach that presents citation as neutral and focuses on citational mechanics rather than politics. A key way our courses can help students grapple with current social and ethical questions posed by the world around them is to explicitly acknowledge source citation as ideological. This begins with rejecting the myth that peer review is free of implicit bias and that "well-regarded" journals are determined to be reliable in ways that are not entangled in normative hegemonies.

My own teaching is aligned with the conclusions of Jessica Edwards (chapter 13, this volume) that students are best able to grasp the need for inclusion measures when writing instruction plainly addresses racism. I talk with students about how the scholarly pipeline is not equally accessible to all. Recently, I have shared Sofia Leung's explanation of the barriers to people of color in Library and Information Systems (LIS) to help them understand the whiteness of scholarly pipelines:

> You need to get into a bachelors and then masters [sic] program, which use standards not meant to be met by Black and Brown folx. You need wealth to pay for those programs and we already know its [sic] harder to get loans for Black and Brown folx. You have to survive those programs, which were not built for you and which operate on white supremacy culture characteristics meant to tear you down. Then you gotta get a job, which again is based on white standards of what is considered experience, knowledge, and professionalism. Once in that job, you're expected to keep your head down, not rock the boat, continue doing things the way they've always been done, and just be fucking grateful that you got a job at all. Once we've finished funneling through this system, what do we have to believe constitutes knowledge?[50]

I use another explanation from Leung to help students understand why a person of color might decide not to put themselves through that process: "We have been told in lots of little and big ways that the very knowledge we have inherited from our families, our ancestors isn't important, is lesser than the knowledge we learn in the US education system and from the LIS profession, that our experiences as BIPOC don't matter and that no one wants to hear our stories."[51] Leung captures here that to get through the system that is designed to keep people of color out, a person of color's identity is impacted.

I have deliberately moved away from specifying how many sources students should cite, asking them to focus on the quality of their engagement with sources rather than on the quantity of sources they use.[52] I often give an assignment I'll describe shortly that engages students in exploring citation practices that push back on white literacy normativity, or I have them write acknowledgments in which they talk about why they chose particular sources. My emphasis is on making citation choices and conscientiously engaging points toward a slower research process, focusing on quality rather than quantity.

Several pedagogy chapters in Barbara J. D'Angelo, Sandra Jamieson, Barry Maid, and Janice R. Walker's collection *Information Literacy: Research and Collaboration across Disciplines* offer inspiration for resisting the white normative hegemony embedded in typical citation practices.[53] For example, Miriam Laskin and Cynthia R. Haller describe having their students map the "web of interconnected texts within which a particular text occupies a single node."[54] This work allows students to see which scholars' voices dominate scholarly conversations and their own representations of the conversations. An instructor could add another layer to such an assignment in which students research the authors of the sources in their network to discover their race, gender, and/or sexual identities and then analyze the diversity or lack of diversity of perspectives represented. Students could reflect on who has dominated the conversations on their research topic and how that may have shaped their own or public perceptions of their topic.

I challenge the idea that source citation can ever be neutral and aim to disrupt existing practices and pedagogies, exposing assumptions that inform current citation pedagogies and make them appear "natural" or "commonsensical." As an example and model, I will describe an assignment I give that asks students to formulate a citation policy for their final research project and then reflect on the implementation of that policy.

I begin by sharing a quote from Adam J. Banks's book *Race, Rhetoric, and Technology*, about citation systems being technologies: "Whether one uses MLA, APA, Chicago or any other citation system . . . that citation system, as a set of rules governing the appropriation and recognition of knowledge from other sources[,] has a technological function in the academy. One's ability to use this 'system' of citation often has direct effects on the kind of access she or he will obtain to academic discourse communities."[55] I then move the conversation around source citation away from economic metaphors—which frame source citation as a way to repay debt, give credit, or make a kind of epistemological payment to an author—and introduce the idea of framing source citation as being about indicating relationships among authors and ideas.[56] Instead of it being a way to "give credit," I suggest it can be a way to indicate who has had an impact on your thinking. I talk about how who an author chooses to cite can be a form of allyship, elevating and highlighting marginalized voices (or having the opposite effect). This leads to a discussion of bibliographic mining strategies. Backward citation searching involves identifying the sources used in the article you are reading, which can reveal what has shaped the current author's thinking. Forward citation searching, in which you see who has cited the source you are currently looking at, can be done through search engines like Google Scholar, which indicate who has cited a source. It allows you to see how the current article shaped thought that came after it. With the context of forward and backward citation searching, students can see the potential for unjust citation practices to perpetuate further oppression.

Next, I share with students Rigoberto Lara Guzman's zine post, "How to Cite Like a Badass Tech Feminist of Color," in which she urges readers to "unsettle expertise" by valuing and citing their own experiences and knowledge and amplifying the work of others who have been excluded by citation traditions.[57] She encourages readers that "there are ways to SHINE without reproducing the systems that exclude us," elaborating on "SHINE" as "a tactic to counter our erasure by acknowledging one another and unsettling who is considered an expert."

Finally, I ask students to build on the concept of citing "like a badass tech feminist of color" by selecting one of their identities and imagining what a citation practice built around "citing like a badass [whatever identifier they chose]" might look like. Using concepts raised by Banks, I ask students to think about how the citation practice they imagine would offer ways to resist excluding minoritized voices.

CONCLUSION

The field of composition and rhetoric is long overdue in examining its complicity in normalizing discourse and practices that support white literacy normativity. In both our own practices and pedagogies, we need to recognize our complicity in a #CitationPedagogySoWhite. This means explicitly acknowledging citation as a site of oppression. Most important, we need to shift the focus of citation pedagogy away from formatting and the assumption that source citation is a neutral activity and toward a pedagogy that engages with the ideologies embedded in the constructions of authority.

NOTES

1. Ahmed, "Declaration of Whiteness."
2. Pritchard, *Fashioning Lives.*
3. Pritchard, "When You Know Better."
4. Pritchard, "When You Know Better," 28.
5. Tuck, Yang, and Gaztambide-Fernandez, *Citation Practices Challenge*; Williams and Collier, "About Us"; Marston, "Introducing #FEAS Cite Club."
6. Vershawn Ashanti Young cautions us in "Black Lives Matter in Academic Spaces" that literacy "pedagogies may actually elicit violent reactions and might be complicit in violence" (8).
7. White, "Beethoven Has a First Name."
8. Pritchard, "When You Know Better."
9. Royster, "Disciplinary Landscaping," 150.
10. Royster, "Disciplinary Landscaping," 149.
11. Royster, "Disciplinary Landscaping," 160–61.
12. Chakravartty et al., "#CommunicationSoWhite," 257.
13. Chakravartty et al., "#CommunicationSoWhite," 260.
14. Rolf, "Navigating Power," 490.
15. Pritchard, *Fashioning Lives*, 103–4.

16. Houdek, "The Imperative of Race for Rhetorical Studies," 294.
17. Powell, "2012 CCCC Chair's Address," 395.
18. Leon, quoted in Powell, "2012 CCCC Chair's Address," 395, original emphasis.
19. Association of College and Research Libraries, "Framework."
20. Rapchak, "That Which Cannot Be Named," 180.
21. Rapchak, "That Which Cannot Be Named," 181; Kendi, *How to Be an Antiracist*.
22. Tuck, Yang, and Gaztambide-Fernandez, *Citation Practices Challenge*; Williams and Collier, "About Us"; Smith, "Our Story."
23. Ahmed, *Living a Feminist Life*.
24. Mott and Cockayne, "Citation Matters," 955.
25. Mott and Cockayne, "Citation Matters," 960; Royster, "Disciplinary Landscaping."
26. Royster, "Disciplinary Landscaping," 964.
27. Mott and Cockayne, "Citation Matters," 965.
28. Walker and Boamah, "Making the Invisible Hyper-Visible"
29. Press et al., "How Do We Intervene," 53.
30. Tuck and Yang, "Journals Make Terrible Time Machines," 3.
31. Russell, "Farewell Editorial," 9.
32. Ewell, "Music Theory's White Racial Frame."
33. Loewe, Twitter moment; Wardle, Twitter moment. I also want to note that *Race, Rhetoric, and Research Methods* by Lockett, Ruiz, Sanchez, and Carter, which explores how race impacts knowledge production in rhetoric, composition, and writing studies, came out after this chapter was drafted.
34. Wanzer-Serrano, "Rhetoric's Rac(e/ist) Problems," 471.
35. Inoue, "Why I Left the CWPA."
36. Blewett et al., "Editing as Inclusion Activism."
37. Cagle et al., "Anti-Racist Scholarly Revising"; University Press of Colorado, "Our Publication Processes and Timelines."
38. Jamieson and Howard, "Phase I Data"; Burton and Chadwick, "Investigating the Practices of Student Researchers"; McClure and Clink, "How Do You Know That?"
39. Kleinfeld, "Just Read the Assignment."
40. Purdue Online Writing Lab, "Research: Where to Begin."
41. Fraser Hall Library, "Engage First-Year Students."
42. Sweetland Center for Writing, "First-Year Composition."
43. Sweetland Center for Writing, "Teaching Citation and Documentation Norms."
44. Robillard, "Young Scholars' Affecting Composition."
45. Robillard, "Young Scholars' Affecting Composition," 258–59.
46. Robillard, "Young Scholars' Affecting Composition," 258.
47. Robillard, "Young Scholars' Affecting Composition," 259.
48. Robillard, "Young Scholars' Affecting Composition," 259–60.
49. Rose, "The Role of Scholarly Citations in Disciplinary Economies," 244.
50. Leung, "Knowledge Justice."
51. Leung, "Knowledge Justice."
52. I acknowledge the tension between engaging deeply with sources, as Pritchard advocates, and reading the volume of available work Robillard explores in "Prototypical Reading."
53. D'Angelo et al., *Information Literacy*.
54. Laskin and Haller, "Up the Mountain," 237–38.
55. Banks, *Race, Rhetoric, and Technology*, 89.
56. For an in-depth discussion of the problems and limitations of theft metaphors for plagiarism, see Robillard, "Pass It On."
57. Guzman, "How to Cite."

REFERENCES

Ahmed, Sara. "Declarations of Whiteness: The Non-Performativity of Anti-Racism." *Meridians* 7, no. 1 (2006): 104–26.

Ahmed, Sara. *Living a Feminist Life*. Durham, NC: Duke University Press, 2017.

Association of College and Research Libraries. "Framework for Information Literacy for Higher Education," 2015. https://www.ala.org/acrl/standards/ilframework.

Banks, Adam J. *Race, Rhetoric, and Technology: Searching for Higher Ground*. Mahwah, NJ, and Urbana, IL: Lawrence Associates and National Council of Teachers of English, 2006.

Blewett, Kelly, Christina M. LaVecchia, Laura R. Micciche, and Janine Morris. "Editing as Inclusion Activism." *College English* 81, no. 4 (2019): 273–96.

Burton, Vicki Tolar, and Scott A. Chadwick. "Investigating the Practices of Student Researchers: Patterns of Use and Criteria for Use of Internet and Library Sources." *Computers and Composition* 17, no. 3 (2000): 309–28. https://doi.org/10.1016/S8755-4615(00)00037-2.

Cagle, Lauren E., Michelle F. Eble, Laura Gonzales, Meredith A. Johnson, Nathan R. Johnson, Natasha N. Jones, Liz Lane, Temptaous Mckoy, Kristen R. Moore, Ricky Reynoso, et al. "Anti-Racist Scholarly Reviewing Practices: A Heuristic for Editors, Reviewers, and Authors." 2021. https://tinyurl.com/reviewheuristic.

Chakravartty, Paula, Rachel Kuo, Victoria Grubbs, and Charlton McIlwain. "#CommunicationSoWhite." *Journal of Communication* 68, no. 2 (2018): 254–66. https://doi.org/10.1093/joc/jqy003.

D'Angelo, Barbara J., Sandra Jamieson, Barry M. Maid, and Janice R. Walker, eds. *Information Literacy: Research and Collaboration across Disciplines*. Fort Collins, CO: WAC Clearinghouse, 2016.

Ewell, Philip A. "Music Theory's White Racial Frame." *Music Theory Online* 26, no. 2 (2020): 324–29. https://doi.org/10.1093/mts/mtaa031.

Fraser Hall Library, SUNY Geneseo. "Engage First-Year Students through Creative Citation Instruction," 2020. https://libguides.geneseo.edu/citationlessonplans.

Guzman, Rigoberto Lara. "How to Cite Like a Badass Tech Feminist Scholar of Color." *Points: Data and Society*, August 22, 2019. https://points.datasociety.net/how-to-cite-like-a-badass-tech-feminist-scholar-of-color-ebc839a3619c/.

Houdek, Matthew. "The Imperative of Race for Rhetorical Studies: Toward Divesting from Disciplinary and Institutionalized Whiteness." *Communication and Critical/Cultural Studies* 15, no. 4 (2018): 292–99. https://doi.org/10.1080/14791420.2018.1534253.

Inoue, Asao B. "Why I Left the CWPA (Council of Writing Program Administrators)." *Asao B. Inoue's Infrequent Words*, 2021. http://asaobinoue.blogspot.com/2021/04/why-i-left-cwpa-council-of-writing.html.

Jamieson, Sandra, and Rebecca Moore Howard. "Phase I Data." *The Citation Project*, 2011. http://site.citationproject.net/.

Kendi, Ibram X. *How to Be an Antiracist*. New York: One World, 2019.

Kleinfeld, Elizabeth. "Just Read the Assignment: Using Course Documents to Analyze Research Pedagogy." In *Points of Departure: Rethinking Student Source Use and Writing Studies Research Methods*, edited by Sandra Jamieson and Tricia Serviss, 227–44. Logan: Utah State University Press, 2018.

Laskin, Miriam, and Cynthia R. Haller. "Up the Mountain without a Tail: Helping Students Use Source Networks to Find Their Way." In *Information Literacy: Research and Collaboration across Disciplines*, edited by Barbara J. D'Angelo, Sandra Jamieson, Barry Maid, and Janice R. Walker, 237–56. Fort Collins, CO: WAC Clearinghouse, 2016.

Leon, Kendall, quoted in Powell, Malea. "2012 CCCC Chair's Address: Stories Take Place, a Performance in One Act." *College Composition and Communication* 64, no. 2 (2012): 383–406.

Leung, Sofia. "Knowledge Justice," September 4, 2020. https://www.sofiayleung.com/thoughts/knowledgejusticekeynote.

Lockett, Alexandria L., Iris D. Ruiz, James Chase Sanchez, and Christopher Carter. *Race, Rhetoric, and Research Methods.* Fort Collins, CO: WAC Clearinghouse, 2021.

Loewe, Drew M. Twitter moment, May 17, 2020. https://twitter.com/drewloewe/status/1262109849371975680.

Marston, Kate. "Introducing #FEAS Cite Club," 2017. http://www.genderandeducation.com/cite-club/introducing-feas-cite-club/.

McClure, Randall, and Kellian Clink. "How Do You Know That? An Investigation of Student Research Practices in the Digital Age." *Libraries and the Academy* 9, no. 1 (2009): 115–32.

Mott, Carrie, and Daniel Cockayne. "Citation Matters: Mobilizing the Politics of Citation toward a Practice of Conscientious Engagement." *Gender, Place, and Culture* 24, no. 7 (2017): 954–73.

Powell, Malea. "2012 CCCC Chair's Address: Stories Take Place, a Performance in One Act." *College Composition and Communication* 64, no. 2 (2012): 383–406.

Press, Andrea, Deb Verhoeven, Jonathan Sterne, and Vicki Mayer. "How Do We Intervene in the Stubborn Persistence of Patriarchy in Communication Scholarship?" In *Interventions: Communication Theory and Practice,* edited by D. Travers Scott and Adrienne Shaw, 53–64. New York: Peter Lang, 2017.

Pritchard, Eric Darnell. *Fashioning Lives: Black Queers and the Politics of Literacy.* Carbondale: Southern Illinois University Press, 2016.

Pritchard, Eric Darnell. "'When You Know Better, Do Better': Honoring Intellectual and Emotional Labor through Diligent Accountability Practices." Education, Liberation, and Black Radical Traditions for the Twenty-First Century: Carmen Kynard's *Teaching and Research Site on Race, Writing, and the Classroom,* July 8, 2019. http://carmenkynard.org/featured-scholar-eric-darnell-pritchard-when-you-know-better-do-better-honoring-intellectual-and-emotional-labor-through-diligent-accountability-practices/.

Purdue Online Writing Lab. "Research: Where to Begin," June 2020. https://owl.purdue.edu/owl/research_and_citation/conducting_research/research_overview/index.html.

Rapchak, Marcia. "That Which Cannot Be Named: The Absence of Race in the Framework for Information Literacy for Higher Education." *Journal of Radical Librarianship* 5 (2019): 173–96.

Robillard, Amy. "Pass It On: Revising the 'Plagiarism Is Theft' Metaphor." *JAC* 29, no. 1–2 (2009): 405–35.

Robillard, Amy. "Prototypical Reading: Volume, Desire, Anxiety." *College Composition and Communication* 67, no. 2 (2015): 197–215.

Robillard, Amy. "'Young Scholars' Affecting Composition: A Challenge to Disciplinary Citation Practices." *College English* 68, no. 3 (2006): 253–70.

Rolf, Harry G. "Navigating Power in Doctoral Publishing: A Data Feminist Approach." *Teaching in Higher Education* 26, no. 3 (2021): 488–507. doi: 10.1080/13562517.2021.1892059.

Rose, Shirley K. "The Role of Scholarly Citations in Disciplinary Economies." In *Perspectives on Plagiarism and Intellectual Property in a Postmodern World,* edited by Lisa Buranen and Alice M. Roy, 241–49. Albany: SUNY Press, 1999.

Royster, Jacqueline Jones. "Disciplinary Landscaping, or Contemporary Challenges in the History of Rhetoric." *Philosophy and Rhetoric* 36, no. 2 (2003): 148–67.

Russell, Connie. "Farewell Editorial: On Open Access, the Politics of Citation, and Generous Scholarship." *Canadian Journal of Environmental Education* 21 (2016): 5–12.

Smith, Christen A. "Our Story." *Cite Black Women,* 2017. https://www.citeblackwomencollective.org/.

Sweetland Center for Writing, University of Michigan. "First-Year Composition," June 6, 2022. https://libguides.utk.edu/c.php?g=882094&p=6921084.

Sweetland Center for Writing, University of Michigan. "Teaching Citation and Documentation Norms," June 26, 2020. https://lsa.umich.edu/sweetland/instructors/teaching-resources/teaching-citation-and-documentation-norms.html.

Tuck, Eve, and K. Wayne Yang. "Journals Make Terrible Time Machines." *Critical Ethnic Studies* 3, no. 2 (2017): 1–11.
Tuck, Eve, K. Wayne Yang, and Ruben Gaztambide-Fernandez. *Citation Practices Challenge*, July 20, 2019. https://goo.gl/forms/rKsYjVWExEFng9pz1.
University Press of Colorado. "Our Publication Processes and Timelines," June 10, 2022. https://upcolorado.com/publish-with-us/our-publication-process.
Walker, Margath A., and Emmanuel Frimpong Boamah. "Making the Invisible Hyper-Visible: Knowledge Production and the Gendered Power Nexus in Critical Urban Studies." *Human Geography* 12, no. 2 (2019): 36–50.
Wanzer-Serrano, Darrel. "Rhetoric's Rac(e/ist) Problems." *Quarterly Journal of Speech* 105, no. 4 (2019): 465–76. https://doi.org/10.1080/00335630.2019.1669068.
Wardle, Elizabeth. Twitter moment, May 17, 2020. https://twitter.com/ElizabethWardle/status/1262147257958309888.
White, Chris. "Beethoven Has a First Name: It's Time to 'Fullname' *All* Composers in Classical Music." *Slate*, October 24, 2020. https://slate.com/culture/2020/10/fullname-famous-composers-racism-sexism.html.
Williams, Brittany, and Joan Collier. "About Us." *CiteASista*, 2017. https://citeasista.com/about/.
Young, Vershawn Ashanti. "Black Lives Matter in Academic Spaces: Three Lessons for Critical Literacy." *Journal of College Reading and Learning* 50, no. 1 (2020): 5–18. https://doi.org/10.1080/10790195.2019.1710441.

12
FILM IN THE INTERDISCIPLINARY COMPOSITION CLASSROOM

Rachel McCabe

As a field, composition and rhetoric has been greatly influenced by its fluctuating location within larger university structures. Political and financial factors have shifted its placement; while larger programs exist as their own departments, many universities house composition and rhetoric courses alongside neighboring fields of literature, creative writing, communication, and education. This interdisciplinary location and the diverse people who teach writing courses have led to the use of interdisciplinary texts.

This chapter explores one such medium—film—and its beneficial relationship to student writing within the interdisciplinary structure of the modern, and future, composition course. To do so, I apply an interdisciplinary methodology informed by theories of identification to illustrate the power and potential of writing about film. Film's ability to help students see the world from another person's perspective, along with its visual complexity, makes it an increasingly important medium within the ever-changing shape of English departments. As departments continue to shrink and shift, composition continues to teach not only writing practices but also the habits of mind developed by the liberal arts. Visual analysis of film allows students to combine their visual knowledge with visual analysis vocabulary; when this prior knowledge is supplemented with new vocabulary, students are able to see the rhetorical construction in these texts. This practice allows students to understand other visual texts not only as capable of communicating arguments but also as actively engaged in argumentation.

The presence and benefits of film in the writing classroom were researched extensively in the late 1980s through the early 2000s, when film was readily available for classroom use through the video rental system.[1] However, the dawn of the digital age has made other audiovisual texts even more accessible: YouTube clips, podcasts, and social media posts are just a few of the multimedia resources frequently brought into the classroom.[2] Despite this plethora of textual resources, film continues to be frequently taught even if its researched use has diminished in the last decade.

Despite its limitations, film's accessibility as a visual text—one students are often engaging with outside the classroom—makes it useful in introductory writing courses.[3] Its narrative structure and visual elements make it a fruitful basis for rhetorical analysis. While the general benefits of using visual texts in the writing classroom have been well-established by scholars such as Ellen Bishop and Joseph Harris, this chapter will consider the benefits of specific levels of cinematic complexity and their benefits to student learners and writers.[4] To do so, I look at two case studies: Quentin Tarantino's *Django Unchained* and Jordan Peele's *Us*.[5] While both films focus overtly on race, their differing levels of visual and narrative complexity provide two vastly different examples of what students can *do* with film.[6] I then explore how the differences in these films work with or against the student writing process. In the case of Tarantino's film, the straightforward narrative and Western genre conventions make his film easy to understand but difficult to complicate. Bringing other voices into conversation with the film can help redirect students' attempts to identify too strongly with the film's protagonist. *Us*, however, is a film layered with ambiguity, and asking students to make and support a claim in interpreting the film can produce fruitful analysis with no additional sources. These examples of the student writing process for film highlight the benefits and the different pedagogical avenues necessary for differing levels of complexity in a film's narrative and cinematography. Complex films require more conversation to help students unpack the details and ideas of the film but can lend themselves to similarly complex writing as students continue this exploration in their written work. In contrast, films that often seem simplistic can be complicated by classroom discussion; by pairing seemingly simplistic texts with complex ideas from secondary sources, students can ultimately arrive at insightful views of superficially simple films.

FILM AS A MEDIUM FOR STUDENT WRITING
A New (Visual) World

In many cases, students come to the writing classroom with significant visual experience. Their familiarity with visual texts allows them to say smart things about what's happening on the screen even when they don't necessarily have the vocabulary to draw out their observations.

Film utilizes the visual experience students are used to from occasional trips to the movie theater along with increasingly common binging of television on streaming platforms and YouTube videos. As Dulce Cruz points out, students are already spending so much of their time watching films that bringing these texts into the writing classroom is both accessible and exciting for them, so much so that they quickly build classroom community.[7] Since the publication of Cruz's piece, students are spending even more time with visual texts: their smartphones and laptops both facilitate and necessitate a significant amount of visual literacy. Cruz's link between engagement and analysis, if anything, has only become more critical to acknowledge with this increase in visual literacy. Because students are still engaged with films, bringing in examples they are familiar with gives them space to ask questions about the films they've seen, which may help them see the overall potential of analysis in ways that aren't always clear with textual analysis. In contrast, bringing in films that are unfamiliar to students but which still rely on the genre conventions they're familiar with can push their analytical skills in new directions. Because many students arrive with cultural understanding of the visual codes around them, film provides a space to explore the context-heavy coding system of the visual elements of the text. In addition, film provides a multisensory viewing experience that typifies the differences between written rhetoric and visual rhetoric.[8]

While film viewing may feel familiar to students, it also requires its own language.[9] Students can often provide a sense of what's happening in a scene, but describing *how* it's happening can sound like a different conversation altogether.[10] The "visual language" that film utilizes can be understood as a sort of terministic screen. Kenneth Burke's *Language as Symbolic Action* considers this term from a social constructivist perspective.[11] To draw out the parallel, film's visual languages of cuts, shots, and content serve as their own terminology; as Burke explains, "even if any given terminology is a *reflection* of reality, by its very nature as a terminology it must be a *selection* of reality; and to this extent it must function also as a *deflection* of reality."[12] Because we each move through reality with our individual "screens" shading our view, "*many of the 'observations' are but implications of the particular terminology in terms of which the observations are* made."[13] It is our often limited way of seeing, hearing, and viewing new information that commits us as speakers and thinkers to our one terministic screen. However, film watching provides a way to expand beyond this one way of understanding the world: it asks us to understand the visual language of the medium. Film specifically crafts a vision for an audience and represents another person's reality, and describing how it does so can require new vocabulary. As a visual medium, the terministic screens offered by film go beyond terminology and can actually allow viewers to see the world from another person's perspective. Moving between these screens constructed by our own terminology provides the flexibility of imagination to see the world from a new point of view.

Identification: The Central Drawback

While students' familiarity with film can be beneficial, it also brings a central challenge: over-identification. While seeing another person's perspective play out on the screen can potentially expand viewer thinking in productive ways, it can also erase critical differences between the viewer and the film's subjects.

Identification, as an experience, happens to us all the time. As Krista Ratcliffe explains, identifications happen every day: we can look at ads in magazines or on television and identify with another person based on gender, age, race, class, and similar factors. In the process, though, Ratcliffe warns that "when people's identities are interpreted as identical in terms of a single identification (e.g., defined in terms of one TV ad) or in terms of a single cultural category (e.g., defined in terms of gender), then opportunities for stereotyping abound."[14] Ratcliffe explains that the process of listening to and identifying with the Other can erase critical and necessary differences between the listener and the speaker. I argue that the same erasure can happen with viewing a text, particularly film. Watching a screen can often leave viewers feeling as though their eyes and the eye of the camera are functioning similarly; while this can be a useful convergence to see the world from a different perspective, viewers can also fuse their identities with the characters they are watching. This seems to come from a desire to align themselves with the "hero" of the story as well as being a result of the passivity with which so many people consume visual texts. In an increasingly visual world, defaulting to passive consumption often brings a passive identification based on simplistic identifying factors.[15]

By looking at two examples, we can see the ways films make it easier or more difficult for viewers to identify with a film's characters. In turn, I'll present different ways to navigate the over-identification that can sometimes take place with more linear film plots and simpler characters as well as to provide students with a foothold to begin the writing process with more ambiguous texts that resist identification.

CASE STUDIES

In considering two film case studies, *Django Unchained* and *Us*, we see two primary types of films that can work effectively in the writing classroom. Tarantino delivers a straightforward narrative with little ambiguity: his commitment to the genre conventions of the Western means we know exactly who the good guys and bad guys are. This binary approach is reinforced by the historical elements of the film, as our hero is also an enslaved man fighting for his and his wife's freedom. In contrast, in *Us*, Peele is invested in challenging our assumptions about heroes and villains. By subverting expectations, the film resists viewers' impulse to identify with any of the characters and forces them to sit with the ambiguities of the film.

While both films address questions of race (primarily by including Black cast members as the films' protagonists), neither film's plot is entirely driven by questions of race: *Django Unchained* is a revenge narrative told through the structure of a German fairytale, and *Us* is a horror film that explores socioeconomic issues and punishment for difference. Race in both films becomes an added complexity to their central questions. However, asking a diverse group of students to respond to these films requires a look at the ways different subject positions inform our interpretation of each film's different aspects. As Elizabeth Kleinfeld illustrates in chapter 11 of this volume, the inability to separate ideas from their speakers or writers necessitates a look at the racial politics of identification in both texts. While some students may feel closer to or more distanced from the texts given their subject positions, both films nonetheless distance themselves from all viewers: the details of Tarantino's 1800s setting and Peele's commitment to the horror genre initially make it difficult to map our reality onto either film.

The differences between these two films necessitate different pedagogical practices. When analyzing and writing about more complex films, students often need help pinning down their content. That said, these films are often easier to write about once students understand the directors' rhetorical goals. Their complex elements lend themselves well to fruitful, nuanced analysis. More straightforward cinematic texts don't require as much support in their initial readings and analysis, but students often require support in complicating these texts. Bringing in outside voices and asking students to extrapolate a film's relationship to larger social questions can often provide the complexity necessary to produce interesting debate from reductive conclusions about the film itself.

Django Unchained

Quentin Tarantino's 2012 film *Django Unchained* serves as both an authorial rewriting of history and a genre mash-up. Set in the antebellum South and Southwest US, the film combines the American spaghetti Western, Tarantino's signature revenge narrative,[16] and a German fairytale. This combination of genres further emphasizes the anachronistic plot line: while the film's depiction of a freed slave seeking revenge against his former owner is plausible, its historical ramifications, if true, would have been widespread and well-known. This means American viewers are aware that the story must be fictional; in the very impossibility of this narrative, the dark history of brutal suppression against multiple attempts for Black people to escape or fight against slavery is brought forward to viewers' attention. While the film can produce fruitful analysis from a race studies perspective, rhetorical analysis looks at the ways Tarantino is utilizing race to complicate genre conventions, using violence in a particular way to convey the content he wants his audience to experience, and rewriting history to demonstrate the ways narrative guides our viewing. These critical moves all serve to both pull the viewer into the plot and distance them from the reality represented by the film, which involves a complex simultaneity in the viewing experience that is perhaps one of the film's most fascinating takeaways.

Django Unchained is overtly a critique of racism. The narrative follows Django Freeman (Jamie Foxx), a slave who is freed by and then partnered with Dr. Schultz (Christoph Waltz). The two work as bounty hunters in search of Django's wife, Broomhilda. Django's heroic escape from the clutches of multiple villains and his victory over Calvin Candie (Leonardo DiCaprio), the film's most notorious slave owner and imprisoner of Broomhilda, make Django a "Black-centered superhero."[17] In teaching this film, I've observed that students, regardless of race, often point out that Django is the character they most identify with or desire to identify with as they watch the film. The only other identifiable character for them is Dr. Schultz, but he dies well before the end of the film, forcing the viewer to start and end the film with Django. There are clear benefits to this identification with a Black character, as it asks all students who hold privilege or power to consider a perspective radically different from their own.[18] However, over-identifying with Django can also lead white students to erase crucial differences between themselves and the character's experiences.[19]

While teaching this film in an introductory writing course in 2018, I noticed that students interpreted its violence as proof of "realism."

Despite discussing the genre conventions Tarantino is using, students often went back to the scenes of brutality against Django and saw them not only as proof of the horrors of slavery but as justification for the violence that befalls the white slave owners and their family members in the film. In early student writing, I saw statements such as "the film represents the true situation in the South during this time" and "Tarantino doesn't sugarcoat slavery, and even shows the most disturbing consequences of the system." Similarly, the ways Tarantino met viewer expectations through genre conventions (many of which students weren't necessarily able to articulate but were nonetheless aware of) communicated a "straightforward" or "candid" tone to the film's content delivery. When we discussed how students arrived at this conclusion, we talked about how the cinematic elements helped them, as audience members, identify with Django. In the process, all moral ambiguity about the violence Django commits was erased, and it became even easier for students to talk about the film purely in terms of the satisfaction they felt when the "good guy" won.

One way to combat the common student impulse of over-identification is to challenge reductive readings of the film and lead students to the more controversial and thought-provoking details. Composition can learn from literature and film scholars who have found ways to help students read and see beyond initial moments of problematic identification. Lynn Makau demonstrates the kind of fruitful conversation available to students when considering this film in "Django Unpacked: A Student Forum on *Django Unchained*." When the film was paired with a larger conversation about racism in American history and contemporary representations of slavery, Makau explained how her literature course's investment in challenging dominant narratives helped students see points of interesting tension in the revenge plot of *Django Unchained*. The students who conducted the forum on the film argued that Tarantino "presents a fictional version of the antebellum South with enough detail of this rarely portrayed period (particularly in context of their peers) as to seem plausible, despite the film's anachronisms and limited depiction of sexual coercion under slavery. They sought to use *Django*'s popularity as a foundation for better-informed discussion of these oversights."[20] Thus, the historical accuracies provided a kind of historicization that students found distracting (and easy to see as entertaining). However, the students integrated this popularity into their discussion, as they ultimately "wished to address the evident discrepancy between the 'acceptable' violence of a truly volatile era and its excessive parody that thrills Tarantino fans, but which may divert attention from the atrocities the film purports to address."[21] Their external knowledge of the history of this time period and the inclusion of other voices on the subject allowed these students to see the problems of justifying violence in this film. Specifically, the students concluded that the film was particularly problematic in its depiction of issues of gender: "Discussion leaders crafted their primary questions around issues of consent under conscription and what they viewed as irreverent or incomplete depictions of gender and sexuality in Django, as well as the film's excessive violence and implied distance from history. This distancing, like spurious claims of postraciality in contemporary media, provides fallacious reassurance that we have moved beyond the effects of American slavery to achieve racial harmony."[22]

Rather than allow the setting, costumes, and time period of Tarantino's film to distance it from the current moment, "the Forum applied close-reading techniques to key scenes in *Django* to demonstrate connections with modern-day race- sex- and class-discrimination."[23] Makau's classroom experience demonstrates the potential of both including problematic texts and, specifically, putting them in conversation with academic pieces that help to parse out the complexities represented in the source of analysis.

While the context of Makau's classroom allowed for these conversations, bringing in scholarly articles that reflect multiple sides of the fraught conversation about the film can similarly model the kind of intellectual debate achieved in the student forum. Although Django is a violent character, his violence is justified to audiences due to the treatment he receives as a slave. As a result, Django's violence becomes understandable.[24] Structuring Django's violence in terms of the revenge narrative allows audiences to root for a historically marginalized character and reconfigure the historical binaries traditionally imposed in fiction, film, and history. Andrew Schopp continues to explain that "just as Tarantino's films draw upon traditional moral binaries in order to explode them, their use of the ex-centric never simply reverses focus or political polls. When the post-modern text plays with center and margin, the center is not destroyed or replaced, but [is] critically examined through the lens of the marginal."[25] This allows the film to explore the complexities of the antebellum South through Django's perspective. In the process, the simplicity of the genre is challenged by inverting the racial allegiances Hollywood relied on for decades, allowing for a meta-critique of the film industry.

In the writing classroom, asking students to combine film analysis with critical sources that argue for differing interpretations helps them contend with and even build in ambiguity in the film. For example, when viewing *Django Unchained* without exploring these opposing conversations, the passive reading of the film as a feel-good revenge narrative is easy to write about. In teaching this film, I noted that the identification with Django and satisfaction with the film's ending led many students to conclude that Tarantino was making an anti-racism film. Unlike our experiences with more ambiguous texts (during which students were invested in complicating the narratives and considering the text from multiple perspectives), students were resistant to challenge Tarantino's film because passive reading was so much more convenient. Only by highlighting the film's controversies and bringing the scholars discussed here into conversation with the film were students able to see and write about its racial politics in a more nuanced way. Bringing in articles like Coetzee's can facilitate conversation about representation in the film industry and, in the case of *Django Unchained,* what it means to have a white director bring us a "Black-centered superhero." Contending with Schopp's claims about the moral ambiguities available in the film can raise important questions about what it means to identify with any of the characters. In this way, we can mirror Makau's class debate by bringing in scholarly sources already engaged in such conversations. This transitioned many students' claims toward statements such as "this scene is a reflection of societal entrapment of Black people and unending psychological effects of slavery, an emotional disparity that the director and actors continue to extend when thinking about who made this film." Reading the voices of scholars who are both critical and supportive of the film had the added benefit of demonstrating scholarly discourse between sources for students, a skill we cultivated in their writing over the course of the semester.

Us

Unlike Tarantino's style of filmmaking, which challenges the genre of historical films, Jordan Peele's films have challenged the genre conventions of horror films. His first film, *Get Out*,[26] was critically acclaimed upon its release for its interrogation of racist tropes through the conventions of horror: the film's protagonist, Chris Washington (Daniel Kaluuya), has a sense that something is wrong when visiting his white girlfriend's family. His instinct alerts him to the eeriness of the "post-racial" space, which, in turn, helps save his life when the family tries to take over his body and erase his consciousness.[27] While Peele's 2019 film *Us* also looks at racial differences within the horror film genre, the film is more invested in interrogating systemic injustice and exclusion. The film follows Adelaide Wilson (Lupita Nyong'o), a wife and mother of two whose traumatic childhood experiences in a funhouse make her reluctant to let her family travel to Santa Barbara for vacation. On this trip, we see the ways the Wilsons—made up of Adelaide, her husband, and her two children—try to compete with their white neighbors. Soraya Nadia McDonald explains, "[The Wilsons] are black, and so they are Americans in a country that does not always fully regard black people as such—and thus are immigrants in their own nation, in a way. For the Wilsons, assimilation is mostly economic, finding ways to signal that they, too, are the American Dream."[28] While settling into their vacation home, the family is attacked by the Tethered, grotesque doppelgangers who have been forced to live underground. Using the Tethered as a metaphor for the arbitrary differences between the privileged and underprivileged in America, Peele uses the horror film to raise questions about social and economic inequality. The Tethereds' weapon of choice is a pair of golden scissors, an apt choice both for its doubled structure and its mundanity. As the Tethered terrorize their aboveground doubles, we increasingly see links between the two worlds and learn more about the injustices experienced by the Tethered. While the Wilsons survive the attacks by the Tethered, killing their underground counterparts, they also see the results of the revolution. As a grand act of resistance, the Tethered hold hands to create a human chain across the country, a reference to the Hands across America campaign Adelaide watched on television as a little girl.

The film's ending is particularly complex: viewers learn that the Adelaide we've been following throughout the film is actually her doppelganger. Having switched places as children, it is Adelaide's double, Red, we've been rooting for. We only learn that we've been watching the "fake" Adelaide throughout the film after she kills her doppelganger, who is the product of life in the underground tunnels ever since her childhood vacation. Peele foreshadows this reversal by showing us the devastation both Red and Adelaide experience when Pluto, Red's son, is killed. The horror film genre is firmly situated in binary opponents: people versus monsters, sane people versus psychotic people, people versus the elements (either supernatural or natural). The Tethered are, at first, presented as monstrous: the way they move is too fast or erratic, many have scars, and they wear identical "prison-style" jumpsuits. However, upon closer examination, they are identical to their aboveground counterpart in every way, and their differences are the result of their lives underground. Peele's doppelgangers, then, present the problems of inequity more than reinforcing the hero/villain line. In examining the importance and implications of mimicry in the film, Harry Olafsen notes that despite the Wilsons' middle-class economic status, "their black identity holds them back from achieving the same standard of living above ground, mirroring that of American society in 2019"[29]—a central socio-political throughline that connects *Us* and *Get Out*.

In discussion, students didn't know where to start. The film's genre led some to default to an understanding of the Tethered as monstrous and to cite the film's horror elements as proof of their difference. Others were confused by the film's ending. Many noted that they didn't know who to "side with" and were surprised by the lack of resolution in the film's last few scenes. Making Adelaide's "success" in killing her doppelganger so complex creates an ambiguous "hero"—in discussion, some students were unsure what events occurred in the final third of the film. Because the Tethered look identical to the main characters (they are played by the same actors), none of the film's murder scenes provide the audience with a catharsis or sense of security. By leaving the viewer with no clear "winner" or "good guy" (unlike *Django Unchained*), there is also no character to easily identify with. These ambiguities, at first, make the film a challenge to write about. Many students were still trying to pin down the film's events and central ideas during our class discussion in the fall of 2019, and at least half of our discussion time was spent sorting through its content.

Much of this difficulty comes from Peele's rhetorical goals for the film. In addition to the lack of easily identifiable characters, the film also shows the difficulties faced by both sets of characters: while the Tethered Adelaide is deprived of all luxury belowground, Red/fake Adelaide must adjust to life aboveground with the knowledge of what's happening to her counterpart. As McDonald points out, "For both Adelaide and Red, assimilation involves erasure and survival."[30] In discussing his goals for the film, Peele makes it clear that the title, *Us*, is intentionally ambiguous: while it conjures up the us/them binary and blurs it, it also refers to the United States. In an interview with Simran Hans, Peele states, "Right now, my country is going through an obsession with the outsider, and the fear of the invader and the Other. This is a movie about the fact that maybe we are our own worst enemy."[31] This again makes the film difficult to process, since seeing oneself as part of a societal problem is a big request to ask of viewers.

As discussion of the film progressed, students were eventually able to make nuanced interpretations of Peele's rhetorical goals for the film. Many students wrote about how the film's horror elements transitioned to first show how scared the Wilsons are when the Tethered arrive to empathy for the horrific conditions the Tethered endure underground. In addition, some students chose to write about the scene in which Adelaide is upset by the death of Pluto. These students noted the "sense of empathy" we see in Adelaide, which, in turn, asks the viewer to be more empathetic toward the Tethered as well. Here, a kind of "complex empathy" began to develop in their writing. Seeing the arguments available in Peele's text also helped students with visual analysis of the other texts we looked at: it showed them the argumentative potential within narrative structure. This was especially helpful for students as we transitioned into analysis of YouTube clips and music videos, as the more condensed narrative structure no longer seemed antithetical to the rhetorical goals of these constructed texts. The choices that led to the creation of these often complex visual texts were more apparent to students, and this shift showed in their writing: they were able to talk about the visual details through cinematic language and could point to the choices the director or content creator made to produce a particular effect on their audience.

CONCLUSION

Once students understood the premise of Peele's film, it became difficult for them to write a response that didn't contend with at least some complexity. There are no likable characters with which to identify, and there is no easy moralization of the plot. The ambiguity prevents students from generating an "easy" reading of the film but also requires more vocabulary so they can stake a claim in their interpretation of the film. In contrast to the experience of discussing and writing about *Us*, *Django Unchained* required much more pedagogical work as I tried to steer students away from reductive readings. While there were fascinating takeaways from the film's representation of American history, students needed help with complicating the text and questioning the "realism" Tarantino seemed to present. The film erased important cultural differences between themselves and the film's protagonist, and this experience needed to be challenged by bringing different scholarly voices into our conversation about the film.

Both films demonstrated the many benefits of working with these kinds of texts in the writing classroom. Visual analysis of either film allowed students to combine their visual knowledge with specific terms, and students were then able to see the ways each film was crafted with specific rhetorical goals in mind. Once the constructedness of these texts was exposed, students were better able to see other visual texts as *composed* objects (these included television shows, YouTube videos, photographs, and other types of visual art). These texts also provided a way into difficult conversations about race, socioeconomic inequality, and identity. In the process, film analysis can also be used to address the ways students identify or don't identify with texts.

Using student language and experiences and building on their interests helps them see their educational experience as a larger narrative rather than a set of hoops to jump through. While student language serves as a great starting point for classroom engagement, providing students with specific language from the fields in which they're operating (rhetoric, composition, and film in this case), they can learn how to incorporate field vocabulary into their current understanding.[32] It's not a matter of erasing one vocabulary for another but rather of incorporating new concepts that often require new terms.[33] Therefore, film works to expand student vocabulary and analytical ability while also allowing them to showcase the visual literacy they arrive with in college. While film shouldn't be used to replace textual analysis, it can build on and underscore the fundamental moves of analysis and writing but in a realm where students are often more comfortable.

Questions about which texts and practices can best serve student development have been a part of the field's conversation for decades and will certainly continue to evolve. As the field of composition continues to question which texts and practices best serve student development, it is hoped that film will continue to be part of the conversation.[34] Much like the question of literature in the writing classroom,[35] film's affective benefits seem clear: seeing the world from another person's point of view becomes increasingly critical as our political world seems more and more polarized. As composition scholarship increasingly turns toward student multimodal production, the value of exploring the perspectives of others only becomes more important. Film asks its viewers to see the world from a new perspective and, in the process, presents new ideas in a familiar narrative structure. These strengths and the ability of both more straightforward and more complex films to help students arrive at critical, rhetorical academic writing make it a worthwhile text in the digital age. Rather than undermine the identity of the composition classroom, writing about film highlights the best qualities and practices we want students to bring forward into their college courses as well as to life beyond the university.

NOTES

1. Ellen Bishop's *Cinema-(to)-graphy*, with its broad reflection on the teaching of film across a multitude of writing courses, can be seen as the height of film use in the composition classroom beyond the cultural turn in the 1980s. However, articles and books on the teaching of writing using film slowly continued to be released into the 2010s, as Colleen Jankovic's "Feeling Cinema" demonstrates.
2. We can see the use of YouTube video clips explored extensively by composition and rhetoric scholars in *Enculturation*'s 2010 issue "Video and Participatory Cultures" (under Carter and Arroyo).
3. Any kind of visual text comes with accessibility concerns for students who have visual impairments. It also requires student focus for an extended period of time, which can be challenging for those with cognitive processing concerns, and often relies on cultural knowledge that is easiest for native speakers of the film's language to understand.
4. Bishop, Cinema-(to)-graphy; Harris, Rosen, and Calpas, *Media Journal*.
5. Tarantino, *Django Unchained*; Peele, *Us*.
6. Just as Elizabeth Kleinfeld notes (chapter 11, this volume), the interconnectedness of race and the ideas produced by marginalized authors mean that race is always part of the identification process (or the lack thereof).
7. Cruz, "Mapping the Use of Feature Films," 101.
8. This emphasizes Barbara Stafford's central point in "A Constructivist Manifesto"— that visual objects utilize different rhetorical elements and should be considered differently than other types of texts.
9. This claim is specific to the context of the composition classroom and Standard Academic American English.
10. While some new vocabulary is often critical for learning about film, it doesn't necessarily require an entirely new way of talking about texts. As Jankovic explains, teaching film in the writing classroom can be done with minimal vocabulary if students are asked to instead rely on conveying their affective relationship to the text. By asking students to write about their analytical and affective responses, Jankovic explains: "I have found that this approach allows introductory film/writing students space to engage with film without necessarily learning the technical vocabulary or interpretive modes of critical viewing, writing, and research typically used in film studies" ("Feeling Cinema," 90).
11. While Burke's theoretical label has been substantially debated, I'm relying here on Paul Stob's understanding from "Terministic Screens."
12. Burke, *Language as Symbolic Action*, 45, original emphasis.
13. Burke, *Language as Symbolic Action*, 46, original emphasis.
14. Ratcliffe, *Rhetorical Listening*, 51.
15. As Wenqi Cui explains in "Rhetorical Listening Pedagogy," multimodal texts can only provide cross-cultural communication when rhetorical listening is employed. This listening and the pedagogical techniques that facilitate it help students avoid problematic forms of identification.
16. We see this narrative in the *Kill Bill* series, *Inglourious Basterds*, and *Death Proof*.
17. Coetzee, "*Django Unchained*."
18. This specifically draws on Scarry, "The Difficulty of Imagining Other Persons," in which she explores the ways literature has enabled readers to break down the separation between themselves and an "Other."
19. In many ways, this over-identification resembles Krista Ratcliffe's critique of Burke's theories on identification in *Rhetorical Listening*.
20. Makau, "Django Unpacked," 437.
21. Makau, "Django Unpacked," 437.

22. Makau, "Django Unpacked," 439.
23. Makau, "Django Unpacked," 439.
24. As Andrew Schopp explains in "Gettin' Dirty," *Django Unchained, Inglourious Basterds,* and *The Hateful Eight* "remind audiences that we might all be capable of atrocity, and they therefore undermine the reductive, binary morality so prevalent in the filmic history upon which his [Tarantino's] films draw and equally prevalent in the years following 9/11, when politicians and cultural leaders asked that Americans embrace a host of oversimplified binaries like 'friend/enemy' and 'good/evil' " (172).
25. Schopp, "Gettin' Dirty," 173.
26. Peele, *Get Out.*
27. The film's title is a nod to a 1983 Eddie Murphy routine on haunted houses in which Murphy explains that if a Black family were situated in the Amityville Horror house and a ghost whispered "get out," he and his family would immediately leave without question or hesitation, unlike the white family in the film.
28. McDonald, "Free to Be You and Me," 44.
29. Olafsen, "It's Us," 22–23.
30. McDonald, "Free to Be You and Me," 45.
31. Hans, "The Lives of Others," 35.
32. In the concluding chapter of Don Bialostosky's *Mikhail Bakhtin,* he states: "As part of a college education designed to initiate students into reflective use of these authoritative languages, the study of college writing should not permit students to conform without struggle to the new academic languages or to retreat from the challenges they present by falling back on languages they already know. If they simply abandon or compartmentalize the language they already have and adopt the disciplinary languages the university offers each in its own department, they will pass their courses but pass through school uneducated" (154).
33. Bialostosky explains that "if, however, they are encouraged to imagine the language they already have as their own authentic language, which the new alien languages threaten from without, they will be deterred from engaging in the struggle of making their own the new resources those languages offer for seeing and saying. The college writing course can cultivate students' understanding of their ambivalent situations and validate their struggles to remake themselves and the language imposed on them" (154).
34. As Robert Scholes noted, there are two central issues that prevent a student from effectively representing the ideas of texts they engage with: "One is a failure to focus sharply on the language of the text. The other is a failure to imagine the otherness of the text's author" ("The Transition to College Reading," 166).
35. Sheridan Blau explores the importance of using literature in the writing classroom in "How the Teaching of Literature in College Writing Classes Might Rescue Reading as It Never Has Before."

REFERENCES

Bialostosky, Don. *Mikhail Bakhtin: Rhetoric, Poetics, Dialogics, Rhetoricality.* Anderson, SC: Parlor, 2016.

Bishop, Ellen, ed. *Cinema-(to)-graphy: Film and Writing in Contemporary Composition Courses.* Berkeley: University of California Press, 1999.

Blau, Sheridan. "How the Teaching of Literature in College Writing Classes Might Rescue Reading as It Never Has Before." In *Deep Reading: Teaching Reading in the Writing Classroom,* edited by Patrick Sullivan, Howard Tinberg, and Sheridan Blau, 265–90. Urbana, IL: National Council of Teachers of English, 2017.

Burke, Kenneth. *Language as Symbolic Action: Essays on Life, Literature, and Method.* Berkeley: University of California Press, 1966.
Carter, Geof, and Sarah J. Arroyo. "Video and Participatory Cultures: Writing, Rhetoric, Performance, and the Tube." *Enculturation* 8 (2010). http://enculturation.net/video-and-participatory-cultures.
Coetzee, Carli. "Django Unchained: A Black-Centered Superhero and Unchained Audiences." *Black Camera* 7, no. 2 (Spring 2016): 62–72.
Cruz, Dulce. "Mapping the Use of Feature Films in Composition Classes." In *Cinema-(to)-graphy: Film and Writing in Contemporary Composition Courses*, edited by Ellen Bishop, 100–115. Berkeley: University of California Press, 1999.
Cui, Wenqi. "Rhetorical Listening Pedagogy: Promoting Communication across Cultural and Societal Groups with Video Narrative." *Computers and Composition* 54 (2019). https://doi.org/10.1016/j.compcom.2019.102517.
Hans, Simran. "The Lives of Others." *Sight and Sound* 29, no. 5 (2019): 34–36.
Harris, Joseph, Jay Rosen, and Gary Calpas, eds. *Media Journal: Reading and Writing about Popular Culture*, 2nd ed. Boston: Allyn and Bacon, 1998 [1995].
Jankovic, Colleen. "Feeling Cinema: Affect in Film/Composition Pedagogy." *Transformations: The Journal of Inclusive Scholarship and Pedagogy* 22, no. 2 (Winter 2012): 86–103.
Makau, Lynn. "Django Unpacked: A Student Forum on *Django Unchained*." *Psychoanalysis, Culture, and Society* 19, no. 4 (2014): 435–41.
McDonald, Soraya Nadia. "Free to Be You and Me." *Film Content* (May–June 2019): 44–47.
Olafsen, Harry. "It's Us: Mimicry in Jordan Peele's *Us*." *Iowa Journal of Cultural Studies* 20, no. 1 (2020): 20–32.
Peele, Jordan, dir. *Get Out.* Universal City, CA: Universal Pictures, 2017.
Peele, Jordan, dir. *Us.* Universal City, CA: Universal Pictures, 2019.
Ratcliffe, Krista. *Rhetorical Listening: Identification, Gender, Whiteness.* Carbondale: Southern Illinois University Press, 2005.
Rosenberg, Stuart, dir. *The Amityville Horror.* Los Angeles: American International Pictures, 1979.
Scarry, Elaine. "The Difficulty of Imagining Other Persons." In *The Handbook of Interethnic Coexistence*, edited by Eugene Weiner, 40–62. New York: Continuum, 1998.
Scholes, Robert. "The Transition to College Reading." *Pedagogy: Critical Approaches to Teaching Literature, Language, Composition, and Culture* 2, no. 2 (2002): 165–72.
Schopp, Andrew. "'Gettin' Dirty': Tarantino's Vengeful Justice, the Marked Viewer, and Post-9/11 America." In *American Cinema in the Shadow of 9/11*, edited by Terrence McSweeney, 169–90. Edinburgh, Scotland: University Press, 2017.
Stafford, Barbara. "A Constructivist Manifesto." In *Good Looking: Essays on the Virtue of Images*, edited by Barbara Stafford, 3–17. Boston, MA: MIT Press, 1998.
Stob, Paul. "'Terministic Screens,' Social Constructionism, and the Language of Experience: Kenneth Burke's Utilization of William James." *Philosophy and Rhetoric* 41, no. 2 (2008): 130–52.
Tarantino, Quentin, dir. *Death Proof.* New York: The Weinstein Company, 2007.
Tarantino, Quentin, dir. *Django Unchained.* New York: The Weinstein Company, 2012.
Tarantino, Quentin, dir. *Inglourious Basterds.* New York: The Weinstein Company, 2009.
Tarantino, Quentin, dir. *Kill Bill: Volume I.* New York: The Weinstein Company, 2003.
Tarantino, Quentin, dir. *Kill Bill: Volume II.* New York: The Weinstein Company, 2004.

13
LEARNING FROM BLACK TEACHERS
Ida B. Wells-Barnett and Implementing Critical Engagement Strategies in Writing Classrooms

Jessica Edwards

I teach technical communication and composition studies, and I find great purpose in connecting the classroom to life outside the classroom. As a Black teacher, I find it difficult to ignore the lived experiences of my people and the people I teach, as those experiences shape who we are and how we navigate the world; it is important to me to be able to write and talk about joy, history, pain, workplaces, and even race in the classroom to inform meaningful choices about our futures—our writings. My approaches to the classroom build on Black teachers and thinkers who promote practices that help students and budding instructors understand themselves in relation to the world and imagine the possibilities of a just world.[1] I echo the work of these educators, asserting that the teaching of writing should intentionally help scholars connect history to the present. This kind of teaching can be inherently anti-racist if it builds on pedagogy developed by Black teachers—teachers who, as early as the nineteenth century, "have been deeply engaged in the work of challenging racial domination in American schools. The traditions of African American teachers provide the country with a model, a vital intellectual resource for more nuanced conversations about the place and possibility of anti-racism in the classroom."[2] Arming students and instructors with tools to build racial literacy, understand history, and write about race can help everyone meet writing situations and communicative instances with more responsibility.[3]

In 2018, I published an essay about developing critically conscious pedagogy in writing classrooms.[4] That essay included data from my research on students and race in two different writing classrooms; I asked students to imagine themselves as workplace supervisors to answer two questions about the changing demographics of higher education based on a study published in the *Chronicle of Higher Education*.[5] Of the questions posed in the study, the second is the more relevant to share here: how does your racial identity and comfort level influence the people you work with, especially people of races other than your own? I analyzed student responses to that question and developed the following categories for analysis: "Hopeful about Race in the Workplace" and "Indifference about Race in the Workplace." From student responses, I concluded that direct conversations about race and racism are needed in the writing classroom to help students understand and actually employ inclusion and equity in the workplace, a request that is becoming not only a part of job descriptions but also the basis for entire jobs in some circles. I extend my points from that essay here and posit that history can teach us a lot about inclusion, especially if we look to Black teachers who have paved the way. Specifically, developing a writing course that includes historical documents—such as pamphlets, flyers, letters, and archival notes composed by Black teachers and leaders from the nineteenth century and beyond—can give us intelligence from a perspective that is often not highlighted in learning spaces. Bringing these documents into classrooms can also help us tighten learning objectives by promoting deep reading, advancing exposure to writing genres and communicative practices, and encouraging thoughtful conversations about race and racism.[6]

BACKGROUND SCHOLARSHIP

Both writing students and instructors alike are in need of more useful spaces and places to talk about race and racism even as conversations and active movements to support Black, Latinx, and other minoritized voices add to national consciousness in writing studies.[7] Organizations like Digital Black Lit and Composition (DBLAC), founded by Drs. Khirsten Scott and Louis Miraj to aid Black and minoritized graduate student communities, along with calls for linguist justice as put forth by Drs. April Baker Bell and Bettina Love and projects like the Black Gaze Podcast, curated by Drs. Kisha Porcher and Sharmaine Bertrand, all help advance justice that builds on what Black teachers model so well: equity. Scholarship that chronicles the need for de-colonial practices as well as proper citation of minoritized scholars to help chart more equitable practices is important to both heed and disseminate, as these ideas need to be made more visible so they can be more frequently employed.[8]

In September 2020, the Conference on College, Composition, and Communication's (CCCC's) task force on Black Technical and Professional Communication published a Position Statement with Resource Guide.[9]

Commissioned by the 2019 chair of CCCC, Dr. Vershawn Ashanti Young, the task force, chaired by Dr. Temptaous Mckoy, put together a list of resources that offer methods, theories, and practices to continue the work of advocacy and inclusion. The authors posit that the guide "contextualizes the experiences and cultures of Black peoples through research, teaching, and scholarship."[10] These advances offer clear ways to "break precedent," to make more visible what can help us implement critical engagement strategies in the writing classroom.[11] They also remind us how the personal is very much tied to the classroom, placing teaching at the heart of humanistic practice.[12] This position statement and resource guide, which includes work composed and developed by Black educators, makes important strides to show how Black people have been doing the important work of equity and inclusion for some time.

WORKING WITH HISTORICAL DOCUMENTS

For this chapter, I look specifically to one Black teacher whom I admire a great deal, Ida B. Wells-Barnett (1862–1931)—investigative journalist, advocate and crusader for social justice, and, I argue, technical and professional communicator. She was born on July 16, 1862—just a few months before the Emancipation Proclamation of 1863—and was raised in Holly Springs, Mississippi, about 30 miles west of my hometown of Coldwater, Mississippi. Early in her life, Wells-Barnett became the head of her family after her parents succumbed to the yellow fever pandemic in the late 1870s. She attended Shaw University, now known as Rust College, a historically Black college in Holly Springs. Wells-Barnett became a teacher to provide for her family. She eventually wrote many works to shed light on how Black people were being treated in cities and counties in America. She championed and called for the just treatment of women and minoritized people around the globe—building on alliances across the world, speaking out against the Philippine-American War in the late 1800s, leading writing projects and press rooms, working in the women's suffrage movement, founding women's groups, and helping to found the National Association for the Advancement of Colored People (NAACP). As a teacher, Wells-Barnett's activism and commitment was not only a job but also a calling.

I have come to understand Wells-Barnett's life and writings as critical for connecting the power of language, what it means to resist, and why it is important to see our lives interwoven. As a grade school teacher in Mississippi and Tennessee in the late 1880s and 1890s, Wells-Barnett saw the need for advocacy just by being a conscious and active citizen. She wrote about her experiences in the *Memphis Free Speech*, a Black newspaper company she was actively involved with. Wells-Barnett was able to publish about the inequities she experienced, noting in her biography how exposing these truths was important to advancing conversations and promoting change. In addition to her lawsuit and subsequent publications on her experience of being made to move from her seat on a streetcar because of the color of her skin, in 1891, she was dismissed from the Memphis, Tennessee, school system for an article she wrote about the board of education's poor funding of Black schools. She also penned an article about three Black men who were lynched for opening a grocery store (the People's Grocery Store) in Memphis. Her use of language to resist oppressive forces in an effort to affirm Black communities and experiences put much attention on the *Memphis Free Speech* office. In fact, the office was destroyed while Wells-Barnett was out of town; she was threatened with lynching by white mobs if she returned to Memphis and was forced to move to another city. Her resistance through language, though risky, exposed the truth of the inequity around her. Wells-Barnett was able to see how words brought about action, and she designed communication that would allow readers to see "the light of truth" in an effort to push toward progressive change.[13] Through her use of public mediums such as the newspaper and pamphlets as technical communication,[14] Wells-Barnett showed how words bring people together. She actively called for and demanded change by showing people just how connected they were and how close these injustices were to their lives.

Wells-Barnett also modeled why it's important for Black people to tell their own stories. With her 1895 report *The Red Record*, Wells-Barnett positioned herself as a teacher who made structural and systemic inequalities more visible, writing about lynching cases not as incidents but as crimes, creating irrefutable and important meaning for Black liberation.[15] This liberation, to borrow from the Combahee River Collective's Statement, noted that the liberation of Black women "necessitates the liberations of all people."[16] In *The Red Record*, Wells-Barnett shared that it "becomes the painful duty of the Negro to reproduce a record which shows that a large portion of the American people avow anarchy, condone murder and defy the contempt of civilization."[17] I deduce, through analysis of the time period, that the recordings of the many lynchings she'd read about in local Chicago newspapers (in contrast to her own writings) were void of agency, giving little voice to the victims or their families involved. They were without context. In fact, in *Lynch Law in All*

Its Phases, Wells-Barnett made known that "those who commit the murders write the reports, and hence these lasting blots upon the honor of a nation cause but a faint ripple on the outside world."[18] In essence, the lynchings were made to look like isolated incidents, and no one was ever charged or convicted of the crimes. Because the story was controlled by those who were actually committing the crimes, their severity was never fully communicated. Wells-Barnett went on to say in *The Red Record* that her report designed to correct the stories was written "in no spirit of vindictiveness, for all who give the subject consideration must concede that far too serious is the condition of that civilized government in which the spirit of unrestrained outlawry constantly increases violence . . . We plead not for the colored people alone, but for all victims of injustice."[19] Wells-Barnett was writing to help communicate the seriousness of these crimes against humanity, noting that if crimes can happen to one of us, they can indeed happen to any of us.

At the NAACP's first meeting in Atlanta in 1909, Wells-Barnett echoed ideas from *The Red Record*. First, she acknowledged three "salient facts" about lynching: that

1. racial prejudice is at the center of these acts of violence;
2. being a criminal is the excuse used to justify acts, but it is certainly not the cause; and
3. "it [lynching] is a national crime and requires a national remedy."[20]

Wells-Barnett's point in writing the report and giving public speeches was to not only make the public aware of the epidemic but also to provide clear underpinnings of the cause. She was not simply responding; she was advocating for justice and providing a roadmap to achieve it. She offered a counterstory that not only tabulated the lynchings but also shared specific information—including names (if able), gender, alleged crime, city, and state—to tell a collective story across perceived boundaries. She used her rhetorical and technical skills to develop the report and made the records clear and accessible to her audience. Wells-Barnett created a history that otherwise would not have been noted. She was doing what effective technical communicators did long before they were called such: she conducted responsible research and curation of data and thoughtfully designed the material for public consumption. Wells-Barnett's writing of history, her technical communication, was political, social, and critical for situating and countering constructed histories of Black people. Ida B. Wells-Barnett's record worked to give a more representative view of how lynchings were literally changing communities by the thousands. Wells-Barnett storied for justice.

To use a modern framework to help make sense of what Wells-Barnett was doing, I look to critical race theory (CRT). CRT helps us understand the relationship among race, racism, and power.[21] Aja Martinez extends CRT for writing studies work, noting that storying "serves the purpose of exposing stereotypes and injustice and offering additional truths through a narration of the researchers' own experiences."[22] As a methodology, counterstory in writing aids in the teaching of historical documents, like those in Wells-Barnett's *The Red Record*, because it pushes us to rethink what counts as a text and gives us the ability to affirm the voices and stories of those who make our history so rich. For writing teachers, engaging historical documents like those of Wells-Barnett through the lens of story creates an opportunity for exploration. When these texts are brought into the classroom and students are asked to think about context, writing practices, writing genres, race, and systemic racism, they have a chance to explore concepts like audience, purpose, and genre to understand more about the lived experiences of writers along with the lasting nature of this writing. Use of story through historical documents also allows for development of racial literacy, as it builds in a guide for understanding histories through language and beckons self-reflection. These practices lead to a practice Gloria Ladson-Billings dubbed "culturally relevant pedagogy." With it, both teachers and students consider how events impact, support, and lead to the current moment. In a study of Black teachers and how they engage Black students, Ladson-Billings concludes that "a culturally relevant pedagogy is designed to problematize teaching and encourage teachers to ask about the nature of the student-teacher relationship, the curriculum, schooling, and society."[23] Through Wells-Barnett's approach to writing and teaching, we can see early notes of what Ladson-Billings asserts here, reminding us that direct study of historical documents such as newspaper clippings, pamphlets, and letters can give us tools to help advance both teacher and student engagement.

By storying, Wells-Barnett influenced many people from all walks of life. The Equal Justice Initiative and the site of the National Memorial for Peace and Justice, both headed by Bryan Stevenson, along with Michelle Alexander's work on mass incarceration, to name a few, are building on the communication skills Ida B. Wells-Barnett modeled for us in the late nineteenth and early twentieth centuries—using critical thinking and rhetorical awareness to make connections that can only be made when a person has the ability and the opportunity to tell their own story and to clearly articulate their own racial identity. As writing teachers, we have the means to carefully and meaningfully infuse documents developed by Black people as well as to continue to add to national consciousness in ways that affirm, enlighten, and empower.

HOW TO

To infuse historical documents developed by Black people into writing classrooms, instructors need to focus more on the teaching of reading and racial literacy in those spaces. By honing in on reading, students can be primed to not only develop their rhetorical reading skills but also to recognize connections across time and space. Instructors, then, can share their reasons for assigning work more clearly and offer explanations about their practices to students to help communicate their teaching philosophy. In so doing, students will also be able to develop their racial literacies as they map how race can be understood through reading. In her work on mindfulness and reading, Ellen C. Carillo offers insights into how students benefit from taking the time to understand the fullness of a reading situation. Carillo shares that "to transfer—or apply—what is learned in one course to another, students need to actively think about—or reflect on—what they have learned. In other words, they need to be mindful."[24] Mara Lee Grayson extends Carillo's point, noting that cultivating "racial literacy, like reading, can be seen as a sort of transfer concept . . . Thus, rather than transferring discrete skills to other classrooms, students transfer ways of thinking practiced in the racial literacy classroom to their experiences and understandings of the worlds they inhabit."[25] In many ways, the teaching of critical reading provides an opportunity for transfer that will aid students as they build their literacies and ultimately help them beyond the classroom.

Encouraging students to practice mindfulness and racial literacy can be done by assigning historical documents as core readings in writing courses. In other words, instructors provide the historical documents as the main texts for the class, scaffolding multiple assignments using those documents. First, instructors can incorporate some of the strategies for reading introduced in Carillo's textbook, particularly as they relate to empowering students to adopt a reading strategy for Wells-Barnett's work (or another historical document). When students understand their instructor's purpose for assigning work, they are more invested in the reading they do. Carillo notes that "determining why you are reading is crucial to choosing the most productive strategy."[26] Once students understand why the reading is being assigned, tracking the reading process through writing becomes a useful tool to help students see the relationship between reading and writing.

Once students see their own purpose for reading, they can do the work of making connections between the reading and the self. If students encounter, for example, Wells-Barnett's *The Red Record*, not only can they investigate the genre of report writing, students can also be empowered to think about context (why is Wells-Barnett compelled to write such a report), purpose (why is Wells-Barnett's report important for readers to engage), and audience (who did Wells-Barnett hope to reach by composing the report). As students read *The Red Record*, they may also consider how report writing has changed or remained the same over time. In addition to closely reading the report, students can look to Bryan Stevenson's National Memorial for Peace and Justice, the first and only site in the United States that publicly recognizes lynchings as crimes; in doing a rhetorical analysis of Stevenson's website, students could spend time looking to how he conceived of the memorial and its museum. A critical reading of the site, coupled with Wells-Barnett's report, would allow for an exercise in mindfulness and racial literacy while also connecting the 1800s to the present. As Zapoura Newton-Calvert asserts (chapter 7, this volume), I am a believer that "writing and reading about racial justice both play important parts in the root systems holding the learning together." Connecting the past to the present through reading and writing about historical documents gives us an opportunity to make important connections.

CONCLUSION

In Paulo Freire's "The Importance of the Act of Reading," he says that "reading the world . . . precedes reading the word and writing a new text must be seen as one means of transforming the world."[27] When we are able to engage a text like Wells-Barnett's *The Red Record*, we cannot dismiss the realities of the time and the ways her work has contributed to the world. One of the best takeaways about studying historical documents is that we can produce thoughtful research, generating productive conversations about just *how* the writer and the text exhibit rhetorical agency and thus encouraging students to think critically about our relationships to the past. Students in writing courses represent many majors and minors, including English. As teachers, we can help them write for justice through study of historical contributions. Building on the works of Black educators like Ida B. Wells-Barnett can teach us a lot about what it means to connect our classrooms to the outside world. Her work, along with the works of many other Black thinkers and communicators, encourages me to foster spaces where students understand collective humanity as I push to story for justice—much like those who came before me—and, I hope, assist my students in doing the same.

NOTES

1. Muhammad, *Cultivating Genius*; Tatum, *Why Are All the Black Kids Sitting Together*; Jones and Williams, "The Just Use of Imagination."
2. Givens, "What's Missing from the Discourse."
3. Sealey-Ruiz, "Racial Literacy."
4. Edwards, "Race and the Workplace."
5. Gomstym, "Minority Enrollment in Colleges More than Doubled in Past 20 Years."
6. Sullivan, "Deep Reading as a Threshold Concept."
7. Porcher, "Teaching While Black"; Griffin et al., "(Re) Defining Departure"; Smitherman, "God Don't Never Change"; Richardson and Ragland, "#StayWoke."
8. Haas, "Race, Rhetoric, and Technology"; Agboka, "Decolonial Methodologies"; Pritchard, "When You Know Better, Do Better"; Medina and Luna, "Publishing Is Mystical."
9. McCoy et al., CCCC Black Technical and Professional Communication Position Statement.
10. https://cccc.ncte.org/cccc/black-technical-professional-communication.
11. Villanueva, "On Rhetoric and the Precedents of Racism."
12. Brock, *Sista Talk*.
13. Wells-Barnett, *The Red Record*.
14. Williams, *From Black Codes to Recodification*.
15. Wells-Barnett, *The Red Record*.
16. Combahee River Collective Statement.
17. Wells-Barnett, *The Red Record*, 1.
18. Wells-Barnett, *Lynch Law in All Its Phases*, 1.
19. Wells-Barnett, *The Red Record*, 1.
20. Wells-Barnett, *The Red Record*, 2.
21. Delgado and Stefancic, *Critical Race Theory*, 3–9.
22. Martinez, *Counterstory*, 17.
23. Ladson-Billings, "Toward a Theory of Culturally Relevant Pedagogy," 488.
24. Carillo, *A Writer's Guide to Mindful Reading*, ix.
25. Grayson, "Information, Identity, and Ideology," 273.
26. Carillo, *A Writer's Guide to Mindful Reading*, 10.
27. Friere, "The Importance of the Act of Reading," 5.

REFERENCES

Agboka, Godwin Y. "Decolonial Methodologies: Social Justice Perspectives in Intercultural Technical Communication Research." *Journal of Technical Writing and Communication* 44, no. 3 (2014): 297–327.

Brock, Rochelle. *Sista Talk: The Personal and the Pedagogical*. New York: Peter Lang, 2005.

Carillo, Ellen C. *A Writer's Guide to Mindful Reading*. Denver: WAC Clearinghouse and University Press of Colorado, 2017.

Combahee River Collective Statement. Boston: Combahee River Collective, 1977.

Delgado, Richard, and Jean Stefancic. *Critical Race Theory: An Introduction*. New York: New York University Press, 2012.

Delpit, Lisa. *Other People's Children: Cultural Conflict in the Classroom*. New York: New Press, 2006.

Edwards, Jessica. "Race and the Workplace: Toward a Critically Conscious Pedagogy." In *Key Theoretical Frameworks: Teaching Technical Communication in the Twenty-First Century*, edited by Angela Haas and Michelle F. Eble, 268–86. Logan: Utah State Univeristy Press, 2018.

Friere, Paulo. "The Importance of the Act of Reading." Trans. Loretta Slover. *Journal of Education* 165, no. 2 (1983): 5–11.

Givens, Jarvis. "What's Missing from the Discourse about Anti-Racist Teaching." *The Atlantic*, May 21, 2021. https://www.theatlantic.com/ideas/archive/2021/05/whats-missing-from-the-discourse-about-anti-racist-teaching/618947/.

Gomstym, Alice. "Minority Enrollment in Colleges More than Doubled in Past 20 Years, Study Finds." *Chronicle of Higher Education*, October 17, 2003. https://www.chronicle.com/article/minority-enrollment-in-colleges-more-than-doubled-in-past-20-years-study-finds-20000/.

Grayson, Mara Lee. "Information, Identity, and Ideology: Reading toward Racial Literacy in a Composition Classroom." *Pedagogy* 21, no. 2 (2021): 259–75. https://www.muse.jhu.edu/article/793511.

Griffin, Kimberly, Meghan Pifer Griffin, Jordan Humphrey, and Ashley Hazelwood. "(Re)Defining Departure: Exploring Black Professors' Experiences with and Responses to Racism and Racial Climate." *American Journal of Education* 117, no. 4 (2011): 495–526.

Haas, Angela. "Race, Rhetoric, and Technology: A Case Study of Decolonial Technical Communication Theory, Methodology, and Pedagogy." *Journal of Business and Technical Communication* 26, no. 3 (2012): 277–310.

Jones, Natasha, and Miriam Williams. "The Just Use of Imagination." *ATTW Blog*, June 10, 2020.

Ladson-Billings, Gloria. "Toward a Theory of Culturally Relevant Pedagogy." *American Educational Research Journal* 32, no. 3 (1995): 465–91.

Martinez, Aja. *Counterstory: The Rhetoric and Writing of Critical Race Theory*. Champaign, IL: National Council of Teachers of English, 2020.

McCoy, Temptaous, Cecilia Shelton, Donnie Sackey, Natasha Jones, Constance Haywood, Ja'La Wourman, and Kimberly Harper. *CCCC Black Technical and Professional Communication Position Statement with Resource Guide*. Urbana, IL: National Council of Teachers of English, 2020.

Medina, Cruz, and Pia Luna. "'Publishing Is Mystical': The Latinx Caucus Bibliography, Top-Tier Journals, and Minority Scholarship." *Rhetoric Review* 39, no. 3 (2020): 303–31.

Muhammad, Gholdy. *Cultivating Genius: An Equity Framework for Culturally and Historically Responsive Literacy*. New York: Scholastic, 2020.

Porcher, Kisha. "Teaching While Black: Best Practices for Engaging White Preservice Teachers in Discourse Focused on Individual and Cultural Diversity." *Journal of Urban Learning, Teaching, and Research* 15, no. 1 (2020): 116–34.

Pritchard, Eric Darnell. "'When You Know Better, Do Better': Honoring Intellectual and Emotional Labor through Diligent Accountability Practices." *Education, Liberation, and Black Radical Traditions for the Twenty-First Century* (Blog), edited by Carmen Kynard. July 8, 2019. http://carmenkynard.org/featured-scholar-eric-darnell-pritchard-when-you-know-better-do-better-honoring-intellectual-and-emotional-labor-through-diligent-accountability-practices/.

Richardson, Elaine, and Alice Ragland. "#StayWoke: The Language and Literacies of the #BlackLivesMatterMovement." *Community Literacy Journal* 12, no. 2 (2018): 27–56.

Sealey-Ruiz, Yolanda. "Racial Literacy: A Policy Research Brief." New York: Teachers College, Columbia University, 2021. https://ncte.org/wp-content/uploads/2021/04/SquireOfficePolicyBrief_RacialLiteracy_April2021.pdf.

Smitherman, Geneva. "God Don't Never Change: Black English from a Black Perspective." *College English* 34, no. 6 (1973): 828–33.

Sullivan, Patrick. "Deep Reading as a Threshold Concept in Composition Studies." In *Deep Reading: Teaching Reading in the Writing Classroom,* edited by Patrick Sullivan, Howard Tinberg, and Sheridan Blau, 123–71. Champaign, IL: National Council of Teachers of English, 2017.

Tatum, Beverly. *Why Are All the Black Kids Sitting Together in the Cafeteria?* New York: Basic Books, 1997.

Villanueva, Victor. "On Rhetoric and the Precedents of Racism." In *Cross-Talk in Comp Theory: A Reader,* edited by Victor Villanueva, 645–61. Champaign, IL: National Council of Teachers of English, 2001.

Wells-Barnett, Ida B. *Crusade for Justice: The Autobiography of Ida B. Wells.* Chicago: University of Chicago Press, 1970.

Wells-Barnett, Ida B. *Lynch Law in All Its Phases.* 1893.

Wells-Barnett, Ida B. *The Red Record: Tabulated Statistics and Alleged Causes of Lynching in the United States.* 1895.

Williams, Miriam. *From Black Codes to Recodification: Removing the Veil from Regulatory Writing.* Baywood's Technical Communications. Abingdon, UK: Routledge, 2010.

Afterword
TIMELY IS TIMELESS

Deborah H. Holdstein

When I first saw the title—but not the content—of this decidedly impressive volume, I was concerned: would scholar-teachers in composition and rhetoric assume that this must be a collection too rooted in its time and place to have long-standing relevance and influence for both scholarship and teaching? Would there be similar judgment by department chairs and others in administration who might otherwise look to this volume to best understand how to think about first-year writing, writing in the disciplines (WID), and their attention to diversity and equity, for instance, at their respective institutions?

On perhaps the too optimistic assumption that our colleagues will read carefully (and I hope some will), *Composition and Rhetoric in Contentious Times* captures long-standing pedagogical and scholarly contexts while flexibly mapping paths forward.

As they have for many years, my concerns—those that directly affect our students, programs, and colleagues—lie uneasily within the institutional and administrative structures in which we live and that we cannot control. For instance, in chapter 4 of this volume, Christopher Basgier notes that vision and strategy must ensure the long-term viability of writing across the curriculum (WAC) and writing in the disciplines (WID) programs, maxims that can be extended to first-year writing and to any campus initiative that explicitly involves writing. Basgier rightly suggests that "strategy names the concrete actions, policies, structures, projects, and services that serve the mission and vision" of these programs. He also cites WAC scholar and pedagogical fore-parent Elaine P. Maimon in her appropriate insistence that there be "peripheral vision,"[1] "an awareness of rhetorical institutional and interpersonal factors" that could affect the long term.

But how effective are vision and strategy in the face of budget cuts where for ease and convenience (as is now the case at my own institution), for instance, administrators attempt to cut the second semester of our very successful and necessary two-semester first-year writing requirement for reasons that have little to do with student success? Maimon (as quoted by Basgier) writes that "strategic thinking, like vision, requires sight and insight—seeing many pathways through a complexity of choices and discovering the best route to success, and curricular change depends on scholarly exchange among faculty members."[2] But whose definition of success? At whose expense? And what if valid scholarly exchange, in the end, doesn't affect the curricular outcome?

As Michael Bérubé pointed out in 1998, "The question . . . is not whether the university will serve the general public; the question is *which* structural and economic segments of the public will be served—and interpolated—by which academic disciplines."[3] In 2001, I wrote an essay published in *Pedagogy* titled " 'Writing across the Curriculum' and the Paradoxes of Institutional Initiatives." I suggest the following:

> It is surprising . . . that scholars so concerned with the economic and other forms of prostitution on the part of universities are so rarely if ever concerned with their contradictory effects on the actual programs that serve students—and the effects on students themselves. Indeed, there has been little scholarly link among institutional agendas and contexts, the movements that fall under the rubric of "university-wide initiatives," and the ultimate effects of these on the students we claim to serve. In this case, I refer to such university-wide concerns as "Writing Across the Curriculum" (WAC) (assessment is another of many), which at times appear to configure and inform the worst institutional attempts to maintain [Jean-Francois] Lyotard's sense of a negative "internal cohesion."[4]

Historian Joan W. Scott argues that "we operate within a rhetoric of crisis in higher education, which upon analysis is rooted in paradox."[5] She articulates four paradoxes, seemingly "contradictory developments":

1. The more the university community has diversified, the more relentless have been the attempts to enforce community;

2. The more individualism is used by those opposed to the institutionalization of diversity, the more advocates of diversity invoke individualism;

3. The greater the need for open-ended research, reflection, and criticism in the production of new knowledge, the more instrumental the justifications for taking new directions have become;

4. The greater the need for theorizing—for the practice of questioning unquestioned assumptions and beliefs—the faster has been the turn to moralism and the therapeutics of the personal.[6]

As I wrote in 2001, those of us involved in composition and rhetoric and in the administration of English and writing programs can readily see the parallels between these paradoxes and composition studies, and I am aware that these concerns are exacerbated as I write this. And I add another composition-related, Scott-inspired paradox: the more dedicated the composition faculty members or some administrators are to the professed goals of good, expansive, and varied forms of instruction in writing at a variety of levels, the more likely they are to believe that they and their students operate in a closed community somehow untouched by these bacterial paradoxes and contradictions. For instance, when faculty members carefully delineate a new curricular focus for a unit in a first-year composition course, to what extent must they incorporate any upper administrative strategic plans or goals that the course doesn't necessarily reflect, even as the curriculum meets faculty-articulated learning objectives?

The *idea* of community ("we are compositionists and administrators of composition programs and English programs; we are good; we try hard; we teach well and with more than just regard for DEI; we're dedicated; we operate within our own sphere")—in Scott's words regarding institutions generally—is "substituted for an analysis of social relationships,"[7] making it easy for us to separate what we do (teach, write) from what others do (administer, draft strategic plans and budgeting priorities, set curricular agendas, deal with boards of trustees, seek funds from state legislatures, and so on). In this light, we must be warned against the use of campus-wide writing efforts as part of a "reductive instrumentalism" that "tailors knowledge to a narrowly specified outcome," the counterpart to our own belief that scholarly-pedagogical community alone will undergird our efforts for our students and that our "social relationships" with the institution will have no bearing on our teaching.[8] As Basgier acknowledges (chapter 4, this volume) despite the success of his institution's particular program, "No WAC program is immune to the contraction of higher education."

But perhaps I'm too pessimistic. *Composition and Rhetoric in Contentious Times* often reignites my optimism with essays that honor the past and broadly sculpt the future: consider Nicole Khoury, Nicholas Behm, and Sherry Rankins-Robertson's essay (chapter 5, this volume) on graduate programs, the need to build an infrastructure that "constructs and supports healthy, egalitarian norms." Even the Jumbo writing classes delineated by Laura Sparks and Kim Jaxon in chapter 6 (the large class, of course, being a writing program administrator's [WPA's] worst nightmare) involves "powerful possibilities for creating and sustaining vibrant, action-oriented communities." The authors argue that "Jumbo design was not a reaction to budgetary or staffing concerns; nor was it imposed on our program by administrators." But what I would want senior administrators to ferret out from the authors' description is *not* that the course has ninety students. Rather, it's essential to note that this curriculum is *pedagogically* effective, *not a cost-effective* or cost-cutting enterprise. As Sparks and Jaxon explain (chapter 6, this volume):

> The design call[s] for the addition of nine embedded peer writing mentors, who would attend every Jumbo class and lead their own ten-person workshops each week. The Jumbo itself meets as a whole class twice weekly for one hour; peer writing mentors (first trained in our department's tutoring writing course) lead weekly workshops, and those workshop groups are maintained throughout the semester. The Jumbo design thus offers both large- and small-scale learning environments. The mentors see and respond to student writing frequently, with opportunities for more feedback and norming in our weekly "mentor meetings." These weekly meetings between the mentors and instructor allow for ongoing course design, feedback opportunities, class and activity planning, and so on.

Sparks and Jaxon caution that the Jumbo "does not address the labor concerns frequent in higher education, especially writing programs, that may rely on contingent and adjunct labor to staff composition courses, offer insufficient notice for course assignments, and even underfund instructors and support staff." Indeed, the authors articulate another concern: "that the Jumbo might displace lecturers by occasioning fewer sections of traditional writing courses." Indeed, my concern won't surprise: that in trying times, it would be decided, and not by WPAs or department chairs, that the structure of the Jumbo would remain with ninety students—but without the extensive infrastructure described by Sparks and Jaxon, one that supports student learning and effective pedagogy.

Of course, the requirements of this afterword prevent my commenting on each chapter in the volume. Word and page limits should not be seen as a judgment of value regarding any of the essays. Rather, as is the case with this type of rhetorical situation, aspects of certain chapters stand in certain relief, reflecting my own projects and current thinking about a variety of administrative and pedagogical issues that, I believe, affect many, if not all, of us. For instance, I am struck by Hannah J. Rule's "A Future without Thesis Statements" (chapter 10, this volume), an essay far more nuanced than the title might suggest. Rule's concluding sentence is, "Let's finally put thesis statements in their place—as a small set of options in the infinite range of writing in the wild, in the world."

If, in fact, we are so worried about the tyranny of the thesis, why, then, do we risk reductivity as a method by which we affirm composition as a discipline? Rule's well-argued piece is ultimately conciliatory, I think, and it takes me to an essay about William Irmscher written by Christine R. Farris, part of a volume I edited titled *Lost Texts in Rhetoric and Composition*. Farris articulates a concern about current trends in composition that shift our emphasis from learning to write to learning about writing, creating "key words" that potentially put us and our students in another type of lockstep from the alleged confines of the thesis statement: "Drawing from principles of educational psychology, rhetoric, genre theory, and findings from a number of empirical studies of students' repurposing of prior composition knowledge . . . the approaches known as Writing about Writing and Teaching for Transfer view the purpose of first-year courses to be the development of that meta-cognitive awareness."[9] Farris continues with her concern about new frameworks and "key words": "I can understand the usefulness of threshold concepts to frame what composition knows in, say, a graduate seminar or as a tool in negotiating conflicting assumptions about writing with faculty across the disciplines . . . I wonder, though, to what extent a focus in an undergraduate course on 'discourse about writing' is a conflation of our agenda as knowledge producers with that of our students."[10]

Farris questions the "requisitioning" of "new frameworks for articulating a disciplinary identity," arguing that we are, as in the past, "privileging the importance of fields other than our own." She continues by citing William Irmscher: "Do we have to abandon the literary and critical values of our discipline in the name of scholarship? By denying these values, whom are we trying to please? Must we continue to be plagued by the scientific nemesis?"[11] Is our drive to disciplinarity and frameworks restricting us, as does, some might argue, the inflexible nature of the thesis statement? Are we relinquishing what "attracted most of us . . . in the first place": navigating the puzzling and the unpredictable in texts, grappling with "what we *don't* know?"[12] Shouldn't we be arguing for writing as the humanities? Indeed, as Kurt Spellmeyer points out, it is "the prospect of a Wall Street of the mind, as critics like Martha Nussbaum . . . have warned."[13]

While the chapters in this volume reflect what I have called in my title both the "timely" and "timeless" nature of this collection, they clearly encourage and demand the ongoing, necessary conversations about pedagogy and the future of our field, tempered by the ever-present constraints of the institutional contexts in which our students learn and in which we teach. In sum, I pose an additional question for the ongoing conversation: what might we ask of our institutions, given that they ask so much of us? Perhaps Zapoura Newton-Calvert's (chapter 7) concluding acknowledgment of the work at Portland State University can articulate an overarching ethos of the volume and of our work as a whole: "As we all work together to grapple with our future's inevitable disruptions, which can surely fracture and destroy us, we also have the potential to crack open the ground and find new places to plant seeds."[14]

NOTES

1. Maimon, *Leading Academic Change*, 12.
2. Maimon, *Leading Academic Change*, 14, 24.
3. Bérubé, *The Employment of English*, 191, emphasis added.
4. Holdstein, "Writing across the Curriculum," 38.
5. Scott quoted in Holdstein, "Writing across the Curriculum," 37–52.
6. Scott, "The Rhetoric of Crisis in Higher Education," 295.
7. Scott, "The Rhetoric of Crisis in Higher Education," 295.
8. Holdstein, "Writing across the Curriculum."
9. Farris, "Possibilities Rather than Certainties," 214–15.
10. Farris, "Possibilities Rather than Certainties," 215.
11. Farris, "Possibilities Rather than Certainties," 215.
12. Farris, "Possibilities Rather than Certainties," original emphasis.
13. Spellmeyer "The Trouble with an Airtight Case," 577.
14. The author wishes to thank Professor Hilary Sarat-St. Peter, colleague at Columbia College Chicago, for her thoughts on this essay.

REFERENCES

Bérubé, Michael. *The Employment of English: Theory, Jobs, and the Future of Literary Studies.* New York: New York University Press, 1998.

Farris, Christine R. "Possibilities Rather than Certainties: William Irmscher's 'Finding a Comfortable Identity.'" In *Lost Texts in Rhetoric and Composition*, edited by Deborah H. Holdstein, 207–18. New York: Modern Language Association, 2023.

Holdstein, Deborah H., ed. *Lost Texts in Rhetoric and Composition.* New York: Modern Language Association, 2023.

Holdstein, Deborah H. "'Writing across the Curriculum' and the Paradox of Institutional Initiatives." *Pedagogy* 1, no. 1 (2001): 37–52.

Irmscher, William F. "Finding a Comfortable Identity." *College Composition and Communication* 38, no. 1 (February 1987): 81–87.

Maimon, Elaine P. *Leading Academic Change: Vision, Strategy, Transformation.* Sterling, VA: Stylus, 2018.

Scott, Joan W. "The Rhetoric of Crisis in Higher Education." In *Higher Education under Fire: Politics, Economics, and the Crisis of the Humanities*, edited by Michael Bérubé and Cary Nelson, 293–303. New York: Routledge, 1995.

Spellmeyer, Kurt. "The Trouble with an Airtight Case: The Rhetoric of Method or the Rhetoric of Urgency?" *Pedagogy* 15, no. 3 (2015): 569–77.

INDEX

Page numbers followed by *n* indicate endnotes.

ableism, 12, 202; able-bodied, 53, 202
adaptation, 169; intentional adaptation, 9, 126, 128–130, 136. *See also* brown, adrienne maree
affect, xii, 4, 51, 53, 58, 61; dimensions of, 50, 57; affective, 50, 57, 61, 62, 84, 92, 101, 104, 227; affective infrastructure, 58, 84, 100–101, 103, 104, 114; affective vulnerability, 91, 95, 96–97, 100–102, 104, 151. *See also* affective rhetorics
affordances, 10, 108, 110–111, 114, 163–165, 166, 167, 168, 169, 170, 174, 175, 183
agency, xiii, 23, 27, 52, 75, 94, 96, 102, 152, 154, 234, 238
anti-racist: anti-racism, 9, 197, 202, 223, 231; course model, 126, 130, 132, 136, 139; educator, 127, 129; efforts, xii; feminist lens, 203; language, 138; practice, 128, 129, 131, 132, 133–134, 135, 136, 204; reading, 137–139; space, 126, 129, 136; teaching, 129, 133, 137, 138, 202, 231; work, 134, 137
arguments, xii, 4, 6, 10–11, 18, 19, 20, 22, 30, 38, 39, 40, 50, 56–57, 60, 79, 147, 150, 151, 174, 184, 185, 187, 188–189, 191, 193, 198, 204, 215, 226; argumentation, 46, 59, 151, 191, 215; argumentative strategies, 46; counterarguments, 19. *See also* Carillo, Ellen
"alternative facts," 6, 36–37, 38, 39, 40, 42, 43, 46; "fake news," 6, 36, 39–40, 42, 43, 46; "junk science," 6, 39, 42, 46
artifacts, xii, 110, 117, 118. *See also* multimodal
authority, 50, 152, 189, 190, 191, 200, 202, 203, 205, 206, 210; authority in the classroom, 116

Banks, Adam, 163, 166, 168, 170, 183, 192–193, 210
Bartholomae, David, 166–167, 174
belief, xiii, 40, 41, 42, 43, 44, 45, 46, 119, 129, 147, 154, 166, 167, 174, 243, 244
Berggren, Anne, 185–186. *See also* thesis

BIPOC (Black, Indigenous, People of Color), xi, 54, 57, 61, 71, 100, 105*n18*, 200–201, 208
binary, 10; binary thinking, 4, 6
black educators, 231–232, 233, 236, 238
Black Lives Matter, xi, 3, 37, 43, 93, 130, 137
black people, 125, 130, 220, 223, 224, 233, 234, 235, 237. *See also* BIPOC
Black Technical and Professional Communication, 232–233
Blankenship, Lisa, xiii
Borrowman, Shane, *Trauma and the Teaching of Writing*, 90–91, 104
brown, adrienne maree, 126, 130–131, 134; emergent strategies model, 9, 128, 140. *See also* intentional adaptation
budget, 70, 77–78, 85, 100, 108, 244; budget cuts, 69, 74, 242; priorities, 244
Burke, Kenneth, 52, 217, 228*n19*
Burrows, Cedric, xiii
Butler, Judith, 91, 92–96, 97, 101, 102, 203. *See also* vulnerability

cancel culture, xii–xiv
capstone, 125, 126–127, 139
care work, 6, 19–20, 24–28, 29, 30
Carillo, Ellen, 38, 44–45, 237
Chakravartty, Paula, Rachel Kuo, Victoria Grubbs, and Charlton McIlwain (#CommunicationSoWhite), 200–201
Chronicle of Higher Education (CHE), 6, 17–18, 30, 231
citations, 11, 198, 199–201, 203, 204, 205, 206–207, 210; citation campaigns, 202; citation conventions, 205; citation policy, 198, 202, 209; citation practices, 10–11, 197–200, 202–204, 208, 209, 232; citation politics, 197, 205
civic life, 143, 146
close reading, 41, 166, 187, 189, 222
collaboration, 30, 36, 112, 114, 115, 119, 157, 208; collaborative, 41, 111, 116, 119, 149, 156, 198; collaborator, 26, 152

250   INDEX

Conference on College Composition and Communication (CCCC), 19, 30, 35, 97, 183, 201, 232–233
colonialism, 53, 56, 59, 64; de-colonial, 51, 58, 60, 232
community, xv, 4, 8, 9, 45, 62, 91, 94, 95, 99, 100, 104, 111, 113, 125, 126, 127, 128, 129, 130, 131, 132, 133, 134, 135, 136, 137, 138, 139, 140, 145, 149, 152, 154, 157, 217, 244; community action, 136, 149; community activism, 136, 144, 157; community-based model, 110; community building, 125; community-engaged education, 139; community engagement, 85; community-interdependent course model, 126, 127, 131, 132, 136, 139; community-interdependent educational space, 126; community learning, 127, 136, 137, 139, 143; community membership, 118, 127, 137; community needs, 137; "community of practice" model, 112; community organizations, 154; community partners, 154, 156; community work, 132, 134, 136, 137, 156, 157; community writing, 138, 144; educational community, 4; learning community, 125, 132, 140, 150; scholarly community, 4, 201, 205, 243, 244. *See also* working-class
competencies, 162, 163, 165, 167, 169, 171, 172, 174, 175; core competencies, 162, 169, 171, 172, 175
complexity, 12, 38, 80, 81, 148, 215, 216, 219, 222, 226, 243
contraction, 38, 188, 189, 243, 244
Council of Writing Program Administrators (CWPA), 35, 97, 204
Covid-19 pandemic, xv, 3, 5, 9, 19, 25, 30, 39, 44, 54, 69, 71, 77–78, 80, 81, 90–91, 92, 94, 95, 99, 103–104, 125, 129, 136, 140, 143, 146, 233
critical race theory (CRT), xii, 4, 7, 11, 58, 59, 61, 236
critical reading, 23, 237, 238
cultural artifacts. *See* artifacts

Digital Black Literature and Composition (DBLAC), 232
disciplinarity, 6, 18, 20–23, 102, 246
discourse community, 200, 206–207
disability, 52, 53–54, 147, 157; disability studies, 58, 59, 92; disability theory, 7, 104–105n9
disenfranchised. *See* marginalized
diversity, xv, 5, 11, 21, 36, 39, 43, 58, 60, 62, 77, 81, 112, 117, 149, 209, 242, 243

Django Unchained (Quentin Tarantino), 216, 219, 220–223, 226, 229n24
Duffy, John, xvi

education, xv, 6, 30, 59, 117, 127, 128, 135, 139, 140, 144, 146, 158, 185, 203, 215; board of education, 234; college education, 12, 69, 70, 139, 146; community colleges, 74; education justice, 137; education models, 135; education system, 127, 131, 132, 208; educational background, 7; educational experiences, 227; educational infrastructure, 6; educational organizations, 136; educational space, 6, 45, 126, 128, 129; educational structures, 155; higher education, xv, 4, 5, 6, 7–8, 11, 22, 29, 30, 36, 43, 69, 70, 71, 73, 74, 75, 77, 80, 84, 85, 92, 108, 111, 139, 145, 148, 149, 152, 200, 231, 243, 244, 245; K-12 education, 9; National Center for Education Statistics (NCES), 70; postsecondary education, 38; secondary education, 186; Standford History Education Group, 35
elaborated prose, 168–169, 171, 172, 173, 174, 176
embodiment, 51, 52, 56, 58, 60, 62, 140, 198, 205. *See also* pedagogy: critical embodiment pedagogy
emergent strategies model. *See* brown, adrienne maree
empathy, 8, 45, 62, 97, 104, 226. *See also* Blankenship, Lisa
enrollment, 5, 8, 12, 69, 72, 73, 83, 107, 108, 114, 146
ePortfolios, 76, 79, 81, 83
essay, xvi, 4, 17–18, 25, 28–29, 50, 117, 162–163, 166, 171, 172, 174, 175, 183–184, 185, 186, 187, 188, 189, 193, 231, 243, 244, 245, 246; academic essay, 184; argumentative essay, 38; exploratory essay, 174; literary essay, 168; "traditional essayistic literacy," 163; essayistic prose, 168; essayistic writing, 184–185, 192; essayists, 185; the logic of, 167–169. *See also* thesis: thesis-driven essay
ethnicity. *See* race
ethos, 43, 45, 46, 48n30, 247
Euro-American: canon, 59; discourse, 185; literacies, 56; tradition, 192
expansion, 69, 75, 107, 108, 119
expertise, 17, 18, 19, 22, 23, 28, 29–30, 103, 110, 113–114, 117, 119, 143, 153, 154, 155, 156, 157, 163, 200, 210; undisciplined expertise, 20, 22, 23, 28

explication, 24, 168–169, 171; logic of explication, 168–169, 171, 173

faculty development, 76, 77, 80, 81, 83, 85
Farris, Christine R., 11, 246
feminism, xii, xv, 52, 58–59, 146, 202, 203, 209, 210
fieldwork, 151
film analysis. *See* visual analysis
first-generation students, 111, 114
first-year composition. *See* first-year writing
first-year writing, 23, 29, 75, 107, 109, 114, 116, 148, 200, 204, 242, 243, 244; first-year courses, xii, 109, 116, 246; first-year students, xiii, 146, 191, 204, 205 (*see also* undergraduate students); first-year writing classroom, 113; first-year writing teachers, 46
five-paragraph theme, 183–184
Flores, Lisa, xiii
FOX News, 37–38, 44

gender, xii, xv, 5, 22, 52, 54, 58, 71, 96, 97, 104–105*n*9, 147, 157, 199, 202, 203, 209, 218, 222, 235
generative combination, 9, 29, 161, 162–163, 164, 165, 167, 169, 172, 173, 174, 175, 176, 194
genre, 9–10, 27, 29–30, 59, 61, 134, 161, 162, 163, 164, 165, 167–168, 170, 172, 174, 175, 176, 184, 193, 204, 216, 217, 219, 220, 222, 223, 224, 225, 232, 236, 238, 246; genre conventions, 219, 221, 223; genre emeritus, 163, 183
Glenn, Cheryl, xii, 133
graduate: courses, 8, 29, 91, 246; labor, 111; level, 157; programs, xii, 58, 84, 91, 92, 95, 96, 97, 99, 100, 102, 103, 104, 156, 244; school, 97, 200, 155; students, xi, 8, 91–92, 93, 95, 96, 97, 98, 99, 100, 101, 102, 103, 104, 114, 143, 155, 174, 232; studies, 145, 155; training, 9

Hesse, Doug, 18–19, 30
High Impact Practices (HIPs), 8, 76, 79, 82, 83; high impact writing activities, 76–77, 82; high impact writing instruction, 78, 80
historical documents, 232, 233, 236, 237, 238, 239
hooks, bell, 24, 25, 126, 140
hyper-visibility, 54, 58, 61

identity, xi, xvii, 3, 4, 44, 46, 51, 52, 53, 54, 57, 58, 59, 61, 92, 93, 99, 111, 127, 128, 129, 132, 134, 135, 138, 139, 140, 143, 146, 147, 153, 155, 193, 198, 205, 208, 209, 210, 218, 225, 227; disciplinary identity, 21, 246; formation, 147; group identity, 55; identification, 11, 57, 93, 95, 172, 203, 215, 218, 219, 220, 221, 223, 228*n*6; identity crisis, 21; identity politics xii, xv
identity work, 127, 128, 133–134, 135, 136, 137; marginalized identities, 201; over-identification, 218, 221; racial identity, 232, 236; scholarly identity, 113; writerly identity, 20, 146
in-person teaching, 127, 130
Inoue, Asao B., 127, 204
Inside Higher Education (IHE), 6, 17–18, 30
interdependence, 54, 145, 149, 150
International WAC/WID Mapping Project, 74, 85
Irmscher, William, 246

Jumbo, xii, 8, 107–119, 244–245; class size, 8; large class, 108, 109, 244

kairotic opportunity, 100
Kimmerer, Robin Wall, xvi
Kress, Gunter, 161, 163–164

labor, 4, 20, 21, 55, 56, 79, 84, 96, 97, 100, 103, 107, 110, 111, 113, 115, 145, 146, 148, 245; adjunct labor, 111, 245; emotional labor, 92, 100, 102, 199; intellectual labor, 198; labor-based grading, 26; labor force, 186; labor insecurity, 95. *See also* graduate student labor
layering. *See* sequencing
literacy, 6, 52, 56, 60, 111, 163, 164, 175, 199; information literacy (IL), 190, 201–202, 208; Information Literacy Standards for Higher Education, 201; literacy activities, 162, 174; literacy challenges, 9, 161, 176; literacy forms, 162, 163, 164, 165, 167, 171, 173–174, 175, 176; literacy justice, 9, 127, 136, 137; literacy normativity, 198, 200, 201, 208, 210; literacy practices, 116; literacy resources, 162, 175, 175, 194; literacy skills, 35, 162, 172, 175; literacy technologies, 164, 168; politics of literacy, 197–198; racial literacy, 231, 236, 237, 238; visual literacy, 217, 227
logic of juxtaposition, 170, 171–172, 174
logos, 35, 43, 45, 46, 48*n*30, 50, 61; logocentric, 50, 53
Long Time Coming: Reckoning with Race in America (Dyson), xiii, xiv
Lost Texts in Rhetoric and Composition (Holdstein), 246

Maimon, Elaine, 80, 81, 82, 242, 243
marginalized: authors, 198, 228*n6*; character, 222; communities, 51, 53, 58, 59, 61, 93, 94–95, 207; identities, 201; non-marginalized group, xiv; people, xiv, 7, 50; voices, 209
material: analysis, 162, 167, 177*n56*; materiality, 52, 53, 164, 169, 175; reality, 143, 149, 151, 152
McComiskey, Bruce, 36, 39, 42, 45
meme, 162, 167, 169–172, 175; rare events meme, 169–170
mentors, 8, 96, 97, 98, 102, 104, 145, 197, 200; peer writing mentors, 107, 108–109, 110, 111, 112–116, 119, 245; mentoring, 81; mentorship, 110, 113
#MeToo Movement, xi, 3
mindfulness, 237, 238
mission, 20, 22, 30, 36, 46, 69–70, 75, 78, 80–81, 82, 83, 84, 85, 242
multimodal, 4, 10, 163, 166, 167, 169, 172, 173, 174, 175, 176, 227; multimodal composition, 29, 165, 166; multimodal literature, 162, 163; multimodal texts, 110, 118; multimodality, 163, 166, 167, 175. *See also* artifacts; pedagogy: multimodal pedagogy

National Census of Writing, 74, 85
National Center for Education Statistics, 70
neoliberal, 30, 95, 144, 152, 153, 155, 158, 203, 205
non-human, 119
non-scalability, 107, 112, 118; non-scalable, 112, 115. *See also* scalablity
Nussbaum, Martha, 246

Obama, Barack, xvi, 36, 40. *See also* optimism
Olson, Gary A., 189, 191
optimism, xvi, xvii, 4, 12, 244
online, 5, 35, 115, 127, 130, 136–137, 186, 188, 199, 205

pandemic. *See* Covid-19 Pandemic
paradox, 188, 243–244
partnership, 78, 81, 82, 127, 137, 144, 148, 153, 154, 155, 156
pathos, 35, 45–46, 48*n30*, 48*n31*, 50–51, 52, 57, 61–61, 63*n48*
pedagogy: of care, 57; of composition, 19; critical embodiment pedagogy, 7, 51, 58, 59, 62; critical pedagogy, 27, 58, 60; culturally-relevant pedagogy, 236; of generative combination, 175; of hope, 126; of kindness, 25–26; of listening, 45; of mix, remix and mixtape, 171; of multiliteracies, 174; multimodal pedagogy, 165–166; of optimism, xvi–xvii; of practical criticism, 166; of self-care, 8, 9; working-class, 143–144; writing pedagogy, 19, 24, 28, 29–30, 133, 161, 163, 166, 168, 175, 193
Us (Jordan Peele), 216, 219, 223–226
plagiarism, 25, 26–27, 211*n56*
polarized, 4, 227. *See also* binary
politics, 35, 37, 39, 44, 46, 53, 207; identity politics, xii, xv; politics of citation, 197, 202–204, 205, 206, 207; politics of self-care, 102; racial politics, 219, 223. *See also* rhetoric: political rhetoric
post-truth, 36, 39, 43, 44–45
power, xi, 4, 11, 40, 43, 50, 56, 61, 93–94, 102, 116, 127, 133, 137, 145, 147, 164, 198, 203, 207, 220, 236; power dynamics, 52, 60; power relations, 93–94, 95, 101, 105*n18*, 205; power of writing, 215, 233
precarity, 71, 82, 90, 91, 92–95, 104–105*n9*; precarious, 69, 95, 145; precariousness, 90, 94
Pritchard, Eric Darnell, 197–198, 199, 200, 202, 204, 211*n52*
privilege, 4, 61, 107, 176, 198, 220. *See also* white privilege
properties, 162, 164, 165, 167, 169, 171, 172, 175
publics, 9, 18, 23, 144, 155, 157; public discourse, 6, 17, 20, 23, 28, 36, 40, 143, 144; public issues, 150, 151, 153, 154, 155, 157; public writing, 19. *See also* rhetoric: public rhetorics

Quality Enhancement Project (QEP), 76, 79, 83

race, xii, xiii, xv, 4, 8, 21, 39, 52, 56, 59, 96, 104–105*n9*, 127, 129, 133, 148, 199, 202, 209, 216, 218, 219, 220, 222, 227, 228*n6*, 231–132, 236, 237; racism, xii, 9, 11, 12, 55, 57, 59, 93, 127, 129, 133, 134, 197, 198, 202, 206, 208, 220, 221, 232, 236. *See also* anti-racist; critical race theory
Ratcliffe, Krista, 12, 218, 228*n19*
Red Record, The, 234–235, 236, 238
re-humanization, 54
relational networks, 52
research methods, 21, 46, 144, 157
resistance, 11, 57, 90, 92–94, 98, 101, 102, 129, 204, 224, 234; Reading is Resistance, 136, 137, 138, 139
revision, 23, 109, 110, 113, 138, 166, 174, 188
rhetoric: affective rhetorics, 56, 57; of

assertion, 189, 191; of crisis in higher education, 243; cultural rhetorics, 51, 52, 53, 54, 55, 57; cultural rhetoricians, 53; of fake news, 46; of impatience, 56; political rhetoric, 36; public rhetorics, 56; rhetorical listening, xiii, xiv, 228*n15*; rhetorical power, 192; rhetorical traditions, 146, 192; of vulnerability, 8
Roberts-Miller, Patricia, 184–185
Royster, Jacqueline Jones, 58, 155, 200, 202, 203, 204

scalability, xii, 8, 107, 111–112, 114, 119, 128, 129. *See also* non-scalability
Scarry, Elaine, 118, 228*n18*
science, 36, 39, 40–41, 42–43, 44, 46, 47; 48*n21*, 246. *See also* alternative facts: "junk science"
Scott, Joan W., 243–244. *See also* rhetoric of crisis in higher education
self-care, 8, 9, 92, 100, 102. *See also* pedagogy of self-care; politics of self-care
self-expression, 145, 166
Selfe, Cynthia, 161, 166. *See also* Takayoski and Selfe
sequencing, 172–176
sexual orientation, 104–105*n9*, 202. *See also* gender
social class, 143, 148–149, 153
social justice, 4, 18, 39, 59, 94, 125, 132, 134, 136, 138, 143, 202, 233; "Social Justice Standards," 137, 138
socioeconomic, 4, 97, 219, 227
source material, 135, 198, 206
standardized, 24, 31*n36*, 79, 83, 117, 186
stigmatization, 100, 102
storying, 51, 52, 236
strategy, 22, 43, 69, 75, 78, 81–84, 85, 170, 186, 237, 242
student-centered: learning environment, 115; pedagogies, 60, 126
sustainability, 8, 35, 46, 50, 74, 75, 83, 84, 92, 100, 190
synergy, 10, 162, 175, 176

Takayoshi, Pamela, and Cynthia Selfe, 163, 165. *See also* Self, Cynthia
Teller, Joseph, 18–19
thesis statement, 10, 167, 183–191, 193, 194, 245–246; logics of, 184–186; thesis-driven, 168; thesis-driven essay, 188, 190; thesis-focused instruction, 185, 188–189; tyranny of, 185, 245–246

trauma, xv, 3, 69, 84, 90–91, 94, 95, 96, 100, 102, 103, 104, 126, 135, 224
Tsing, Anna, 107–108, 112, 113, 119. *See also* non-scalability

undergraduate: courses, 111, 246; enrollment, 72–73; majors, 75; students, xi, 155
unsustainability, 97. *See also* sustainability

Villanueva, Victor, 50, 53, 61–62
vision, 6, 11, 22, 60, 69–70, 75, 77, 78–80, 81, 83, 84, 85, 126, 138, 191, 218, 242–243; visioning, 128, 135, 139
visual analysis, 215, 226–227
vulnerability, 104–105*n9*. *See also* affect; rhetoric of vulnerability

Wells-Barnett, Ida B., 11, 233–237, 238
whiteness, 57, 197–198, 200–201, 203, 206; of scholarly pipelines, 208; white-bodied, 127; whitestream, 7, 51, 53, 55, 57, 59, 62; white subject, 54. *See also* authority
white privilege, 57. *See also* privilege
white supremacy, 9, 53, 125, 129, 132–133, 201–202, 204, 208; white language supremacy, 138
working-class, 9, 144, 145, 146, 147, 148, 149, 151, 152–153, 155, 158; working-class community, 147, 149, 153, 154, 155, 156, 157, 158; working-class ethos, 143; working-class publics, 144, 147, 152–153; working-class students, 145, 146, 148, 149, 151, 155, 157. *See also* pedagogy: working-class
Writing Across the Curriculum (WAC), xii, 7–8, 69, 74–75, 76, 78, 80, 81, 84, 85, 242, 243, 244
writing centers, 75, 76, 77, 80, 81, 83, 85, 186; writing center consultants, 76; writing center directors, 7
Writing in the Disciplines (WID), xii, 74, 78, 85, 242
writing intensive: courses, 8, 74, 76, 81, 82; pedagogy, 127
writing program administrators (WPA), 7, 18, 99, 244, 245. *See also* CWPA
writing programs, 8, 21, 29, 74, 75, 92, 100, 103, 105, 111, 154, 156, 243, 245
writing textbook, 23, 48*n30*, 184, 185, 186, 199, 237
writing to learn, 165–166, 169

ABOUT THE AUTHORS

Jacob Babb is an associate professor of English at Indiana University Southeast. He is co-editor of *WPA: Writing Program Administration*. He publishes on composition theory and pedagogy, writing program administration, and rhetoric. He has published articles in *Composition Forum, Composition Studies, Harlot,* and *WPA: Writing Program Administration* as well as chapters in several edited collections. He is the co-editor of *WPAs in Transition: Navigating Educational Leadership Positions* and *The Things We Carry: Strategies for Recognizing and Negotiating Emotional Labor in Writing Program Administration*.

Anna Barritt is a PhD candidate in rhetoric and writing studies at the University of Oklahoma, where she teaches college writing and serves as assistant director of first-year composition. Her primary research interests include disability studies, twentieth-century rhetorical theory, and working-class identities in academia.

Christopher Basgier (he/him/his) is acting director of university writing at Auburn University. He helps faculty integrate writing and high-impact practices such as ePortfolios and undergraduate research into courses and curricula and leads professional development experiences for writing center consultants. His scholarship focuses on WAC, writing program administration, threshold concepts, and rhetorical genre theory.

Christina V. Cedillo is an associate professor of writing and rhetoric at the University of Houston–Clear Lake. Christina's research draws from cultural rhetorics and de-colonial theory to focus on embodied rhetorics and rhetorics of embodiment at the intersections of race, gender, and disability. Their work has appeared in *College Composition and Communication, Rhetoric Society Quarterly, Journal for the History of Rhetoric, Composition Forum,* and various other journals and edited collections. Christina's current project examines the multimodal rhetorics of twentieth- and twenty-first-century women of color activists. They are the lead editor of the *Journal of Multimodal Rhetorics*.

Nicholas Behm is a professor of English and director of the Center for Scholarship and Teaching at Elmhurst University, where he teaches first-year composition, rhetorical theory, and business and technical writing courses. He also frequently teaches in the Honors Program.

William Duffy is an associate professor of English at the University of Memphis, where he teaches courses in composition, professional writing, and rhetorical theory. His scholarship has been published in such journals as *Present Tense, Composition Studies,* and *College English,* as well as in the recent edited collections *After Plato: Rhetoric, Ethics, and the Teaching of Writing* and *Explanation Points: Publishing in Rhetoric and Composition*. His book *Beyond Conversation: Collaboration and the Production of Writing* was recently published by Utah State University Press.

Jessica Edwards is an assistant professor of English at the University of Delaware. Her work centers on writing studies and critical race studies. Her scholarship has appeared in *Computers and Composition Online* as well as *Key Theoretical Frameworks: Teaching Technical Communication in the Twenty-First Century*.

ABOUT THE AUTHORS

Deborah H. Holdstein is a professor of English at Columbia College Chicago. From 2007 to 2014, Holdstein served as dean of the School of Liberal Arts and Sciences at Columbia and, among numerous initiatives, started the institution's first Honors Program. She is a past editor of *College Composition and Communication*. Holdstein has also published widely in composition/rhetoric and in film studies, including the coauthored textbook *The Oxford Reader* and the scholarly volume *Lost Texts in Rhetoric*. She actively consults with the Modern Language Association/Association of Departments of English, colleges and universities, and is a consultant-evaluator for the Council of Writing Program Administrators.

Kim Jaxon is a professor of English (composition and literacy) at California State University, Chico. She is a featured contributor for the Connected Learning Alliance, where she writes about digital pedagogies. She is also the coauthor of *Composing Science: A Facilitator's Guide to Writing in the Science Classroom*.

Matthew S. S. Johnson is a professor of English and director of first-year writing at Southern Illinois University Edwardsville and specializes in composition and rhetoric, digital literacies, and videogame studies/ludology. He is reviews editor for the *Journal of Gaming and Virtual Worlds*. His scholarship often focuses on dismantling boundaries between work and play.

Jennifer Juszkiewicz is the director of the Writing Proficiency Program and the Writing & Tutoring Center at Saint Mary's College, Notre Dame, Indiana. She is also on the faculty of the English department. Her research centers on spatial theory, writing program administration, writing across the curriculum, and computational rhetoric. Her work has been published in *enculturation*, *Kairos*, and *Teaching Theology and Religion*.

Nicole Khoury holds a PhD in rhetoric and composition from Arizona State University and is a founding member of the Non-Western/Global Rhetorics CCCC SIG. Her research focuses on Arab feminist traditions, analyzing rhetoric and discourse on gender, politics, and religion; it has been published in *Women Rising: Resistance, Revolution, and Reform in the Arab Spring and Beyond*; *Global Women Leaders: Studies in Feminist Political Rhetoric*; *Women, War and Violence* with Rita Stephan; and *In Line with the Divine: The Struggle for Gender Equality in Lebanon*, as well as in *Al-Raida Journal* and *Peitho Journal*.

Elizabeth Kleinfeld is a professor and director of the Writing Center at Metropolitan State University of Denver, where she teaches rhetoric, writing center studies, and composition theory and practice. Her research focuses on citation practice, undergraduate research, and anti-racist pedagogy. Her work is informed by disability studies, feminism, and social justice theory. She is coauthor of *The Bedford Book of Genres*, and her work has appeared in edited collections, *Praxis*, and *Computers and Composition Online*.

Rachel McCabe is an assistant professor and director of writing at La Salle University. Her research focuses on the affective experience and its importance to the reading and viewing of texts and how doing so impacts the student writing process. She also considers how positions of power and privilege influence the interpretation process. Her scholarship has been published in *Composition Studies*, *Studies in Documentary Film*, and *Pedagogy*.

Zapoura Newton-Calvert is a faculty-in-residence for community engagement for Portland State University's Office of Academic Innovation and serves as a member of several PSU teams dedicated to integrating community-based learning experiences into online teaching and learning. As part of her community-based teaching and mentoring, Zapoura writes an education blog that incorporates student and community writing to educate the public on educational equity in Portland.

Matthew Overstreet is an assistant professor of English at Khalifa University in Abu Dhabi. He has a PhD from the University of Pittsburgh and has taught writing and writing pedagogy on three continents. His research explores how technology shapes the way we think, write, read, and relate.

Kalyn Prince is a PhD candidate in rhetoric and writing studies at the University of Oklahoma. She has served as an assistant director of first-year composition and teaches first-year writing. Her dissertation interrogates the role of nostalgia as place-based ethos in political movements and public argumentation.

Sherry Rankins-Robertson is chair and professor of writing and rhetoric at the University of Central Florida. Her research includes community-engaged writing, writing program administration, and teaching in online learning environments. She has co-edited two book collections. Sherry is an officer for the Council of Writing Program Administrators and a member of the executive committee of the Conference on College Composition and Communication.

Krista Ratcliffe is a foundation professor and chair in the Department of English at Arizona State University. Her research focuses on intersections of rhetoric, feminist theory, and critical race studies. Her books include *Anglo-American Challenges to the Rhetorical Traditions: Virginia Woolf, Mary Daly, and Adrienne Rich* (1996); *Who's Having This Baby?* (2002); *Rhetorical Listening: Identification, Gender, Whiteness* (2006), which won numerous awards in the field of composition and rhetoric; *Performing Feminist Administration in Rhetoric and Composition Studies* (2010), co-edited with Rebecca Rickly; *Silence and Listening as Rhetorical Arts* (2011), co-edited with Cheryl Glenn; and *Rhetorics of Whiteness: Postracial Hauntings in Popular Culture, Social Media, and Education* (2017), co-edited with Tammy Kennedy and Joyce Middleton, which won a 2018 CCCC Outstanding Book Award. Most recently, she published *Rhetorical Listening in Action: A Concept-Tactic Approach* (2022) with Kyle Jensen. Her work has also appeared in edited collections as well as noted academic journals. She served as president of the Coalition of Women Scholars in the History of Rhetoric and Composition (CWSHRC) and the Rhetoric Society of America (RSA), of which she is also a fellow.

Hannah J. Rule is an associate professor of English in composition and rhetoric at the University of South Carolina. Her scholarship focuses on the material and embodied dimensions of writing and its pedagogies, a focus reflected in her recent book, *Situating Writing Processes* (2019), as well as articles and chapters in various venues including *CCC* and *Composition Studies*.

Laura A. Sparks is an associate professor of English at California State University, Chico, where she teaches courses in writing studies and human rights rhetorics. Her current research focuses on the relationship between rhetoric and interrogational torture. She has recently published work in *Present Tense, Journal of Contemporary Poetics, Screen Bodies,* and *Trace*.